"This book tells the story of an amazing academic career, building on talent and commitment, while at the same time revealing the significance of working together with people in order to 'get the job done'. The really intriguing story running through this book tells about the people Russell Lansbury met and worked together with at home in Australia as well as abroad."

—*Soren Kaj Andersen, Associate Professor and Director of the Centre for Research on Work and Employment Relations, University of Copenhagen, Denmark*

"By masterly weaving in of personal anecdote with economic and political trends, Russell Lansbury identifies key events in Australia's employment relations system in an engaging and insightful analysis. This excellent book, by one of Australia's most outstanding industrial relations scholars of his generation, benefits from his deep understanding not only of Australia but also of developments in other advanced and emerging market economies."

—*Janice Bellace, Samuel A. Blank Professor Emeritus of Legal Studies and Business Ethics, The Wharton School, University of Pennsylvania, USA*

"Russell Lansbury's approach to scholarship and life shine through the pages of this wonderful book. Generosity, curiosity, intelligence and warmth are a rare combination in a scholar and these qualities, as well as his internationalism and commitment to public service, explain the enormous impact he has had throughout his distinguished career. As those of us who have been mentored by Prof Lansbury often say – 'be like Russell'"

—*Rae Cooper AO, Professor of Gender, Work and Employment Relations, University of Sydney, Australia*

"In *Crossing Boundaries* Russell Lansbury provides both a personal memoir and an intelligent, perceptive discussion of the changing world of industrial relations over the last 50 years. Few people have been so central to developments in Australia and worldwide. Over time, Russell developed a network of key academics and actors in the field and this facilitated the unique insights he shares with us here. The book is a clearly written, human account – a 'must read' for those working in industrial relations and related fields."

—*Dexter Dunphy AM, Emeritus Professor UNSW and University of Technology Sydney, Australia*

"*Crossing Boundaries* is the story of an internationally renowned scholar who crosses borders and cultures, exploring the meaning of work and indeed humanity, not only through his research but also through his exploration with people of all nationalities and walks of life. Russell Lansbury's memoir will reignite, deep within us, the desire and hope of connecting with people for building a better future for work and life."

—*Dr Chang-Hee Lee, Country Director, International Labour Organisation, Vietnam*

"In this fascinating book Russell Lansbury provides a wealth of insights into the changing nature of work and the challenges and opportunities society faces adjusting to those changes. Lansbury provides powerful lessons from a remarkable career that mixed path breaking academic work with an insider's engagement with the practical world."

—*Harry C. Katz, Jack Sheinkman Professor and former Dean, Cornell University, USA, and President-elect, International Labour and Employment Relations Association (ILERA)*

"Russell Lansbury is the supreme internationalist. In a truly distinguished career, Russell draws deep respect from scholars around the world for his impressive body of industrial relations knowledge, his facility across disciplines and for his perfect collegiality. All this, combined with warm insights to Russell's family and personal life, make this a most engaging book."

—*John Niland AC, Emeritus Professor and former Vice-Chancellor, UNSW, Australia, and Former President, International Labour and Employment Relations Association*

"This is a must-read book for everyone interested in work and employment relations – as a field of study, and as an important part of contemporary society. It tells the fascinating story of the life, adventures and work of a world-class scholar, and a curious, generous, and kind friend and colleague. The book serves as an inspiration to undertake international and comparative research, and to engage in dialogue with social partners, governments and other stakeholders to promote a fair and just future of work."

—*Mia Rönnmar, Professor and Dean of the Faculty of Law at Lund University, Sweden, and President of the International Labour and Employment Relations Association (ILERA)*

"I thoroughly enjoyed this memoir which not only provides fascinating glimpses of Russell Lansbury's rich academic life but is also highly illuminating about the history of Australian industrial relations. I was riveted and I'm sure many others will be too."

—*Judy Wajcman, Anthony Giddens Chair of Sociology, London School of Economics, UK*

"Russell Lansbury's intriguing memoir perceptively reminds us that the key characteristics of a good society remain much the same through time. It is the road that we must travel down to approach it that changes most. There has never been a better time to put this insight definitively at the centre stage of public debate."

—*Keith Whitfield, Professor of Human Resource Management, Cardiff University, UK*

Crossing Boundaries

This book provides thoughtful insights into the developments in work, organisations and employment relations in the last 50 years. In a semi-autobiographical approach, the author reflects on important contributions by other scholars, practitioners, and policy makers to work and employment relations.

The book covers a variety of themes which have been the subject of research undertaken by the author over his career and explores these themes over a period of time with examples drawn from various countries. It also emphasises that countries and regions cannot be understood in isolation from each other. The author seeks to convey the importance of crossing disciplinary boundaries in the social sciences in order to interpret changes in work, organisations and employment relations.

Drawing on the author's rich experience and research, the book is engaging and accessible to anyone who wishes to learn more about the rapidly changing workplace and employment relations.

Russell D. Lansbury is Emeritus Professor of Industrial Relations at the University of Sydney where he was Head of Department and Associate Dean of Research in the Faculty of Economics and Business. He was the Foundation Director of the Australian Centre for Industrial Relations Research and Teaching at the University of Sydney. He was joint editor of the *Journal of Industrial Relations* for ten years. He holds an MA from the University of Melbourne and a PhD from the London School of Economics and Political Science. He was awarded honorary doctorates by Lulea Technical University in Sweden and Macquarie University in Australia. He has been a Senior Fulbright Scholar at MIT and Harvard University, a Visiting Fellow at the Swedish National Institute for Worklife Research in Stockholm and a Visiting Fellow at the International Institute for Labour Studies at the International Labour Organisation in Geneva. He was President of the International Labour and Employment Relations Association. He is a Fellow of the Academy of Social Sciences Australia and was awarded an Order of Australia (AO) for services to industrial relations and higher education.

Routledge Studies in Employment and Work Relations in Context
Edited by Tony Elger and Peter Fairbrother

The aim of the *Employment and Work Relations in Context Series* is to address questions relating to the evolving patterns and politics of work, employment, management and industrial relations. There is a concern to trace out the ways in which wider policy-making, especially by national governments and transnational corporations, impinges upon specific workplaces, occupations, labour markets, localities and regions. This invites attention to developments at an international level, marking out patterns of globalization, state policy and practices in the context of globalization and the impact of these processes on labour. A particular feature of the series is the consideration of forms of worker and citizen organization and mobilization. The studies address major analytical and policy issues through case study and comparative research.

Human Resource Management in Emerging Economies
Piotr Zientara

The Origins of Worker Mobilisation
Australia 1788–1850
Michael Quinlan

Transnational Management of Globalised Workers
Nurses beyond Human Resources
Tricia Cleland Silva

Contesting Inequality and Worker Mobilisation
Australia 1851–1880
Michael Quinlan

Crossing Boundaries
Work and Industrial Relations in Perspective
Russell D. Lansbury

For more information about this series, please visit: https://www.routledge.com/Routledge-Studies-in-Employment-and-Work-Relations-in-Context/book-series/SE0840

Crossing Boundaries
Work and Industrial Relations in Perspective

Russell D. Lansbury

LONDON AND NEW YORK

First published 2021
and by Routledge
2 Park Square, Milton Park, Abingdon, Oxon, OX14 4RN

by Routledge
52 Vanderbilt Avenue, New York, NY 10017

Routledge is an imprint of the Taylor & Francis Group, an informa business

© 2021 Russell D. Lansbury

The right of Russell D. Lansbury to be identified as author of this work has been asserted by him in accordance with sections 77 and 78 of the Copyright, Designs and Patents Act 1988.

All rights reserved. No part of this book may be reprinted or reproduced or utilised in any form or by any electronic, mechanical, or other means, now known or hereafter invented, including photocopying and recording, or in any information storage or retrieval system, without permission in writing from the publishers.

Trademark notice: Product or corporate names may be trademarks or registered trademarks, and are used only for identification and explanation without intent to infringe.

Library of Congress Cataloging-in-Publication Data
A catalog record for this title has been requested

ISBN: 978-0-367-40802-2 (hbk)
ISBN: 978-0-367-80914-0 (ebk)

Typeset in Galliard
by codeMantra

For my wife, Gwen, our children, Nina and Owen, and our grandchildren, Maya, Dane, Jarrah and Theo

Contents

Foreword by Marian Baird   x
Preface   xii

1 Starting out (1940s and 1950s)   1

2 The world opens up at university (1963–1967)   16

3 Nordic exposure (1967–1970)   32

4 The best of British experience (1970–1973)   44

5 Monash University in the Whitlam and Fraser eras (1974–1980)   54

6 Transition to Sydney: the Hawke/Keating era begins (1981–1986)   79

7 New horizons at the University of Sydney (1987–1999)   101

8 A broader role in academic research and leadership (2000–2009)   128

9 Research and travels in retirement (2010–2020)   140

10 Concluding observations on Work and Industrial Relations   158

Afterword by Thomas A. Kochan   169
Acknowledgements   171
Bibliography   174
Index   183

Foreword

Russell Lansbury is undoubtedly one of Australia's, and the world's, most highly respected industrial relations scholars. His memoir tells how that came to be. Russell's intellectual curiosity and insatiable appetite for travel and conversation shine through in his memoir. Over a period spanning 50 years, he provides key insights on the changing world of work and the part played by governments, unions and employers in Australia and internationally. Throughout, Russell has a keen sense of fairness and justice, and his concluding comments advocating a new social contract for Australia using the lessons of COVID-19 are well worth noting.

The reader will be astonished to read of the people Russell met and worked with, but I particularly like one of the opening vignettes of Russell as a very little boy travelling to kindergarten by bus, talking to a girl and missing his stop as a result, only to later be driven home by the bus driver. This tells you a lot about Russell. Timing and good fortune may have favoured Russell, but Russell also has a tremendous work ethic and always makes the most of any situation. He is also the most generous and energetic of colleagues, endlessly sharing personal connections and ideas.

Russell's enthusiasm for crossing boundaries – disciplinary boundaries, country borders, political divides and labour-management frontiers – are clearly described in his narrative. Russell not only comments on industrial relations policies in Australia, the United Kingdom, Germany, Sweden, South Korea and the United States, he also has a remarkable degree of insight into company level industrial relations issues. The world of academics and politicians that Russell mixed with was very much comprised of men and it must be recognised that Russell could not have travelled and achieved what he did without his wife Gwen, herself a very accomplished woman, to maintain the family and home structures.

I had the pleasure and privilege of being one of Russell's PhD students, and in one trip to the United States and the United Kingdom very early in my own career he introduced me to many of the places he loved and the academics he admired. I am forever grateful to him for sharing his world of industrial relations with me and I am honoured to have become a colleague and a friend of Russell.

I doubt there will ever be another academic like Russell and I am sure that as you read his memoir you will also enjoy learning about his life, his academic and policy contributions to industrial relations.

Professor Marian Baird AO FASSA
Head, Discipline of Work and Organisational Studies
The University of Sydney Business School

Preface

During the early stage of my academic career, I met a retired head of the Australian Department of Labour who had been an influential figure in industrial relations for many years. 'Young man', he said, 'you are very fortunate to be entering the field of industrial relations. For most of the general public, industrial relations is like a black box, full of mystery and intrigue. But you and I know what is in that box'. Alas, I never got to see and understand everything in the industrial relations box. However, I did get some occasional glimpses of the mystery and intrigue of industrial relations during almost five decades of involvement in this field.

In this book, I hope to share some of what I discovered as a teacher, researcher and participant in industrial relations. Furthermore, I will seek to explain why I believe that industrial relations continue to play a crucial role not only in the economy and society but also in the democratic process. I also hope to convey the pleasure and excitement of being an industrial relations scholar. It has been a privilege to meet many inspiring people in the trade union movement, employers' associations, management in private and public sector organisations and members of a wide range of political parties. I have also derived great enjoyment and inspiration collaborating with students and academic colleagues.

When I began this book, it was intended to be a review of the past 50 years of developments in work and industrial relations. I planned to examine a key theme in each chapter, including the changing roles of unions, employers and government, labour market regulation and deregulation, and the future of work. I was going to begin with a brief autobiographical chapter showing how I became involved in the field of work and industrial relations. However, once I began writing, the book became more of a story about my own journey from school days through university followed by my life as an academic engaging in research, teaching and interacting with unions, employers and governments in Australia and around the world. So this book became more autobiographical, examining the key issues in industrial relations through the lens of my experience in various roles, particularly via research and engagement with participants in the everyday world of industrial relations as well as with those who make public policy. Hence, I hope that this book will provide a more personal, albeit partial, view of what is in the 'black box' of work and industrial relations.

In past years, I have co-authored and jointly edited a number of books with various colleagues and enjoyed the process of collaboration. This is the first book I have written as a solo author since the publication of *Professionals and Management: A Study of Behaviour in Organisations*, based on my doctoral thesis, in 1978. Hence, it was a challenge to write this book by myself with relatively little interaction with others. However, once I had completed the first draft, I asked several colleagues and friends to critically review what I had written. This was like the process I observed when I was a visiting scholar at MIT in the mid-1980s when *The Transformation of American Industrial Relations* (1986) was being written by Tom Kochan, Harry Katz and Bob McKersie. As they completed each chapter, they would circulate their work and then hold an informal 'brown bag' seminar at lunchtimes to which students and staff would attend and argue about the merits of what had been written. I emulated this with 'virtual brown bag' exchanges with various people who I thought might be interested in the subject matter of this book. I am most grateful for the advice and constructive criticism which I received but take full responsibility for what I have written.

In the conclusion, I argue that it is time for a new social contract at work. The COVID-19 pandemic is likely to have a long-term effect on the economic and social conditions of many countries. In Australia, there is a need for a new social partnership between government, business and the trade union movement. This would be a reversal of political trends over the past two decades but one that Australia sorely needs. A new social contract at work must rest on three pillars: restoring full employment and providing more secure jobs; revitalising post-secondary education including an easier transition between vocational training institutions and universities; and reforming industrial relations based on fairness and equity. With these principles in place, genuine productivity and prosperity will follow.

1 Starting out (1940s and 1950s)

Recently, someone asked me what was my main field of interest during my academic career. When I replied 'Industrial Relations', the person remarked: 'Oh yes, we used to have something called Industrial Relations. What happened to it? And why were you interested in such an esoteric subject?'

This book is my attempt to provide answers to these and other questions. I began writing this book with considerable trepidation. Who will be interested? What have I learned that I can pass on to others? What can I say about the future of Work and Industrial Relations?

I have also used this book as an opportunity to review my life and try to discover what led me to follow particular interests and drew me towards the fields of Work and Industrial Relations. I have relied on memories, which can be misleading. According to Janan Ganesh (2019) 'our favourite memories are actually memories of memories. Each time we recall an event or an era, another coat of varnish goes on until the original is romanticised out of all recognition'. However, the late Joe Isaac, a pioneer scholar of Industrial Relations, once told me: 'the memory part of our brain is like an onion. As we grow older, our recent memories peel away like the outer parts of the onion leaving the core where our earliest memories are stored and remain clear'.

This book commences with chapters on my family, school days and undergraduate years at the University of Melbourne. These early years shaped my values and beliefs which influenced my choice of Work and Industrial Relations as an academic career. Postgraduate studies in Sweden and England broadened my knowledge and connected me with people who shaped my future interests. My boundaries were expanded as visiting researcher at various institutions around the world including the International Labour Organisation in Geneva, the Swedish Centre for Worklife Research in Stockholm, the University of Wisconsin-Madison, Harvard and MIT in the United States. My appointments at Monash and Macquarie universities provided me with a sound foundation for my later career in Work and Industrial Relations at the University of Sydney.

My chronological account is 'blended' with descriptions of research projects in which I participated during the past 50 years. The book concludes with my speculations on the possible future of Work and Industrial Relations, as the

2   *Starting out*

world enters a dangerous period with the COVID-19 virus, which may cause fundamental changes to the world of Work and Industrial Relations.

I came to Industrial Relations virtually by accident when I applied to the London School of Economics (LSE) to enrol for a PhD either in Sociology or Political science, which I had studied as an undergraduate at the University of Melbourne and in graduate studies in Sweden and Denmark. Having obtained a research fellowship from British European Airways (BEA), to work in their Personnel Planning and Research Department, I was offered a place in the doctoral programme in Industrial Relations at LSE.

Industrial Relations proved to be a field which matched my interests and values. At the LSE and BEA, I learned that Industrial Relations incorporated a number of issues that interested me as well as enabling me to apply what I had learned from my previous studies. Industrial Relations, as a field of study, can be defined in simple terms as analysing the factors which shape the relationship between employers and employees.

An inter-disciplinary field of knowledge, Industrial Relations draws on a wide range of social sciences. Industrial Relations incorporates insights from Psychology to understand factors which influence the behaviour of people at work; from Sociology, to investigate how employers and unions negotiate the terms and conditions of work; from Economics, to analyse how labour markets work; and from Political Science, to examine the role of institutions and the development of public policy as they apply to the regulation of work and employment relations. Other disciplines such as Law, History and Geography are also relevant. But equally important, in my view, is that Industrial Relations applies the principles of fairness and equity to the study of work and employment.

The title *Crossing Boundaries: Work and Industrial Relations in Perspective* was chosen for this book for several reasons. The term 'boundaries' denotes not only in a geographical sense of borders between countries, but also as it relates to different academic disciplines. As noted above, Industrial Relations is an inter-disciplinary field of knowledge which draws on a wide range of social sciences and crosses a number of disciplinary boundaries.

Having studied and researched systems of Industrial Relations in countries around the world, it is my intention that this book will demonstrate why and how we should learn from each other's experience by crossing boundaries or borders between countries. Furthermore, within the workplace, there are often boundaries not only between workers and managers but also between various crafts and professions.

Industrial Relations academics and practitioners can help to resolve conflicts between various groups in the workplace through negotiation, consultation and mediation. Hence, there are practical as well as theoretical contributions which Industrial Relations can make as an inter-disciplinary field which crosses various boundaries.

The subtitle *Work and Industrial Relations in Perspective* was chosen because this book provides a *perspective* on both continuity and change which have occurred in the workplace. The term *Industrial Relations* is deliberately used because it reflects our deep historical roots to the work of Sidney and Beatrice Webb in the United Kingdom and John R. Commons in the United States, who were the founders of this field more than a century ago (Kaufman, 1984). It is sometimes argued that *Employment Relations* can be substituted in place of *Industrial Relations* on the grounds that it deals with both unionised and non-unionised workplaces and also provides a broader perspective of relations at work. However, Industrial Relations can be viewed in more expansive terms involving the parties to the employment relationship (including employers, unions and government), the processes by which the employment relationship is governed, and the outcome of these processes (see Heery, 2008). In a recent paper to the Association of Industrial Relations Academics of Australia and New Zealand (AIRAANZ), Lewer and Larkin (2020) make a persuasive case that 'the death of industrial relations is greatly exaggerated'.

Work is a major theme of this book because it occupies a central part of most people's lives. While not everyone enjoys their work, or every aspect of it, most of us are required to work in order to gain the means to survive. However, work also meets many other needs of people such as feelings of worth and identity, social interaction and a sense of purpose. In the words of a character in Joseph Conrad's *The Heart of Darkness*: 'I don't like work - no man does, but I like what is in the work - the chance to find yourself, your own reality - for yourself, not for others - what no other man can ever know'.

It is commonly stated that the nature of work is being fundamentally changed by technology. While it is true that many aspects of work are currently undergoing significant changes, this has occurred throughout history: from the agricultural revolution to the latest applications of artificial intelligence. However, in recent decades, there has been a shift in advanced economies from stable employment being the norm to a labour market where up to half of the workforce may be in contingent or insecure work. These changes have major implications for Work and Industrial Relations and feature strongly in this book.

Sources of inspiration

This book has been inspired by the writing of several authors and friends who have adopted an autobiographical approach while addressing major issues in their fields of interest and expertise. Bob McKersie's superb book *A Field in Flux: Sixty Years of Industrial Relations* (2019) not only covers historical events in the United States, which he helped to shape, but also discusses the challenges which face the future of Work and Industrial Relations. McKersie's book provided me with a useful 'template' but I have sought to extend his analysis to describe developments in Work and Industrial Relations in Australia and elsewhere through the lens of my own research. I first met Bob McKersie when I was a Fulbright Scholar at MIT in 1984 and he has been an inspiration to me ever since.

In *Born at the Right Time* (2019), labour lawyer Ron McCallum powerfully relates how overcoming disadvantages during his early life shaped his advocacy of social justice and fairness at work. Ron became the first blind person to hold a professorial position and Dean of Law at the University of Sydney. Ron has been Senior Australian of the Year and held prominent national and international roles improving the lives of people with disabilities. Ron and I began our careers together at Monash and we have been colleagues and long-standing friends at the University of Sydney.

In *From the Whangpoo to the Wollombi* (2017), international relations specialist, Tony Palfreeman, traces his life from China, where he was born in Shanghai on the Whangpoo River in the 1930s, through his schooldays in South Africa and England, to his university education in Switzerland and finally, his academic career in Australia. Palfreeman draws on his personal journey when arguing that a social contract between government and the people should be the cornerstone of a properly functioning political system. In his retirement, Tony Palfreeman is our friend and neighbour on a farm outside the village of Wollombi in New South Wales, where we have had a weekend cottage for the past 30 years.

Two other excellent autobiographies which influenced me are by contemporaries from my student days at the University of Melbourne. Both books demonstrate how the authors' early lives influenced their later careers in public life. In *Speaking Out*, Gillian Triggs focuses on her period as President of the Australian Human Rights Commission. *Incorrigible Optimist: A Political Memoir* by Gareth Evans describes his experiences at a long-serving Australian Foreign Minister and other international roles.

Finally, the late Alan Davies, who was my teacher and mentor at the University of Melbourne, had a profound influence on my thinking. In *Private Politics* (1966), Davies emphasised the importance of biography for gaining insights into an individual's political beliefs and behaviour. Davies' approach, which was based partly on his experience at the Tavistock Institute of Human Relations in London, made sense to me because it enabled me to apply what I had learned from both Psychology and Political Science to people's working lives. Davies supervised my Master's thesis and influenced my doctoral research at the LSE, which focused on the changing roles of IT and other technical specialists in management services at BEA.

In this book, an autobiographical approach has been used to show how my early life and education influenced my later perceptions of Work and Industrial Relations as well as the values which I have brought to my research in this field. It begins with an account of the influence of my parents and extended family. I then revisit my school days and discuss the impact of my teachers and other experiences which led me towards my later studies and academic career.

The influence of my parents

For most of us, family provides us with basic values in life. Although the experience of education and work influences our development, early childhood and adolescent shapes our individual character. Hence, I believe that the foundations of my later interest in Work and Industrial Relations as a field of knowledge were laid in early life by the influence of my family, education, organisations to which

I belonged and early experiences in the workforce. This chapter examines aspects of my early life in order to demonstrate the importance of these childhood and adolescent years in shaping the values and sense of curiosity that influenced my later academic career.

I was born in 1945 in the Melbourne suburb of Malvern, the only child of Len and Freda Lansbury, in a two-bedroom timber house that was built by my grandfather in the early 1900s. My parents earned only a modest income from their respective jobs. We did not have a car until my father later acquired one as part of his job, during my late teenage years, so for most of my childhood we travelled mostly by public transport. The highlight of each year was two weeks holiday staying with friends at the beach, a couple of hours from Melbourne. On our side of the street the houses were small and of weatherboard construction, built for working-class families, while on the other side they were large brick villas with expansive gardens, in which lived families with professional and managerial employment. But I never felt deprived or disadvantaged.

Both my parents left school around 14 or 15 years of age. This was a common experience for many of their generation when access to secondary schools was limited and university education was restricted to those students who could afford to pay fees or gain a scholarship. My parents worked hard all their lives and were keen for me to gain higher education and find a secure job. They did not aspire for me to become a lawyer or doctor or businessman because these jobs looked too ambitious and were not for 'the likes of us'. However, they encouraged me to become a school teacher because this would be a 'respectable, safe and secure' job.

Freda

My mother Freda was born in Launceston, Tasmania, in 1912. After completing primary school, she began work in an office as a trainee typist. Later, Freda became a bookkeeper, assisting the company accountant. She left Launceston in her late 20s seeking adventure in Melbourne and, in her words, 'to search for a husband'. She met Len just as he was enlisting for the Army at the beginning of the Second World War and they married during the war years. Freda worked for the same small company over 40 years. The company manufactured flavours, fragrances and colour additives for the food, beverage and cosmetic industries. Although the firm changed ownership several times, Freda always had a close working relation with her boss and the company accountant to whom she reported. Freda used to joke that she kept declaring her age as 50 for about 20 years until she finally retired in her early 70s.

Freda worked part-time during my pre-school years but she did not want others, apart from close friends, to know that she worked. There were several reasons for this. Relatively few middle-class women worked after they married and had children. I think Freda also felt it might reflect negatively on my dad if it was known that she worked as it could appear that Len did not make enough money to support our family and the lifestyle to which they aspired. I recall

Freda sitting at the dining room table with large ledgers and an adding machine as she worked at home doing bookkeeping in my pre-school days. She worked from 10.00am to 3.00pm when I was at primary school and I would spend quite a lot of time at the office and in the factory during school holidays. There were only about 10 employees with the office and the factory all on the same site. I recall enjoying being at Freda's workplace, where I would occasionally run errands. The factory was located in a semi-industrial section of the city along with other small workplaces. These have now all gone and been replaced by expensive apartments.

Despite her lack of formal education, Freda had a lively mind and strong intellect. From my primary school days, Freda took a close interest and assisted me with my education. During my university studies, Freda typed my essays, would read every sentence and require me to rewrite anything she thought was not sufficiently well explained. Her view was that essays should be written in plain English which the average person could understand. She would tell me that 'If I cannot follow your argument, you are not writing clearly enough so it needs to be re-written'. Freda applied this logic as much to my first-year university essays as to my PhD thesis. I think her interest in typing my work was not just to assist me but because she was intensely interested in ideas and wished she had access to higher education.

When Freda was in her early 70s, and living alone in Melbourne, my wife Gwen generously suggested that we invite her to move to Sydney in order to live near us and her grandchildren. Freda readily agreed. After we found her an affordable apartment in Avalon, Freda sold her house in Melbourne and moved north. Freda quickly became part of the community, volunteering at the local library where she typed cards for the catalogue and became a key member of the library volunteer group. She also had regular guests from Melbourne as friends came to visit her.

I was at Macquarie University and began to attend international academic conferences. Gwen suggested that I take Freda with me to the conference venues and she enthusiastically agreed. Hence, during the final decade of her life, Freda became a well-known figure at Industrial Relations conferences around the world! She loved the social events at conferences and would chat happily with people of any age or nationality. I recall an elderly distinguished Japanese professor asking my permission to invite Freda to go out with him to dinner. She was delighted. By this stage of her life she was quite deaf and, despite wearing hearing aids, found it difficult to understand people, particularly in crowded places. But she would smile and agree with what anyone said to her and it seemed to earn her many friends!

Len

My father Len was born in Melbourne in 1910. He worked as an insurance clerk for the same company for his entire career of more than 40 years, although the ownership of the company changed a number of times during this period. At 15,

Len became an 'office boy', and later a clerk, in the Batavia Insurance Company. He briefly attended a technical school intending to become a carpenter, like some other members of his extended family, but found that he had no aptitude for this kind of work. Len often spoke of his 'lost opportunities' leaving school too early and insisted that I study hard and gain a good education.

Len joined the army in 1940, at the outbreak of war, when he was 30. He spent the next five years in army camps in Alice Springs and Darwin in the Northern Territory. For 20 years after the war ended, Len petitioned the Department of Veterans Affairs seeking recognition as a 'returned serviceman' on the grounds that he had been assigned to Darwin during the Japanese bombing raids on that city. Eventually he succeeded and it gave him access to a low interest 'war service housing loan' and other benefits available to returned service personnel.

Len regarded the time he spent in the army as both the best and worst years of his life. He enjoyed the camaraderie with other men and achieved the rank of Warrant Officer. But he claimed that boredom from life in the army caused him to take up drinking and smoking, when he had previously been a keen athlete and teetotaller. After his premature death at 59, due to a heart attack, my mother gained a war service pension as the widow of a returned serviceman. This gave her an important sense of security although she continued to work part-time until her early 70s.

Politics was rarely discussed at home. However, the Vietnam War became a controversial topic once the Australian government introduced conscription of young men over the age of 18 years of age. This was in order to raise sufficient troops to send to assist the American led alliance in South Vietnam. I was among the first group to be placed in the ballot, which was a 'lottery' system, to determine who would be 'called up' and sent to Vietnam. Opposition to sending Australian troops, particularly conscripts, was mounting and I recall having disagreements with my dad about the Australian government's conscription policy and its justification for joining in the Vietnam War. Like many other Australians, after initially supporting Australia's participation in the war, Len gradually changed his views as the war as it dragged on and became an increasingly divisive issue. Len and I eventually finished up on the same side of the Vietnam debate, opposing the Australian government sending conscripts to Vietnam.

A photograph of my father in his early 20s sits in the living room of my son's home. Len is standing in front of a surfboard, looking fit and muscular, tanned and smiling. The photo was taken when Len was in his 20s, before he entered the army, when his life was still before him. It is wonderful that this image of my dad is the one which my son and grandsons see each day. It is exactly as Len would have wished to be remembered.

I am sad that my father died before I realised how much he had given me. Looking back, I realise how much he encouraged and supported me. Len was an accomplished sportsman having been a prize-winning athlete in long distance running, shot put, discus and javelin. Yet he urged me to study hard saying that he had 'wasted his youth' focusing on sport instead of schoolwork. He was an excellent golfer and tried without success to teach me some of the fundamentals, which I am still trying to grasp. Len attended some of the first lectures which I gave at the University of Melbourne and I was told by some of his colleagues, after he died, that he called me 'the professor', even though I was only a tutor at the time.

My extended family

My maternal grandparents lived in Launceston, Tasmania. I saw them mainly during the school holidays when I would be sent to them to stay for a few weeks. Launceston and its surroundings were exciting to me. My grandparents lived in a small house only a short walk to the centre of town. They had no telephone or car and told me that there was no need for such extravagances as anywhere you wished to go was in walking distance, and most of their friends lived close by in the neighbourhood.

My grandfather, Johnny McQueen, made a great impression on me. He was a small man who was constantly joking and singing. I have a photo of young Johnny appearing in amateur vaudeville with his father. He was keen on musical theatre and even constructed a makeshift stage in the backyard for performances. He taught me songs from the era of the First World War which I can still remember. His father was born in Scotland and Johnny loved to sing patriotic Scottish songs which mentioned Bonnie Prince Charlie and other Scottish heroes. Each birthday, I would be given a book about some historical Scottish figure, such as Rob Roy. I am sure that Johnny would be delighted to see the Scottish National Party in government and would have enjoyed visiting Glasgow, his father's birthplace, but his farthest journeys were to Melbourne to visit us.

Johnny started his working life at a young age as a labourer in a foundry. An industrial accident meant that he needed to find work which required less physical activity and so he became a pharmaceutical chemist's assistant. It was common for people on a modest income to go to the pharmacist rather than a general practitioner for basic medical treatment. Johnny became known as the 'baby doctor' because women would consult him about their pregnancies. As he had no medical training, I wonder what kind of advice he gave them.

My grandmother, known as 'Sissie' (short for Sister) had quite a serious demeanour. She was born Mary McCrory and her parents were from Northern Ireland. Sissie would always be formally dressed in a hat and gloves when we walked downtown to do the shopping. But she also liked a 'sing song' and we would visit one of the neighbours on a Sunday night and stand around the pianola and join in the choruses of well-known songs of the era. We still own an old pianola and our grandchildren enjoy playing old piano rolls, some of which are from my grandparents' era.

My cousin Margaret, five years older than me, was also an only child and like an older sister. We saw each other mainly at Christmas and on other family occasions. In many ways, Margaret was my role model when I was growing up as she was the first of our extended family to attend university. Margaret gained a

Commerce degree from the University of Melbourne and worked in higher education as well as government. She was always very active in community activities and remains so. Margaret was always very supportive of me although later we held differing views on social and political issues. Margaret's father, Frank, was my father's elder brother and had a successful career in the public service.

Much of Frank Lansbury's working life was spent in the Australian Industrial Relations Commission where he became a Commissioner towards the end of his career. This was a significant achievement given that he left school early and had studied at 'night school' to gain further education and qualifications. Frank also played a major role as a volunteer administrator in the Victoria Lacrosse Association and the grandstand at the Malvern lacrosse ground is named in his honour. Although Frank provided me with encouragement to play lacrosse from an early age, I was never a competent player but did manage to play intermittently at school and university. Frank would regularly turn up to watch me and must have been disappointed with my performances. But he was always very warm and supportive of my studies and career. It was coincidental that I chose Industrial Relations as my field of academic specialisation but this was after Frank retired. I regret that Frank had passed away by the time I realised that I should have talked more to him about his life-long experience in the Industrial Relations field.

My wife and children

In later life, I have been deeply influenced by my wife, Gwen, and children, Owen and Nina. I met Gwen in Melbourne in 1968, soon after I returned from a year as a graduate student at the University of Lund in Sweden. After our marriage, in November 1969, we travelled to Denmark and then moved on to London for the next four years. Gwen changed her occupation several times to accommodate my career, finally becoming a lecturer in the Department of Physiotherapy at the University of Sydney where she specialised in community health. Gwen's love and support has been central to my life and happiness. She endured my frequent absences while providing a happy and stable environment for our children. We have shared many wonderful adventures in life and work.

While parents clearly have an important influence on their children, the reverse is also true in my case. I continue to learn a great deal from both Owen and Nina. Each has forged impressive careers while bringing up their own children in an admirable way. Owen gained a degree in Fine Art from the University of New South Wales (UNSW) and spent several years in the United States during the formative era of digital design. He is the co-founder of a leading digital company PreviousNext and a Director of the global Drupal Association Board, an educational non-profit organisation which fosters the Drupal software project.

Nina also gained degrees in Arts and Science from UNSW and a PhD in Environmental Studies from Macquarie University. She is currently a Senior Lecturer in the School of Public Health at the University of Queensland and is a lead

Australian author and member of the UN Intergovernmental Panel on Climate Change (IPCC). Nina previously worked as a research scientist at the CSIRO and with various NGOs in the environmental field.

Gwen and I are immensely proud of our children, their partners and our grandchildren: Maya, Jarrah, Dane and Theo.

Primary school years

One of my earliest memories is from pre-school days when I took a short bus ride to 'kindergarten' each day. My mother would take me to the bus stop. I would pay a penny to the bus driver who would deliver me and the other children to the entrance of the school. The bus driver was Mr Stanton, and one day, I forgot to get off the bus and went all the way to the terminus. I must have been distracted while talking to his daughter, whom I recall was very nice. Amazed at finding me still sitting there, Mr Stanton asked where I lived and drove me to my home. I can remember my embarrassment at forgetting to get off at my bus stop but I may have quite liked the idea of the bus taking me all the way home.

Two things strike me about this incident, both of which reflect the high level of trust that seemed to exist in suburban Melbourne in the late 1940s. First is that young children under five years of age were permitted to take the bus by themselves to kindergarten. Certainly, I was not the only one to do this. Second, we knew the bus driver by name and that, at least on this occasion, he would take the trouble to drive an errant pre-schooler like me to my home, which was several kilometres from the bus terminal.

I attended the local primary school which was only a short walk across High Street (as it was aptly named) and later the adjacent 'Central school' which catered for the first two years of secondary education. Malvern was a comfortable middle-class area, and the children attending the local government schools were mostly of English-speaking backgrounds. There were several Catholic schools in the area which were attended by a number of children of Irish and Italian backgrounds. Sectarian conflict was still common, and there was a fair amount of name calling between the children from the two school systems. Although my parents were not religious and rarely attended any church, I was cautioned against playing with children from the Catholic schools but not really given a reason other than they were 'not like us'.

There was 'streaming' in the primary school so that children were put in rows within the classroom according to how well they performed in various tests. In second grade, when I was aged about six years, our teacher reserved one row for students whose performance was poor or who behaved badly. She ignored them and concentrated on the 'good students'. I was inclined to talk too much (and still do) and found myself banished to the 'bad students' row.

Two students were allocated to each desk, and I was placed next to a friendly boy called Geoff. He had worked out an ingenious game with a multisided pencil which he rolled up and down the desk and investigated how many times one side would appear. I think Geoff must have been working on probability theory because he later became a successful management consultant and businessman running large companies. However, my mother was horrified by my demotion and came to school the next day to ask the teacher to restore me to the 'better behaved' rows in the class. The teacher agreed but I wonder, if I had stayed with Geoff, could I have later become his business partner and very rich?

Behaviour in the school grounds during lunchtime and recess was quite friendly but there were 'gangs' with tougher boys as leaders. One of the gangs was led by a boy with the nickname of 'Pluto'. He was a bit older and bigger than most of us because he had to repeat one or two years due to poor performance. Pluto had learning difficulties and I remember giving him some help with schoolwork. I probably regarded this as 'insurance' in case I needed Pluto's assistance when hassled by one of the other gang leaders or members. There was no major bullying problem but just enough to make one careful to be on the 'right side' of the bigger boys. Perhaps, it is not surprising that such 'tribal' behaviour begins so early and then continues into other spheres of life.

One day Pluto told me that he would leave school as soon as he legally could. True to his word, Pluto disappeared after year 6. Later, I would sometimes pass by the local soft drink depot and see him loading bottles onto trucks. Pluto seemed to be a lot happier than he had been at school. But Pluto remains in my memory as someone who the school system failed. Perhaps, he did make progress later in life, like Geoff in business, but I think he would have found it hard to get ahead with only a primary school education.

Entering Central School for years 7 and 8 did not require a change of school as it was part of the same school building. Ours was a 'feeder school' for other primary schools in the area and this meant meeting students from a wider geographical region. Some of the 'new' students had parents from non-English speaking backgrounds, mostly from Europe. David, for example, was the son of Jewish immigrants from Eastern Europe. He was an outstanding student who would later gain a PhD in the United States and pursue a distinguished international career as an economist and philanthropist. David stood out from the rest of us not only for his intellectual ability but also because he excelled at sport and was a popular classmate.

I recall one day when we were asked to write an essay on a sporting event. The teacher read out the first sentence of David's essay in which the opening line was something like 'The footballer leapt into the air like a ballerina to take the mark'. I remember being amazed that football could be compared to ballet, while I had written something prosaic like 'The umpire bounced the ball and the game began'. Clearly, David was demonstrating how to write with an imagination that most of us lacked.

Adolescent years at high school

In the 1950s there was only a handful of selective high schools in Melbourne to which entry was based on academic achievement at primary school. I was fortunate to be accepted by Melbourne Boys High where I spent four years.

The Principal of Melbourne High, Bill Woodfull, was a former Australian cricket captain who led the team against England during the infamous 'bodyline' series during the 1930s. I remember walking with my friend Tom through the gates of the school on our first day at Melbourne High, just as the Principal arrived in his car. Tom said: 'Let's go and say hello'. I replied, 'We can't do that'. But Tom intercepted the Principal and said: 'Hello sir, we're new students'. I cannot recall what Bill Woodfull replied but I imagine he said something like: 'Welcome boys. Enjoy the school'. Despite his fame as a cricketer, Bill Woodfull was a reserved man but would probably have welcomed the approach by enthusiastic new students like Tom and me.

In the foreword to Alan Gregory's excellent book *Woodfull: Gentleman and Scholar* (2011), Jeremy Ludowke, Principal of Melbourne High, wrote that Woodfull would be remembered 'for humbly refusing both a knighthood and initially the captaincy of the Australian team as matters of principle'. Woodfull's obituary in the *Sunday Times* of London in 1965, by the legendary Jack Fingleton, stated: 'He preferred to be known more as a successful headmaster than as a Test captain or player. In all capacities he was eminently distinguished'.

Bill Woodfull appeared to be a modest man and did not boast about the school's achievements or give long-winded speeches. As a prefect in my final year, I saw quite a lot of him at school functions and he seemed quite aloof. However, my friend Gordon Broderick, who was Vice Captain of the school, told me that he was occasionally invited to share a sandwich at lunchtime with Woodfull who wanted to know what the students thought about issues at the school. I think that Woodfull was concerned to keep his 'finger on the pulse' without being too intrusive. However, I recall an incident when some swastikas were daubed on the school walls, and Woodfull addressed the school assembly with a forceful speech stating that such behaviour would not be tolerated. No swastikas ever reappeared. Woodfull's retirement event, held in my final year, was attended by both the Prime Minister and Governor, demonstrating the high esteem in which he was held. Bill Woodfull remains my ideal of a quiet and effective leader.

Melbourne High had a high percentage of students from non-English speaking backgrounds who had been selected on academic merit. A considerable number of students were of Jewish origin whose parents were refugees from the Nazi regime in Europe. Not only were many of these students highly intelligent but their parents were ambitious for their children to do well and encouraged them to work hard. Coming from a predominantly middle-class suburb with few immigrant families, I had to adapt to the fact that many of my classmates had names which were other than Anglo-Celtic origin. It was my introduction to an increasingly multicultural society in Australia.

After the first two years at Melbourne High, we had to choose between science and other groups of subjects for the final two years. My weakest subjects were Science and Maths but I was persuaded by my form master to choose these subjects because, in his view, 'you can learn about the humanities subjects just by reading the newspapers'. It was an unfortunate choice for me as I failed Physics and only barely passed the other science and maths subjects. However, I was able to switch to humanities and social science subjects in the final year and did much better. It was a great relief to be reading and writing about history and social studies rather than trying to understand the mysteries of science.

Teachers

There were many outstanding teachers at Melbourne High, to whom I am indebted. Graham Worrall taught history in a way that made the past seem very relevant to the present. I recall in my first year Worrall showing us facsimiles of newspapers from the early days of the Australian colonies. He read us salacious reports of crimes and misdemeanours by the convicts and others, which had us transfixed. Worrall later became a lecturer in history at Monash University. He later told me that he was disheartened by the obsession with publishing in academic journals and lack of interest in teaching and the students at University. I reconnected with Worrall at a school reunion when he was in his 80s and later corresponded with him. In retirement, he taught courses in history and opera for the University of the Third Age in a country town. He told me that was enjoying teaching as much as he had at Melbourne High, more than 40 years before!

Graham Worrall was in charge of debating and, to my surprise, chose me to be in the school debating team during the final two years of high school. My team mates included David Morawetz, who became an eminent international economist, Les Rowe who was a senior Australian diplomat and retired as Australian ambassador to Russia, and Gareth Evans who became one of the most distinguished and longest-serving Australian Foreign Ministers.

My membership of the debating team gave me a great deal of enjoyment as well as public speaking experience. We appeared on a popular TV debating programme at the time called 'Parliament of Youth' competing against a top private school. We travelled interstate and we had friendly competitions against a number of other schools. Graham Worrall never instructed us in what to say but would listen to our arguments and tell us when we needed to do more preparation. I remember one occasion when we were in Adelaide to compete against Adelaide High. I rehearsed my speech with Worrall and the team. 'That's not bad', he said, 'but give it to Gareth to polish it up a bit'. Gareth Evans was the captain of the team and brilliant debater, as evidenced by his long and successful career in the Australian Senate as well as leading the International Crisis Group in Brussels. I should have welcomed Evans improving my speech. We won the debate!

Graham Duke was another notable teacher who later became Vice Principal of Melbourne High. Graham was form master and taught Social Studies in my final year. Some teachers tended to 'spoon feed' the students, telling us what to expect on the final exam paper and what arguments to use when answering the questions. Duke never did this but taught us research skills and how to think for ourselves. Social Studies was essentially an introduction to politics in Australia and Southeast Asia, which most of us had never studied before. Instead of assigning us a textbook, Duke gave us questions to research in the library. I still remember visits to the State Library of Victoria and reading academic journals for the first time. Duke would go through our essays and ask us to do more research until he felt that we had adequately addressed the question.

Years later, I visited Graham Duke, shortly before he retired from Melbourne High and thanked him for what I had learned from his method of teaching. He told me that it was the first time he had taught Social Studies and it was beyond his area of expertise, which were Latin and the Classics. He decided that his best option was to send us off to find out the answers from research we did in the library! After his retirement as Deputy Principal of Melbourne High, Duke returned to university and completed a doctorate.

Another influential teacher was James Mollison. He taught art at Melbourne High and later became the inaugural Director of the National Art Gallery in Canberra, where he had a major influence on Australians' appreciation of art. Mollison was one of the youngest teachers and was full of enthusiasm for his subject. He encouraged students to use the art room after school and, although I showed no artistic talent, I was a regular at the 'after-school art session'. Mollison was friendly and encouraging. I recall him giving me a copy of 'Catcher in the Rye' by J.D. Salinger to read and invited me to discuss the ideas in the book with him. The conversations which I had with Mollison challenged me to think more deeply about a wide range of issues, including questioning my religious beliefs which were rather dogmatic at the time.

Mollison could be temperamental and quick to castigate students who misbehaved. One day, when Mollison was late to class, one student did a hilarious imitation of him losing his temper, not realising that Mollison had arrived and was standing behind him. Mollison reacted to the performance with good humour and continued with the lesson. For several years after finishing high school, I would visit Mollison at the Victorian Art Gallery where he was an education officer, before he was appointed to the National Art Gallery, and continue our discussions.

Influences outside school

During my adolescent years, two of my central interests were the YMCA and the local Presbyterian Church. My parents encouraged me to become a member of the YMCA which was located in the city and had an active programme for young boys. My father withdrew me from the Australian Boys Choir and the local scout group because he believed that both had been infiltrated by 'homosexuals'. The YMCA gave me opportunities to mix with boys from a wide range of socio-economic backgrounds, access to sporting activities, camping holidays and leadership experience. I remained involved with the YMCA until my early years as a lecturer at Monash University and occasionally taught at the YMCA Leadership College in Melbourne.

During the 1950s and 1960s, churches played an important role in many communities as a place for people to meet socially. Many churches had active youth groups and hosted dances on a weekend where young people could meet.

Many secondary schools during this era were segregated by gender, so any opportunities to meet girls were greatly welcomed. My local Presbyterian Church was a focus of social activity many of us had our first flirtations there. But I was also interested in the religious aspects of the church and for a time during my teenage years, I thought seriously about becoming a minister. Fortunately, however, the local minister at my church advised me to consider training in another field and then consider entering the ministry when I had some experience of the world. This was good advice as I had a number of friends who began theological studies at university but dropped out before completing their education.

My religious zeal had diminished by the time I left school and I became disillusioned with the evangelical approach which appeared to be taking over student Christian organisations with which I had been associated. I also became sceptical about many of the teachings of the church, particularly as I came into contact with people of other faiths at university. My break with organised religion came slowly and I retain a respect for other people's religious beliefs. I look back at my church-going years, and the friends I made through church-related activities and the YMCA, with gratitude. Yet I am appalled at the consequences of religious prejudice and the role which some religious leaders and institutions have played in the sexual abuse of young and vulnerable people.

When I review my childhood and adolescence, I realise that my parents imparted a number of values which have influenced my life. They both had a strong work ethic and were not materialistic. They treated people with respect and equality, irrespective of their wealth or status. However, they did reflect some of the prejudices which were common to their era. Whilst not religious, they were anti-Catholic. Yet my parents were not racially prejudiced, welcomed guests who I invited to our home from all parts of the world. This had some humorous aspects. On occasion, I informed my parents that I wished to invite my new girlfriend home for dinner but said that there was something I should tell them about her. 'Don't tell me she is Catholic' asked Len. 'No, she is Chinese', I replied. 'Well that's a relief' he said. But I did not tell him that she had attended a convent when at school in Hong Kong.

I was fortunate to grow up in an era when greater tolerance and rights were gained, after hard won struggles, in regard to religion, race and sexuality. There are still many barriers to gaining human rights around the world, but these are now more achievable due to the campaigns which were waged at great cost by activists and reformers in recent decades. I had the privilege of education and exposure to a greater range of information and experience than was available to my parents. My later curiosity to explore the world beyond my origins was supported by my parents who also embraced the friends I made at university from other cultures and countries. Hence, my early life and education were crucial influences which led to my later academic career in Work and Industrial Relations.

2 The world opens up at university (1963–1967)

I entered the University of Melbourne in 1963 after completing my final year of high school with first class honours in Australian History and Social Studies. I received a teaching scholarship from the Victorian Education Department which paid my tuition fees and a living allowance. On completion of our undergraduate degree, we were required to complete a Diploma of Education and then teach for three years.

I recall that many high achieving students at Melbourne High opted for teaching for several reasons. The teaching scholarship offered a modest but adequate allowance and this made it particularly attractive to students from less affluent backgrounds. However, teaching was also regarded as a worthy career. Many of us at Melbourne High admired our dedicated and gifted teachers and saw ourselves following their example. I aimed to become an educational psychologist and enrolled in a Bachelor of Arts with majors in Psychology and Political Science.

My choice of academic studies was largely determined by the terms of my teaching scholarship. To become a school counsellor required a three year major in Psychology followed by a Diploma of Education. I also needed to choose subjects that would be useful for classroom teaching. Hence, I undertook a second major in Political Science and a minor in English. However, an Arts degree at the University of Melbourne in the 1960s also required one year of a foreign language. I chose Swedish simply because there were few options for starting a new language and I did not wish to continue with Latin. I was told that Swedish was an easy language to learn and, while this was not true in my case, the choice of Swedish turned out to be a significant decision in terms of my later life and career. I subsequently became a graduate student at the University of Lund in 1967–1968 and undertook a number of research collaborations with Nordic colleagues during the next 50 years.

Finding my feet at university

My academic record during my first three years at the University of Melbourne was lacklustre. I did not find Psychology as interesting as I had anticipated and only managed to gain ordinary passes in Political Science subjects. However,

I was fortunate to take a unit in Political Sociology with the late Alan Davies during my third year. This was a fascinating subject and Davies was a wonderful teacher. His course was a combination of Psychology and Sociology applied to the study of politics. One of the exercises he gave us was to interview people about their early political experiences. The person I interviewed had been involved in the 'mass observation' movement in Britain during the late 1930s, which trained volunteers to anonymously record people's conversations on the street and at various public occasions. In many ways this was the forerunner of gathering and studying public opinion. Davies liked the report I wrote of my interview and read parts of it to the class as it illustrated some of the concepts which he was teaching us. It was the first time that I received recognition for anything I had written at university and it boosted my confidence.

I also recall taking a mind-expanding course in Political Philosophy with Max Charlesworth, one of Australia's most eminent philosophers, who enjoyed and encouraged student engagement in the subject. Our tutor was Father Eric D'Arcy, a Jesuit priest who later became Archbishop of Hobart. D'Arcy had doctorates in Philosophy from both Oxford and the Gregorian University in Rome and was an authority on the work of Thomas Aquinas. The course covered a wide range of political philosophies from Marx to Aquinas, which could have been very heavy-going material, but Charlesworth and D'Arcy made it all accessible and interesting. Our tutorial was in the late afternoon and one of the students, Neil Watson, suggested that we continue the discussions at his house nearby over a flagon of claret (the cheap student choice of that era). D'Arcy joined us and both wine and discussion flowed freely into the evening. It was a revelation to me that academic discussions could actually be so enjoyable. Neil Watson became a life-long friend and colleague in the labour movement and our political philosophy debates continue to this day!

I am greatly indebted to Alan Davies. He awarded me first class honours for Political Sociology, which was the first time I had gained honours for any subject during my first three years at university. More importantly, Davies revealed to me how Psychology and Sociology could be applied to Political Science. At last, I had found a subject which inspired me. When I thanked Davies for his class, he suggested that I should pursue further honours subjects. On his own initiative, Davies contacted the Education Department and asked that I be given an extra year to complete the final year's honours subjects. Fortunately, permission was granted, and I was admitted to the honours programme with the continuation of my teachers' scholarship for an additional year.

This was my most exciting year at the University of Melbourne. I was required to take all of the honours units that I had missed during my three years of undergraduate study plus a final year honours unit and then write a thesis during the following year. I studied these units with great relish and was pleased when I completed the year with first class honours in three units and shared the Jeanette Kosky prize for International Relations. There were a number of excellent students in the final honours year, two of whom remain my friends to this day. David Hegarty became an academic at the University of Papua New Guinea and subsequently a senior adviser to the Australian ministers of Trade and Foreign Affairs and High Commissioner in the Pacific. Derek McDougall gained a PhD from Duke University in the United States and became a leading academic in International Relations at Melbourne University. I successfully applied for a Rotary International Graduate Scholarship which enabled me to spend the following year at the University of Lund in Sweden. Alan Davies agreed to supervise my comparative research project on Australia and Sweden for a Master's degree in Political Science from the University of Melbourne.

Alan Davies was a remarkable academic who had a wide range of interests and expertise. His first book to have a major impact was *Australian Democracy* (1958), which became a standard work, in which he coined the much quoted phrase 'the characteristic talent of Australians …is for bureaucracy'. Like Donald Horne's reference to Australia as a 'Lucky Country', Davies did not mean his aphorism to be taken literally! He was a prolific author with a range of books on a variety of topics including: *Private Politics* (1966), *Images of Class* (1967), *Politics as Work* (1973). According to James Walter, in his entry on Davies in the *Australian Dictionary of Biography* (2007), his masterwork was *Skills, Outlooks and Passions* (1980) in which Davies showed 'how individuals work, think and perceive (are) the integral components of politics'. Walter nicely sums up my experience of Alan Davies' supervisory style: 'Davies encouraged people to articulate their projects and to discover their own potentials and impediments, while also suggesting fresh insights, different angles and apposite readings… He was also a pioneer of interdisciplinary dialogue' (Walter, 2007).

Sadly, Alan Davies died in his early 60s.

Life beyond the classroom

It is difficult to imagine the transformation of universities around the world during the 1960s. In 1962, when I commenced my studies at the University of Melbourne, only about 10 per cent of young people in my age group attended university. Australia was a very conservative society during the 1950s and 1960s, governed by a Liberal-Country Party coalition government, led by Prime Minister Robert Menzies. Universities were elite institutions drawing their students primarily from private schools and selective government high schools. It was not uncommon for lecturers to wear academic gowns when they taught and for male students to wear ties and jackets, particularly those studying law. Women were a small minority of students, particularly in professional degrees such as Law and Medicine. However, the conservative or apolitical mood on campus was to change dramatically during the second half of the 1960s with protests against the Vietnam War. Opposition to the war escalated once the federal government introduced conscription of young men to be sent to Vietnam to serve in the Australian armed forces.

My studies at the university were augmented by participating in several student clubs and societies, including the Debating Society, the International Club and the World University Service (WUS). The International Club was the first student organisation which I joined. The purpose of the club was not only to discuss international issues but also to enjoy social activities involving local and international students. I made several long-lasting friendships with students from Asia and became President of the club. I recall my first experience of organising the annual residential conference when I invited various academics to speak, including Professor W. Macmahon Ball, head of the Department of Political Science at the University. It was held during a weekend at a beach-side guest house and attended by about 50 students.

We put up posters around the university with Macmahon Ball featured as a keynote speaker. I was surprised when I received a note from his secretary telling me that the professor wanted to see me urgently. He was quite upset and said that he had only given a provisional acceptance to speak and was now not available. I was devastated, particularly as I was taking his class in International Relations. However, he told me that he had arranged for his friend and prominent journalist Denis Warner to attend in his place. Warner proved to be an fascinating speaker on emerging conflicts in Southeast Asia and stayed on after his talk to engage with the students. I doubt that Warner would have spoken to our small student conference unless Macmahon Ball had asked him to do so. The conference was a great success but taught me a lesson to make sure I confirm speakers before publicising their attendance! I subsequently enjoyed good relations with Macmahon Ball, and he admitted me to honours programme in Political Science, which set me on the path to an academic career.

This was the first time I had organised such an event and, apart from my mistake with Macmahon Ball, I was surprised at how willing academics were to attend and speak at functions organised by the International Club. One person whom I contacted to speak at the first conference, Jamie Mackie, became a life-long mentor and friend. I remember going to Mackie's office to invite him to speak and being surprised when he asked me my opinion about some international issue at that time. I could not imagine that an academic would be interested in the views of a student. Mackie became head of the Centre for Asian Studies at Monash and later a professor at ANU. He demonstrated to me the importance of showing a genuine interest in students and seeking to understand their view of the world rather than assuming that all knowledge resides with the teacher.

Towards the end of my undergraduate degree, interest in International Relations led me to apply to be a graduate entrant into the Australian Department of Foreign Affairs. I was interviewed by an official from the Australian Security and Intelligence Office (ASIO) who informed me that I would not gain the necessary security clearance because I had been involved with the International Club, which was deemed to be 'a Communist front' organisation. He based this assertion on the fact that the International Club received newsletters and magazines from the embassies of countries such as the Soviet Union and China. I pointed out to him that we also received publications from the United States and Germany, a practice which had started well before my time. However, the ASIO official stated that I could 'clear my name' if I could keep him informed about

20 The world opens up at university

the activities of certain student activists. I declined to assist him and thus ended my attempt to join Foreign Affairs. I am sure that one of the students which ASIO had in their sights was Gareth Evans, with whom I shared a house. Evans was President of the Student Council at the University and active in various campaigns such as anti-apartheid movement. He would later become a highly successful Australian Foreign Minister and Chancellor of the Australian National University.

WUS was active on campus raising funds to assist students in third-world universities. WUS began in the 1920s to assist students facing hardship after the First World War, mainly in Europe. By the 1960s the focus of its main activities was in Asia, Latin America and Africa. WUS still has operations in over 50 countries but is less active at Australian universities. One of the reasons that its fund-raising activities may have declined in Australia is that its main source of income was holding the 'Miss University' contest on campuses. However, the contest was not a beauty pageant but was based on a candidate's academic and other achievements. Faculties and residential colleges would select a candidate and hold fund-raising events with the successful candidate announced at the annual 'Miss University' Ball. This seems to belong to a long-ago era of gender stereotyping. However, one successful candidate was Gillian Triggs, who would later become an eminent lawyer, academic, President of the Australian Human Rights Commission and senior UN official.

Another fund-raising event undertaken by WUS was an International Concert at Wilson Hall at the University of Melbourne. We were fortunate to gain the services of an experienced organiser who donated her time and ensured the success of the event. Such multicultural events are commonplace these days as we now have a rich array of immigrants, as well as students, from around the world. But in the mid-1960s it was relatively unusual to bring together a wide range of students from Asia and Africa, as well as from Latin America and Europe, for such a venture. I recall seeking an appointment with the Vice-Chancellor, Sir George Paton. I asked him if he would let us use Wilson Hall without charge and invited him to open the concert. He agreed to do both. When I entered his office, instead of finding him at his desk, he was seated at a roaring fire reading a book. I imagine that the VC was just taking time out of a busy schedule but the image of academic administration in those days was more genteel and relaxed than it is today! Our international concert gained feature articles in the media and a full house. It was a great success and fund raiser.

My involvement with international students led to some part-time work with Radio Australia which was a section of the Australian Broadcasting Commission (ABC) which transmitted programmes to Asia. I was involved with writing and delivering short programmes of topical interest such as the construction of the Sydney Opera House as well as some Australian history topics which were deemed to be of interest to listeners in neighbouring countries. I met a number of staff at Radio Australia from various parts of Asia. I became particularly friendly with the Indonesian broadcasters, spending time at their homes and enjoying their company. This opened my eyes to a different culture to my middle-class Anglo-Australian background.

This was a delicate period in Australian-Indonesian relations as it was during President Sukarno's policy of 'konfrontasi' or confrontation between Indonesia and its Malaysian neighbours. Australian troops were deployed to assist the Malaysians, and there was the risk of armed conflict between Indonesian and Australian forces. This was embarrassing for the Australian government as a number of Indonesian military personnel were being trained in Australia at the time. Indonesian staff at Radio Australia were also broadcasting the Australian government's perspective on the conflict.

Up for debate

Another major activity at university during my undergraduate years was with the Debating Society. I joined one of the many teams which the University of Melbourne fielded in the Victorian Debating Association. We competed against teams from a wide range of debating clubs including one from Melbourne's Pentridge jail. The team from Pentridge was called 'LaTrobe', which was confusing as there was a university with the same name! I was elected to the executive of the Melbourne University Debating Society and became Assistant Secretary to Gareth Evans who was Secretary. The President was David Kemp. Evans and Kemp were contemporaries in the Law School and both were outstanding scholars. Kemp won a scholarship to Yale University in the United States where he obtained a PhD while Evans won a prestigious Shell Scholarship to Oxford University. Both would later become Senators and Government ministers on opposite sides: Kemp with the Liberal Party and Evans for Labor. Both were formidable debaters and were on the same side of victorious teams representing the University of Melbourne in Intervarsity competitions.

The first time I tried out for the Melbourne University Intervarsity team I was unsuccessful, but I was selected as a reserve member for the competition which was held at the University of Adelaide. When we arrived in Adelaide, I discovered that one of the universities had failed to send a team as planned. I spoke with the reserve members of the Monash team and we proposed to the organisers that we be permitted to replace the missing team in the programme under the name 'Melbash' (i.e. Melbourne and Monash combined). We were accepted on the basis that we were just filling a vacant spot and were not expected to win. But to everyone's surprise, we won our first couple of debates and found ourselves facing the University of Adelaide team in the semi-final. Our team was judged to be the winner, but a protest was lodged by the captain of the Adelaide team, John Bannon. His protest was successful, and we were not permitted to contest the final round. Bannon would later become Labor Premier of South Australia. I think he must have felt a little shame-faced because I remember being driven by him in his battered car to some wild parties during the week of the competition.

Although I was active in various student organisations, I was not affiliated with any political party and initially remained aloof from the emerging opposition to the Vietnam War. I was invited by David Kemp, whom I knew through the debating club, to attend a Liberal Party gathering at his home where a young up-and-coming Liberal MP, Andrew Peacock, was speaking. I was shocked to

22 The world opens up at university

hear Peacock announce at the meeting that the federal government was considering the introduction of conscription of young men to be sent to the emerging conflict in Vietnam. I raised my concerns but these were brushed aside by Peacock, who would later become Minister for the Army. It was not until I spent a year in Sweden in 1967–1968, and was exposed to more information about the war, that I became actively opposed to Australia's participation in the conflict. The Swedish Social Democratic government had extended recognition to the National Liberation Front of Vietnam, and there was much greater coverage of the war from the North Vietnamese perspective in Sweden than I had seen in Australia.

Leaving home

In 1966, at the end of my third year at university, I left home and rented a room in a house in Carlton owned by a former student, Bruce Pollard, whom I had met through the International Club. He had just started an academic career teaching English Literature at what became Swinburne University. He would later establish Pinacotheca which became one of Melbourne's leading avant-garde art galleries for more than 30 years. Pollard bought a pair of old terraces in Drummond Street Carlton. He lived in one of the houses upstairs and I shared downstairs, with Gareth Evans in the front room and me in the back. Pollard rented the next-door terrace to female university students and felt it was best to segregate the sexes. However, we shared the backyard, and there was a free flow of activity between the houses.

This was an exhilarating year having left home and catching up on three years of honours subjects in Political Science. At last, academic progress had been achieved. Evans was in his final year of Law and would win the Supreme Court prize, as the top student of his year. There was a constant stream of people involved in student politics passing through the house. One visitor I recall was Richard Walsh, who was a prominent student activist from Sydney University, a co-editor of *Oz* Magazine and would later become a major force in publishing, including a period as head of Australian Consolidated Press. Another visitor was John Paterson who preceded Gareth as SRC President. Paterson was a brilliant and dominating personality who would become one of Australia's most influential public servants. John was born with diastrophic dwarfism which restricted his height but not his fierce intellect.

One of Gareth Evans' important initiatives, in which I had a minor involvement, was starting a version of the Oxford Union debates at the University of Melbourne. Issues of current significance were debated with major political and community figures as well as students represented in each team. The student audience would vote to determine which team won the debate. The Union Debates were a great success. One of the emerging issues of the time was Australia's participation in the Vietnam War. I recall a vigorous debate with Dr Jim Cairns, a leading Labor Party opponent against the war, leading one side while the Minister for Aviation, Peter Howson led the other. Howson had served as a pilot in Britain during the Second World War and had a long scar on his face from being shot down by German aircraft. There was no doubting Howson's courage as he withstood heckling by students opposed to the war. However, he was dropped from the Ministry by Prime Minister John Gorton for misusing VIP aircraft early the following year. Jim Cairns, on the other hand, led major demonstrations against the war and became Deputy Prime Minister in the Whitlam government.

I took part in a Union Debate just before the 1967 referendum on changes to the constitution to improve the rights of Indigenous Australians and to include them in the national census. The debate was on 'Integration versus Assimilation'. I spoke on the side led by Gordon Bryant who would later be the Minister for Aboriginal Affairs in the Whitlam Labor government, along with Colin Benjamin who became a leader in social welfare policy and social change. I was inspired by Gordon Bryant who had been a passionate supporter of indigenous land rights since the mid-1950s and was subsequently instrumental in the Whitlam government's historic granting of land rights to the Gurindji people in the Northern Territory. However, it now seems shocking that we did not have an Indigenous speaker on our side in that debate. This reflected our failure to identify people who could have taken that role and the rather paternalistic approach among those of us who were seeking to promote Indigenous people's rights.

At the end of the year, Gareth Evans vacated his room in Drummond Street and was replaced by Bruce Hartnett, who was his successor as President of the SRC. Hartnett had also been a student at Melbourne High and was studying Engineering. Like Evans before him, Hartnett won a Shell Postgraduate Scholarship to the University of London while Evans went to Oxford. All three of us would find ourselves as postgraduate students in the United Kingdom in 1970. Hartnett had a significant career in the trade union movement, becoming a policy adviser to Labor ministers and holding senior positions in both the public and private sectors. We have remained friends since that time.

I was also fortunate to meet Harvey Williams towards the end of my undergraduate studies. He was undertaking a double degree in Arts and Commerce, and we had a common interest in international relations. While I travelled to India and Southeast Asia on my first trip overseas, Williams went with a university student group to China. He was there during winter at the height of the Cultural Revolution and brought back first-hand accounts of the situation. Harvey Williams and I would be each other's 'best man' at our respective weddings and have continued to be close friends. While I entered academia, Williams spent his career with General Motors Holden, becoming the Fund Secretary of the Holden Employees Superannuation Fund. He provided me with valuable insights and contacts in the automotive industry, which became a focus of my research.

Learning and earning

Like many students of my generation, and is even more common today, it was necessary to work during the long vacations as well as have a part-time job during the academic year. Even though I was fortunate to have a scholarship from the Victorian Education Department, which paid my fees and provided a modest weekly stipend, it was not sufficient to pay for the maintenance of a car and pay rent. I remained at home for the first three years of my undergraduate course. However, I had to pay board to my parents and I also bought an old second-hand car which always seemed to need repairs. The car enabled me to travel to my job on Friday and Saturday evenings as a waiter at a fashionable Palm Lake 'Outrigger Room' overlooking Melbourne's Albert Park Lake. It also had a wonderful jazz combo on Saturday nights and I enjoyed working there.

I obtained the job at Palm Lake at the end of my first year at university and worked there for the next three or four years. I learned a great deal from this experience, starting as food waiter and 'moving up' to a wine waiter role. Most of the full-time kitchen staff and waiters were recent immigrants from various parts of Europe and it took me quite a while to win their acceptance. The head waiter was Danish and seemed to regard me with such disdain that I was amazed that I survived in the job. We were supposed to address him as 'sir' and I always felt under scrutiny as he waited to find fault with my work. After a year or so I became reasonably competent and he left me alone. However, it was a relief when he left and was replaced by Arthur who had been head waiter in his earlier days at one of the most prestigious restaurants in Melbourne at the 'Hotel Australia'. As head waiter, Arthur transformed work at the restaurant and made my life a lot easier. Even before he became the head waiter, Arthur would occasionally take me aside when he saw I was struggling and say: 'Russell you have a lot of customers tonight, let me give you a hand' and would then show me some of the short cuts and techniques to make the job easier.

My experience as a waiter provided me with some important lessons which I later found useful in my later life when I had to manage people in the workplace. The first head waiter taught me the importance of being competent at the job, but his sarcastic and disdainful treatment of the kitchen staff and waiters created considerable resentment and soured relations. By contrast, his successor won respect and affection from the staff due to his collaborative approach. When there were crises due to a staff shortage or large numbers of customers, we would put in extra effort to clear the backlog, with Arthur working among us and leading by example. I later read the classic sociological study by William Foote Whyte *The Social Structure of the Restaurant* (1949), based on participant observation of restaurants in Chicago in the 1940s. I realised that I had possibly missed a great opportunity to undertake an Australian follow-up study!

I also sought a part-time job as a waiter at University House on campus. This was a 'club' for academics where they could frequent the bar, have meals and hold meetings without the interference of students. I sought out the manager Mr Pavlos and explained my experience as a waiter. He told me that they never employed students at the club as that might make the academics feel uncomfortable. Nevertheless, he arranged for me to be interviewed by the President of University House who was a Professor of Geography. He repeated the advice I had received from the manager that students were not regarded as suitable employees as they might overhear confidential discussions between academics. However, he agreed that I could be hired as an 'experiment' as long as I agreed to keep the content of any private conversations to myself.

Mr Pavlos was Hungarian and had run a successful restaurant in Carlton which was popular among academics from the University. When the committee that ran University House was looking for a new manager, they approached Pavlos and offered him the job. He agreed as long as he could bring his staff with him. Most of the staff were Hungarian, and the signature dish was goulash. Perhaps, the reluctance of Pavlos to hire students might have been that he wanted to preserve the jobs in University House for Hungarian speakers?

It proved to be an interesting casual job as there were a number of functions involving visiting dignitaries. On one occasion, I was asked to look after Mr Lee Kwan Yew, then Chief Minister of Singapore, which was still part of Malaysia, and his wife. Lee was in his early 40s at that time and just emerging as a major international political figure. Lee asked for a beer but I spilled it when serving him. 'Are you an Australian?' he inquired. When I responded yes he asked 'But you don't know how to pour a beer properly?' He then proceeded to show me how to tilt the glass to prevent the beer from frothing over. Unfortunately, I did not get the chance to ask him about the political situation in Singapore at the time!

On another occasion, I was asked to wait on the Chancellor, Sir Robert Menzies, who was presiding over a small private function. Menzies was very fond of oysters and kept asking me to replenish his supply but I spilled some on the table. As expected, I was reprimanded by Mr Pavlos who told me that there had been a complaint. However, it was not that I had spilled the oysters but that I had been hovering around and listening to the conversation. Unfortunately, this was true. However, as I recall, nothing of significance was being discussed. After several months, Pavlos said that my services were no longer required. I was not sure if I had failed in my waiting duties or that students were not welcome as employees. Perhaps both factors led to the end of my brief career at University House?

A passage to India and South East Asia in 1965

My involvement with Asian students in the International Club and WUS made me keen to visit Asia. The National Union of Australian University Students (NUAUS) had just begun to organise trips to Asia during the long summer vacation commencing. In December 1965, I travelled to India by ship and then returned to Australia via several South East Asian countries. There were about 20 of us from various Australian universities on the trip to India, and it was the first time many of us had travelled outside Australia. International travel was still an expensive undertaking in the mid-1960s, and most people travelled by ship as this was much cheaper than flying. We had the cheapest tickets in the lower deck of the *Canberra*, which would later take troops from Australia to the war in Vietnam. The voyage to Colombo took about 10 days, and we entertained ourselves by having students give informal talks on various aspects of India. I recall that George Michel, an architecture student whom I had known at Melbourne High, gave some fascinating talks on Indian art and culture. He later became a well-known author of books on Indian architecture.

We travelled across to India by ferry from Sri Lanka (then known as Ceylon) and then began a long journey by train from the south to the north of India. We had initial accommodation arranged at Indian universities as well as home stays which had been arranged before we left Australia. We travelled as a whole group for the first week or so and then split into smaller groups which we informally arranged while on the voyage from Australia. I teamed up with Emma, an architecture student and Philip with whom I had studied Psychology at Melbourne University. We had many adventures as we travelled as far north as Nepal and visited many places en route. Our visit coincided with conflict between India and Pakistan, and we encountered soldiers returning from war zones on the border when we stayed as guests of a military family in the Delhi cantonment. It was a continuous culture shock and sometimes quite gruelling as we travelled in third class rail coaches and slept in railway stations to economise on accommodation. I was robbed in Kanpur and entered Nepal without my passport which caused problems when I tried to re-enter India. But our experiences were overwhelmingly positive as we received generous hospitality from many locals on our travels. Philip left us in Calcutta to travel on to England.

Emma and I flew from India to Thailand and then travelled by local buses across to the Angkor Wat in Cambodia. This was the calm before the storm which engulfed Cambodia as the war in Vietnam escalated. After Emma returned to Melbourne from Bangkok, I spent another few weeks travelling to Malaysia, the Philippines and Hong Kong. In each of these places, I met with friends who had studied at Melbourne University and then returned to their home countries. It was interesting to meet friends in their own environment in which we effectively changed places as they were 'at home' and I was the foreigner having to adjust to a new environment. Having been involved with Asia at a distance through my roles in the International Club and WUS as well as studying politics and international relations, I was now confronted by the reality of Asia in all its complexity.

An unexpected shock awaited me in Hong Kong where I looked forward to meeting the family of my friend Anna, with whom I had studied in Melbourne. I attended the wedding of her brother and felt welcome until I learned from her sister that Anna's Chinese parents were very unhappy that she had an Australian boyfriend. Anna was to return to Melbourne University to complete her teaching qualification but was prevented from doing so as her parents disapproved of her relationship with me. This was a case of prejudice directed at me by her parents who wanted to avoid the possibility that their daughter might marry a foreigner and remain in Australia.

After returning from Asia, during my final year as an undergraduate, I was increasingly involved with NUAUS. I became the local coordinator of Australia Overseas Student Travel and assisted in promoting and organising an expanding programme which extended beyond India to China, Japan, Malaysia and Indonesia. I was also elected as the director of overseas student welfare for NUAUS. The number of overseas students was still small by current standards and a large proportion was on Colombo Plan and other scholarships funded by the Australian government.

The President of NUAUS was Geoffrey Robertson who would later become an internationally famous human rights lawyer as well as a TV celebrity though his programme 'Hypotheticals'. Robertson had a keen interest in expanding aid and support to international students. When I attended my first executive meeting of NUAUS, Robertson interrogated me on what initiatives I had taken and was not impressed with my answers. I experienced something of what it would be like being cross-examined by Geoffrey Robertson QC in his later career. He was correct in his admonition of me and I proceeded to put greater effort into my role. Robertson was one of several impressive NUAUS Presidents during my undergraduate years who would later make significant contributions to society. They included Michael Kirby on the High Court, Tony McMichael in the World Health Organisation and Peter Wilenski in public administration and its reform.

Journey to Sweden via the United States and Europe: 1967–1968

During my fourth year at university, I began to look for postgraduate study opportunities and applied for a Rotary Foundation Graduate Scholarship which offered a year of study in an overseas university. There was a special category for students who were competent in a foreign language which would enable them to study at a university which no Rotary scholarship students had previously attended. The University of Lund in Sweden was on the list. Having studied Swedish was now a great advantage! I am grateful to my Swedish teacher at the University of Melbourne, Marianne Harry, who encouraged me to apply for the scholarship and insisted that I maintain my Swedish language. I was sponsored by Box Hill Rotary Club whose President, Dr John Booth, enthusiastically supported my application. I also gained permission from the Victorian Department of Education to suspend studies for my Diploma of Education for one year. Hence, in May 1967, I made my way to Sweden via North America and parts of Europe. The Rotary Foundation generously allowed me to take a couple of months to travel to Sweden on the basis that I would visit a number of universities on the way which would assist my research for my postgraduate studies.

The United States

My experiences in the United States were overwhelming. When I landed in Los Angeles, the 'black ghettos' across the United States were ablaze and the civil rights movement was entering a more radical phase. I sought accommodation in a student residence on the campus of the University of California Los Angeles (UCLA) and was invited to attend a rally in the main football stadium which was addressed by the charismatic Afro-American student activist Stokely Carmichael.

The stadium filled to capacity with students listening to Carmichael spell out the demands of the Black Panther Party, for which he was 'Prime Minister'. He was one of the original 'Freedom Riders' who sought to gain voting rights for Afro-Americans in the Deep South of the United States. He was only 26 years old at the time I heard him at UCLA and spellbinding. From UCLA I travelled to the University of California at Berkeley where there was even greater student unrest. I recall sitting on a bus going to Berkeley and trying to strike up a conversation with a young Afro-American women who told me that she did not speak with 'white guys'. I naively stated that I was Australian and would like to understand more about racism in the United States and she then became more friendly and explained the situation to me. Later at Berkeley I attended parties where black and white students mixed freely. It was a time of ferment with the simultaneous emergence of the 'hippie' movement, black rights and anti-Vietnam War campaign.

In 1967, the conflict in Vietnam was increasing and would culminate in the Tet Offensive in early 1968 in which over 500 US soldiers were killed and more than 2,500 were wounded. Students on campuses throughout the United States were demonstrating against the drafting of conscripts. In 1970, there occurred the tragic shooting of students at Kent State University. The first Australian military had just begun operations in Vietnam and Australian opposition to the war was increasing. The activism and radicalisation of students in the United States was greater than in Australia at this time. The student rallies on US campuses from Berkeley to Harvard made a big impression on me at the time.

I was grateful for the hospitality I received from students and others during my month in the United States. In Berkeley, I stayed for a week in a house with a number of graduate students. One of them was Mel Bloom who was doing a PhD in Education and invited me to stay with his parents in Boston. He had recently returned from a period with the Peace Corps in Venezuela and explained to me that he had written a critique of the way the programme was run and had made an appointment with Senator Edward Kennedy to discuss his concerns. I was incredulous that he would gain access to Kennedy. But he was adamant: 'Of course he will see me. He is my Senator (from Massachusetts) and his brother (JFK) set up the Peace Corps, so he will want to hear what I have to say'. I don't know if he succeeded but I was impressed at the confidence that Bloom expressed about the access that he could obtain to Kennedy.

Introduction to elite US universities

True to his word, Mel Bloom's parents accepted me as 'a member of the family', and I stayed with them at their house in Mattapan. His dad was a meat cutter at the Boston market and I travelled in early with him and saw how the market came alive in the early hours of the morning. I also visited Harvard and discovered that it was 'Commencement Week' when students graduate and thousands of parents and friends descend on the campus for celebrations. There were many eminent academics, writers and public figures giving lectures and I was able to simply walk into lecture theatres and listen to them. I heard lectures by John Kenneth Galbraith, Daniel Patrick Moynihan and several other major academic and political figures in the United States at the time.

While at Harvard, I took the opportunity to contact the eminent Harvard sociologist David Reisman. He was about 60 years old at the time and was one of the most influential social scientists of that period. Reisman had published an iconic book *The Lonely Crowd: A Study of the Changing American Character* (1950) in which he argued that American society was shifting from one based on production to one fundamentally shaped by the market orientation of a consumer culture. Reisman cited modern suburbia as having a strong influence on individuals to conform to their neighbours' approval due to fear of being outcast from their community. This was a highlight for me as the focus of my Master's thesis was a comparison of suburban life and leisure in Australian and Swedish suburbs. Reisman was gracious and remarked that he had just read an interesting book about Australia called *The Fern and the Tiki* (Ausubel, 1960), which dealt with national character and social attitudes. Alas, I had to correct him that this book was about New Zealand rather than Australia but this did not seem to disturb him!

I gained a great deal from the weeks I spent in the United States. I stayed mainly in campus accommodation which was far more luxurious than the equivalent student housing in Australia. I was fortunate to be there at the end of the academic year when students were just commencing their summer holidays. I received generous hospitality wherever I went, with invitations to stay with people, eat at their homes and be shown around campuses and adjacent towns. I met a number of academics who provided insights into my research topic. Philip Ennis at the University of Chicago had written extensively on suburbanisation in the United States and pointed out the obvious fact to me that much of this trend was due to 'white flight' from the inner cities where poorer black families were moving into decaying inner cities replacing the departing whites. While the US situation was more dramatic, there were parallels in other countries like Australia and Sweden where poorer recent immigrants were moving into urban centres while the suburbs were being populated by more affluent residents.

My last stop in the United States was New York City where I stayed in a student residence on the campus of Columbia University. I visited Colin Williams who was, at that time, the Director of the National Council of Churches (NCC). He took me on a tour of some of the most deprived areas in New York City and told me about the urban renewal activities which were being driven by the NCC in collaboration with some of the black churches. I had briefly met Williams when he was Professor of Theology at Queen's College at the University of Melbourne. He became a reforming Dean of Yale Divinity School. I gained an introduction to Colin Williams by his brother Morris who was in charge of teaching practice for social studies in the Faculty of Education at Melbourne University when I was studying for a Diploma of Education. Morris Williams sent me for teaching practice to one of the more economically deprived areas of Melbourne as well as to an elite private school, Wesley College, where he had been a teacher before joining the University of Melbourne. Another brother was Bruce Williams who was the Vice-Chancellor at the University of Sydney but had retired by the time I arrived there many years later.

Little did I realise that I would later return on sabbatical leave and on short visits in the years that followed to some of the best US universities, including the University of Wisconsin-Madison, MIT, Harvard, Cornell and the University of California at Berkeley and Los Angeles. This brief introduction in the summer of 1967 revealed the wealth of scholarship which exists at these remarkable academic institutions. I have also gained from generous collaboration with American academics. Yet the deep racial conflict and inequality which I observed in 1967 not only continues but has increased during recent years, particularly during the Presidency of Donald Trump.

Europe

I arrived in London in early June 1967 and linked up with my friend Phil Badger with whom I had travelled in India two years previously. Badger had made his way overland to England and was working as a psychologist at an institution just out of London. In Badger's car, we travelled around the main sights in the south of England, including the West Country and Oxford, staying in hostels and occasionally in parks. Although this was supposed to be the 'Swinging Sixties' era in Britain, the country seemed very despondent compared with the United States. This may have been due to the problems facing the Labour government, led by Harold Wilson, which had imposed austerity policies in order to prevent the economy sinking deeper into recession. I visited a friend who was at Oxford who showed me around the university but it seemed 'other worldly' compared with the vibrancy which I had experienced on American campuses. Nevertheless, I would be very grateful three years later when I was admitted as a PhD student at the London School of Economics on a scholarship initiated by the Wilson Labour government through its training and research levy on British industry.

I made my way across the English Channel to Paris and Geneva and felt the limitations imposed by my lack of French. I visited a friend at the Australian embassy whose parents lived in Geneva, and he invited me to stay with them. He told me that this would be the first of many visits I would make to Europe over the course of my life but at the time I believed that this would probably be my one and only visit as Australia seemed very far away.

Arriving in Geneva, I headed to the headquarters to gain a glimpse of the United Nations, which I had admired for many years. By chance, I discovered that the UN was conducting a summer intern programme for potential recruits from an array of countries. The person in charge of the programme told me that successful applicants had been chosen from a wide range of candidates many months previously. However, as there were no Australians in the intake, he offered me the opportunity to be an 'observer'. This enabled me to 'unofficially' participate in the programme. I was able to stay with the rest of the participants in student accommodation at the university and to attend lectures and discussions by a wide range of UN officials and consultants. This was a great experience and sharpened my ambition to one day join the UN or one of its affiliated institutions.

Looking back on my undergraduate university days, I feel extremely fortunate to have had the opportunities to participate in so many extra curricula activities and to have travelled extensively around the world. The teachers' scholarship provided me with free education and a basic income while studying plus the guarantee of employment when I finished my studies. However, the intervention of Alan Davies in securing the additional year of support from the Department of Education enabled me to embark on a Master's degree and gain a scholarship to Sweden. Davies also opened my eyes to the application of my studies in Psychology and Political Science to graduate research in Sociology. This was a crucial 'crossing of boundaries' not only of a geographic kind, to make a comparative study on leisure in Australia and Sweden, but also widened my knowledge of social sciences. The Master's thesis introduced me to studies of work and provided the foundation of my later academic career in Work and Industrial Relations.

3   Nordic exposure (1967–1970)

I arrived in Sweden in late July having made my way by ferry from Copenhagen to Lund. I had a booking at International House and was immediately made welcome by other students in residence. While I would live there for the rest of my period at the University of Lund, I had been granted a place in an advanced Swedish language course at the University of Uppsala and so travelled north to begin a three-week programme. Most of the other students were from Europe and I quickly felt out of my depth as most seemed to be far more competent than me. I fell in with a group of students from Czechoslovakia and established a life-long friendship with Franta Cermak. Little did we know that the 'Prague Spring' would erupt little over a year later. Franta would suffer for his support of the uprising in 1968 but would eventually become Professor of Linguistics at Charles University in Prague after the end of Soviet domination in 1989. We would visit Franta and his family many times over the next 50 years and his daughter, Anna, stayed with us in Sydney while she was studying English and Australian literature at Charles University.

My year in Lund commences

Returning to Lund, I enrolled in two courses in the Sociology programme. The approach taken at Lund was to take one of two influential books and study them in depth. One of the books was Robert Merton's *Social Theory and Social Structure* (1968). It would have far-reaching influence on my thinking. I was enrolled for an MA degree at the University of Melbourne and planned to conduct a survey of leisure patterns in a Swedish suburban community which I could compare with the results of survey I had undertaken in a Melbourne suburb. I was fortunate to find that Harald Swedner, an Associate Professor in the Department of Sociology in Lund, was interested in this field and had established a research group focused on leisure studies.

Harald Swedner welcomed me into his research group and showed interest in my project, discussing the issues of leisure and work and helping me identify areas around Lund where I could undertake my survey. Swedner was passionate about the need to provide working-class people with access to education and cultural activities. He later became the foundation Professor of Social Work at the University of Gothenburg and is remembered for his advocacy of a broader sociological and social reform approach, in contrast to the narrower individual case study orthodoxy of the time. In Lund, Swedner was very successful at gaining funding for his research and had a team of graduate assistants who occupied desks in a large room. There was always a long line of students waiting outside his door to discuss their projects with him, and he always appeared to have time to talk with them. I was surprised that Swedner would spend time assisting me when he was already so busy, but he had genuine enthusiasm for all of his research students.

Harald Swedner was closely involved with the Social Democrats and was in regular contact with senior politicians, including Olof Palme (even when he was Prime Minister) to raise his concerns about social reforms which he felt needed greater attention. Swedner was the son of missionaries and had spent much of his early youth in China, returning to Sweden in his teenage years. This may explain some of his reformist zeal. He later became the head of the Sociology Department during the student rebellion of the late 1960s when there were demands by some of the Maoist-leaning students for more Marxist-oriented courses. This greatly distressed Swedner who was a committed Social Democrat but had witnessed the excesses of the 'Great Leap Forward' under Mao. He advocated more humane and democratic reforms of the Swedish system.

At the end of my studies in Lund, I was invited home to have lunch at home with Harald Swedner and his wife, who was also a prominent Social Work academic. He seemed surprised that I had actually completed my project and he was interested in the results from the surveys I conducted. I remain grateful for the support that Swedner gave me when I was simply a passing international student who added to his workload!

Leisure in the new suburbs: Australia and Sweden compared

I was drawn to studying leisure in the new suburbs through my involvement in a survey conducted by Alan Davies of approximately 100 families in a newly settled suburb of Boroondara in Melbourne. The survey sought to investigate leisure patterns and community-centredness within this suburb. The research had been stimulated by two prevailing views at the time. First, it was commonly asserted that advanced industrial societies were on the verge of an era of mass leisure made possible by technological changes which would relieve workers from arduous labour. Second, it was argued that as people became more affluent, they would move away from over-crowded and polluted cities to more pleasant suburban communities where they could spend their newly acquired leisure.

In retrospect, it is evident that neither of these predictions was fulfilled. There were successful campaigns by workers and their unions, during the 1980s, to reduce working hours but these resulted in only minor reductions and there has even been a reversal of these trends with working hours actually increasing. While there has been a shift to the suburbs in many countries, there has also been a rejuvenation and gentrification of the inner cities as more affluent people moving back there from the suburbs.

However, our comparative study did reveal some interesting findings. The Australian and Swedish suburban dwellers were fairly similar in their level of participation in leisure activities. Most were 'home-centred' and focused their activities on their immediate family. Weekend activities centred around their house, garden and car. There was a fairly low level of membership and activities undertaken within community organisations and most of their organisational links were outside their immediate neighbourhood. Although most residents shopped within the local area, interest in their immediate community was fairly low. Unlike some findings in relation to American suburbia, Australian and Swedish suburbs were not 'hot beds of participation'.

While the Swedes were more likely than Australians to join community organisations, there was not a significant difference between them. This was contrary to the prevailing literature which suggested that Swedes were more likely to participate in voluntary organisations than many other nationalities. The reason for our contrary findings may have been due to the fact that many of the Swedes in our sample had recently moved from high rise apartments in the city to suburban houses where they were more likely to be engaged in home-related activities.

Although my Master's thesis did not break any new ground in terms of its findings, it did provide me with an important learning experience in undertaking research and writing a long essay. It also provided me with my first academic publications, in the *Australian and New Zealand Journal of Sociology* (Lansbury, 1970a) and a *Danish Journal of Sociology* published by the University of Copenhagen *Sociologiske Meddelelser* (Lansbury, 1970b).

It is interesting to speculate what might be the results if such a study were replicated today. It is likely that the typical worker in each country these days will to be more 'time poor' than in the 1970s. The appeal of the suburbs has declined, particularly as fuel and private transportation costs have increased, and many cities have been rejuvenated. But the popularity and relevance of debates surrounding the impact of new forms of technology on the future of work give new relevance to research on both work and leisure.

The relationship between where people live and work is also of utmost importance. In some respects, developments in IT have made it possible for some people to work in remote locations, often in rural areas, without the need to commute. But many organisational and institutional policies and practices have been slow to permit flexibility in the way people organise their work and leisure, particularly if this reduces managerial control over how people work. It remains to be seen if restrictions on movement by COVID-19 changes attitudes to remote working from home instead of commuting to the office.

There appears to be a cyclical pattern to the discussions about the future of work and leisure. Comments by Bertrand Russell (1935) are still relevant today: 'Modern methods of production have given man the possibility of ease and security for all, yet he has chosen, instead, to have over-work for some and starvation for others'. Russell also argued that 'a great deal of harm is being done in the modern world by belief in the virtues of work'. In Russell's view 'the road to happiness and prosperity lies in an organised diminution of work'. While there has been considerable research in recent years focusing on the future of work, which forecasts that many existing occupations and jobs may cease to exist in the coming years, little attention has been given to how leisure can play a positive role in maintaining social cohesion, particularly if means can be found to provide financial security for those who are unable to find work.

Philip Ennis at the Center for Leisure Studies at the University of Chicago, whom I met on my way to Sweden, lamented that social problems, such as poverty and rising unrest in urban centres, had made the study of leisure appear to be a 'frivolous self indulgence'. Yet, once again, it is important to focus on the importance of leisure as work becomes transformed by technology.

Rotating with Rotary

The Rotary Club of Lund met weekly for lunch at the Grand Hotel in Lund and I was invited to join them. Apart from the free lunch, it provided me with the opportunity to meet people working in a variety of fields and to hear some interesting speakers. One was Gunnar Jarring, who had been UN envoy in the Middle East and provided insights into the negotiation processes between the Arabs and Israelis. Another was a former diplomat who had worked with Raoul Wallenberg who rescued Jews from Nazi-occupied territories but later disappeared, suspected to have been murdered by the Soviets. I was fortunate to be 'adopted' by Gillis Bjork who was a strong advocate for 'internationalism' in the Rotary Club. Gillis had been a leader of the campaign to establish International House in Lund as a student residence where Swedes and foreign students would each comprise 50 per cent and which would be a location for international discussions and events. A photograph in the entrance shows former UN Secretary General, Dag Hammarskjold, opening the House and the street in which it is located is appropriately named after him.

I was the recipient of Gillis's generous hospitality. He was the 'Kronofogde' (or Town Bailiff) in Lund and connected with people in various fields. After learning that I wished to study leisure patterns in new suburbs, Gillis introduced me to the head of Liljenberg's construction company who suggested that I might like to study a new housing development which had recently been established in Bara, located mid-way between Lund and Malmo. On the advice of Harald Swedner, I added two more suburbs to my study to give a broader range of locations: one being an old railway village and the other an upper-class suburb of Lund. I also gained assistance from the head of the Bibliotektjanst which sold books to libraries and provided some financial support if I included questions on people's reading habits, including a question on how much pornography they read.

The combined support I received from these sources paid for the printing and postage of questionnaires to residents in three different areas and also for the preparation and processing of data (which was on punch cards in those days) by IBM in Malmo. Gillis Bjork also organised an interview about my research which appeared on the 'Lund section' of the *Sydsvenska Dagbladet*, the regional newspaper.

I was invited to give talks on Australia at various Rotary clubs around the southern region of Sweden. Towards the end of my time in Lund, Gillis called and said that he had organised a visit to the far north of Sweden with Linjeflyg, the domestic airline belonging to SAS. In return for a free air-ticket, I would only have to write a short article in their Inflight magazine about my impressions. The highlight of the trip was a visit to Sweden's largest iron ore mine in Kiruna. I was accompanied by Gillis Bjork's son Lars, also a student in Lund.

We visited various Rotary clubs in the far north as well as Arctic regions where the Indigenous Sami people still retained semi-traditional life-styles. Almost 50 years later, I revisited the LKAB iron ore mine in Kiruna as a member of an EU research project on sustainable mining. In 2016, I received an honorary Doctor of Technology from Lulea Technical University as a result of collaborative research with Jan Johansson and Lena Abrahamson.

Life in Lund and beyond

International House in Lund lived up to its Dag Hammarskjold legacy. It was largely student-run with a great many academic and social activities. There was a constant flow of celebrity speakers with whom one could discuss and debate issues, including: President Senghor, the poet and President of Senegal; David Halberstam, the American author of 'The Best and Brightest' and Pulitzer Prize winner, the President of the University of Lund; Philip Sandblom, a Professor of Medicine; and French film maker, Chris Marker, who showed and discussed his anti-war film 'Far from Vietnam'. I gained some acting experience in a play by Edward Albee, 'The Zoo Story', produced by a Pakistani student. There was great diversity among the students who came from Asia, Africa, the Middle East, Europe, North and South America, but only three from Australia. The only negative feature of living at International House was that the lingua franca was English and my Swedish proficiency definitely declined.

The University of Lund had active cultural and political programmes in the historic student union building. Speakers included the Swedish Prime Minister, Tage Erlander, German student leader Rudi Dutschke, pioneer feminist and architect of the Swedish welfare state, Alva Myrdal and exiled Greek politician (and later Prime Minister) George Papandreo. International musicians included the legendary US singer Frank Zappa as well as dissident Greek musicians Mikos Theodorakis and Nana Mouskouri.

I joined the swimming team from the South Skane Nation, one of the regionally based student clubs, and trained in a leisurely fashion on Thursday night at the local swimming pool. The focus seemed to be more on the drinking that followed the training session each week than swimming. But to my surprise, our team won the annual intra-university swimming competition and our photo was on the front page of the student newspaper.

The proximity to the European continent meant that travel was easy and relatively cheap. Copenhagen was only an hour away by train to Malmo and then ferry across the 'Oresund'. This was before the bridge was constructed between Malmo and Copenhagen. I spent many weekends during my first months in Lund visiting a Danish girl friend who was studying at the University of Copenhagen. My most exotic trip was to Moscow for the fiftieth anniversary of the Russian revolution. I joined a small youth delegation which enjoyed a semi-official status because our group was sponsored by the Swedish Communist Party. We shared university accommodation with an amiable Cuban delegation whose members seemed more interested in partying than attending military processions in Red Square! Our Russian student colleagues also invited us to parties where much vodka was consumed and we danced to Beatles records which were banned in Russia at that time.

Our interpreter, Nadezda, was a Swedish-speaking Russian in her late 20s who was the former wife of the international chess champion Boris Spassky. She was clearly more than just a simple student as she had her own car and wore stylish Western clothes. I invited Nadezda to a party hosted by an Argentinean embassy official whom I had sat next to on the flight from Copenhagen to Moscow. However, he was concerned that bringing a Russian into a foreign embassy compound could cause diplomatic problems. But Nadezda also spoke excellent Spanish and quickly charmed our host. After I returned to Lund, I wrote an account of our visit to Russia in a student newspaper. I was surprised to receive a letter from Nadezda a few months saying that she had read my article. I presume that the Swedish Communist Party must have monitored any writings about our visit in the newspapers and sent these to our Russian hosts.

I spent Christmas holidays in Paris as the guest of South Vietnamese students whom I had met while hitch-hiking back to Lund from the language course in Uppsala. My French was very limited, as was my hosts' English. They greeted me one morning with a newspaper in French with a photograph of the Australian Prime Minister, Harold Holt, dressed in a wet suit and indicating that he had gone missing in the sea. I was unable to provide a satisfactory explanation to my Vietnamese hosts as to how and why our Prime Minister would disappear at the beach.

During my last few months in Sweden in 1968, I was approached by a doctoral student in Political Science, Goreh Hyden, who asked if I would edit his thesis in English so that he could submit it for publication. Hyden had studied the formation of political identity and affiliation with Julius Nyere's TANU Party among Tanzanians at the village level (Hyden, 1968). He had written a fascinating thesis in near perfect English, so there was very little for me to correct. Hyden had been the President of the Conservative Student Association in Lund but was an admirer of President Nyere. He later had a distinguished career as a specialist in African politics, spending many years in East Africa and becoming a professor at prestigious US universities. Although I did not maintain my connection with Goran Hyden, he impressed me as a committed academic who was deeply engaged in the study of African politics but not bound by political ideology.

I took advantage of a programme offered by Rotary International to travel back to Australia visiting and speaking to Rotary clubs, particularly in Asia. I was provided with contact details of clubs to visit and additional funds for the journey. I stopped briefly in Rome and Athens and then travelled to Israel where I was hosted by Rotary clubs in Tel Aviv and Jerusalem. I was not to know that I was visiting Israel just prior to the devastating Six Day War. I spent a week in Pakistan in Peshawar, Lahore and Chittagong, all of which became embroiled in conflict many years later. I was generously hosted in Bangkok, Singapore and Jakarta.

The most surprising stopover was in Jakarta where I contacted the head of the Indonesian YMCA whom I had met in Melbourne at an Asian Regional conference of YMCAs. I had volunteered to assist with the conference and drove various officials around Melbourne, one of whom was the President of the YMCA of Indonesia and his wife. He had given me his name and address and invited me to stay with him anytime I visited Jakarta. I was surprised when I arrived at the airport and was ushered through the VIP entrance to a waiting military vehicle. I soon discovered that my host was an Army General and that his role in the Indonesian government was to oversee all the youth organisations, particularly those with foreign connections. He also revealed to me that one of the reasons he had been appointed to this position was that his wife was a good friend of Mrs Suharto, wife of the Indonesian President. Despite the generous offer of hospitality to stay in his family compound, I kept my visit brief and arrived home in Melbourne earlier than planned.

Returning to the University of Melbourne

I returned home to Melbourne to complete a Diploma of Education, expecting to be posted to a school by the Victorian Education Department. I also planned to complete my Master's thesis based on the data I had collected in Sweden. The teaching qualification included full-time study as well as assignment to schools for teaching experience. As I intended to become a school counsellor and psychologist, I was sent to a centre for training in this field. These were most useful experiences in addition to classroom teaching practice.

While visiting Alan Davies for advice on my Master's thesis, I met Leon Peres who had recently joined the Department of Political Science from the Commonwealth Scientific and Industrial Research Organisation (CSIRO), where he had held a management position in the administration. Peres had recently completed a Master's degree at the John F. Kennedy School of Government at Harvard and decided to make a mid-career move into academia in order to teach Public Administration. Peres asked me if I had met Stefan Dedijer at Lund University where he headed a research centre in Science Policy. In fact, I had attended a series of lectures given by Dedijer on the Sociology of Science which I found fascinating. This must have impressed Peres as he invited me to be the tutor in Public Administration. The unit was taught in the evening as many of the students were full-time public servants undertaking a degree or diploma specialising in this field. I had no prior knowledge of the subject area but I found the unit fascinating, particularly when Peres discussed issues related to the management of scientists and scientific institutions based on his experience at the CSIRO.

I owe a great deal to Leon Peres who not only gave me my first academic appointment as a casual tutor but also opened my mind to policy issues involving science and technology. My choice of a topic for my PhD at the London School of Economics was directly attributable to ideas I gained while tutoring for Peres and listening to his lectures. Sadly, Leon Peres died in his mid-50s from cancer just when he was becoming active as a consultant with UNESCO assisting developing economies with science policies.

Towards the end of 1968 I met the person who would have the greatest influence and impact on my life. Gwen James was working as a first-year graduate physiotherapist at the Bendigo Base Hospital and was visiting Melbourne for the weekend. I was having lunch in the university cafeteria with my housemate Bruce Henry who introduced me to Gwen when she walked into the cafeteria. She was a friend of Bruce's brother and I had briefly met her at the home of Bruce's parents. Gwen announced that she was planning to leave Australia in the following year to travel the world with her girlfriend and fellow physiotherapist, Kathy, and hoped to work in places like Scandinavia and Canada. I was immediately attracted to Gwen's sparkling personality and offered to share my experiences of living and travelling in the Nordic countries. A few weeks later, I took Gwen to visit then Swedish cultural centre in Melbourne. It housed the Swedish church where we would marry a year later. However, it would take some months of persuasion to convince Gwen that rather than travelling on a ship to Europe with her friend Kathy, she should marry me and we would travel overseas together. I am forever grateful that Gwen made the decision in my favour. However, at that stage I had no idea of where or when we would travel and how we would get there.

Teaching a course in Swedish politics

I was surprised and delighted, in December 1968, when Alan Davies offered me a one-year appointment as a tutor in the Department of Political Science. I was also offered a residential tutor position at Queen's College at the University of Melbourne. A major hurdle, however, was that I was bound by the requirement to teach for three years for the Victorian Department of Education. However, once again Davies interceded with the Department on my behalf and I was granted permission to complete my teaching obligations within the University instead of at a school. I was also fortunate that a visiting academic who had agreed to teach a unit on Italian politics was unable to fulfil his commitment. Davies then asked me if I could teach a unit on Sweden to replace Italy. Somewhat ambitiously, I thought that I could expand the unit to include other countries in the Nordic region.

Accordingly, I contacted embassies in Australia from the Nordic region and received an enthusiastic response from a representative in the Danish Embassy who invited me to visit them in Canberra. When I met him and explained that I had spent a year in Sweden as a graduate student, he asked if I would like to be a visiting scholar in Denmark for six months. I readily accepted his offer and we moved to Copenhagen a year later. The Victorian Education Department was once again generous and allowed me to take leave of absence to study in Denmark. Eventually, when we did return to Melbourne at the end of 1973, I was permitted to complete my three years teaching obligation at Monash University.

In the meantime, I discovered that teaching a half-year unit on Nordic politics was too ambitious and decided to confine it to Sweden. This was a challenging experience as I had no previous lecturing experience but I enjoyed preparing the unit and delivering the lectures. The Swedish embassy were not as forthcoming as the Danes, with an offer of a scholarship, but they did agree to let me know if there were any Swedish politicians visiting Australia who might be willing to speak to my students. I presented a positive view of the Swedish government's policies at the time, including their support for a generous welfare state as well as their neutral foreign policy which had prevented Sweden becoming involved as a combatant in wars for the past few hundred years. However, to my surprise, the Swedish politician who came to speak was from the Conservative Party, then in opposition, and he presented a contrary view to mine. He criticised the high taxes and generous government spending on health, education and welfare. He also expressed the view that Sweden should end its policy of neutrality, join NATO and become more closely allied with the United States. This certainly made for some interesting discussions with the students and demonstrated that the so-called 'Swedish model' was not embraced by all political parties.

Visiting scholar at the University of Copenhagen in Denmark

In January 1970, Gwen and I flew to Copenhagen on a one way ticket. We discovered that Japan Airlines (JAL) had just opened a new route from Sydney to Copenhagen via Tokyo and Moscow in association with Aeroflot and were offering a significant discount to students. The first leg of the flight was by JAL to Tokyo and we were greeted by a Japanese friend, Yutaka Okino, whom I had met when he spent a year as a visiting student in Political Science at Melbourne University. Yutaka worked with a travel agent taking Japanese tourists to various parts of the world but lived in a one room apartment with his grandmother near Haneda Airport, then the main international airport in Tokyo. They lived in very modest circumstances by Australian standards, and we were shocked when Yutaka and his grandmother gave up their 'two tatami' (or two sleeping mats) sized room for us to sleep while they slept elsewhere. Yutaka took us to the local bathhouse where Gwen went on one side with grandmother while Yutaka and I went to the other side. There was only a low partition separating the two sections of the bathhouse. I looked up and to my surprise saw Gwen, grandmother and other women looking at me and laughing. I imagine that it must have been very amusing to see a naked pink man trying to navigate his way between the various pots of hot baths which comprised the local 'onsen'.

The next day, on Yutaka's advice, Gwen and I took the train to the beautiful mountain town of Nikko where we spent a very enjoyable few days walking around ancient temples in deep snow. This first experience of Japan introduced us to the generosity of our Japanese hosts also showed us how the ordinary Japanese lived such a modest life. The next few decades would see Japan become a major global economic power but the standard of housing remained low for much of the population. In recent years, we have made several return visits to Japan and taken enjoyable cycling holidays in Hokkaido and Kyushu.

The trip from Tokyo to Moscow by Aeroflot was quite a Spartan affair. We arrived in cold, dark and snowy conditions in Moscow and were transported from the airport to our hotel in a minivan with two other Australians. Barry Jones and Philip Adams were both relatively young but well known in Australia in 1970 and would subsequently become major 'public intellectuals' in the decades ahead. They told us that they were on a 'mission' for the Prime Minister, John Gorton, to locate an inaugural director for a new national film and television school, and were focussing their efforts on Eastern Europe. This surprised us as Australia had tended to look towards the United Kingdom for cultural leadership.

John Gorton was an unusual politician and Prime Minister, who would later vote himself out of office. Gorton also appointed the relatively unknown and young James Mollison, my former art teacher at Melbourne High, as his advisor to establish a new national art gallery. Phillip Adams had already had a highly successful career in advertising and was playing a key role in the revival of the Australian film industry. Barry Jones would become Minister for Science in the Hawke Labor government in the 1980s.

Barry Jones later contacted us in Copenhagen and told us that he and Philip Adams had met with an accident after hiring a car in Moscow and Jones had to spend a brief period in jail before being released following assistance from the Australian embassy. Adams and Jones finally accomplished their objective after recommending a Pole as the inaugural director of the National Film and Television School.

After we settled in Copenhagen, the Danish Ministry of Education provided me with a modest scholarship. Gwen immediately gained work as a physiotherapist in the Danish health system. Every week the postman would knock on our door and deliver my stipend in cash from a pouch he carried around his waist. I thought it was remarkable that there were no robberies of postmen or women as they went around the back streets of Copenhagen laden with cash! I recently told this story to a Danish colleague who said that cash deliveries by postal employees still occur in rural areas of Denmark.

At the University of Copenhagen, I was welcomed by the Professor of Sociology, Kaare Svalastoga, whose research on social class in Denmark was cited by Alan Davies in his book *Images of Class*. I was permitted to enrol in a couple of subjects, one of which was 'Industrial Sociology' taught by Reinhard Lund. I was in the process of applying to PhD scholarships in North America and the United Kingdom in the field of Political Science. I sought a doctoral grant from British European Airways (BEA) in Personnel Management and Industrial Relations which was tenable at the London School of Economics. To my surprise, I received an invitation to fly to London to be interviewed by Keith Jackson who was head of Personnel Management research at BEA. The interview was successful, and I was offered a three-year scholarship and admission to the PhD programme in Industrial Relations at the LSE.

The six months in Copenhagen was a formative experience for Gwen and me. We began our married lives together in this wonderful city, learning Danish and travelling to nearby countries while working and studying. We lived in modest accommodation in the 'red light' district not far the central station. It was located behind a hotel for the hotel staff. The apartment was old but inexpensive and was obtained for us via the Rotary connections of my old benefactor, Gillis Bjork, in Lund.

Our street, Saxogade, had been the location of the Danish underground movement against German occupation of Copenhagen during the Second World War and was a long-standing working-class district with plenty of colourful characters still resident. Fifty years later, it is gentrified, but in the early 1970s, there was still a feeling of the wartime resistance which ended only 25 years previously. The government medical clinic where Gwen worked had many older patients who came for their weekly therapeutic massage, which was available under the Danish National Health Service. Many of the older residents had lived through the difficult war years of German occupation and would tell Gwen stories about the history of the area.

We attended weekly Danish classes at an Adult Education centre where we met a number of friendly classmates, many of whom were also foreign students. We became friends with a Bulgarian couple who urged us to take a trip to Eastern Europe. They provided us with names and addresses of friends in a number of Eastern European cities. During an extended Easter vacation, we took an extensive rail journey on cheap student fares. We travelled through Poland, Hungary, Bulgaria, Romania, Czechoslovakia and Yugoslavia meeting many interesting people along the way. Occasionally we met with hostility from people who thought we were Russians but most were hospitable once we explained we were from Australia. The trip opened our eyes to the diversity and richness of Eastern European countries and the generosity of people we met along the way.

One of the other students in our Danish class, Ken, was working for the US Army purchasing eggs and other farm produce to supply the US bases in Germany. Ken invited me to accompany him on a visit to some farms outside Copenhagen. At each farm, we were given food and drinks (beer or coffee) while my American friend 'inspected' the produce. These inspections seemed rather perfunctory and took less time than we took for our 'refreshments'! Ken explained that the eggs and other produce was always of the highest standard and did not require close inspection. But I never gained an adequate explanation as to why the US Army did not purchase their eggs in Germany for their bases there. Perhaps, it was part of a deal between the United States and Denmark to support Danish farmers and keep the Danes in NATO?

At the Institute of Sociology at the University of Copenhagen, I was fortunate to take a Master's degree seminar in the Sociology of Work with Reinhard Lund. He had conducted comparative research on Danish and British shop stewards, and his seminar provided me with an introduction to industrial relations. I was also able to use the seminar to develop some ideas for my doctoral thesis which I initially envisaged as a comparative study of technical specialists and professionals in British and Scandinavian airlines. Reinhard provided me with valuable advice and also suggested that I attend the World Congress of the International Industrial Relations Association in Geneva in June.

The period I spent at the University of Copenhagen coincided with ongoing conflict between students and the university administration. The student unrest which began in France and Germany in 1968 persisted in Denmark and the other Nordic countries during the early 1970s. Students were demanding long-overdue changes in curricula and governance structures at universities. Sociology at the University of Copenhagen became a battle ground between the Marxist and non-Marxist reformers. This led to a split and two departments of Sociology being formed, a division which lasted about a decade. A major conflict at LSE also erupted in the late 1960s but had ceased by the early 1970s. There was strong justification for educational reforms during this period, which were needed to modernise the systems and broaden access to higher education to students from lower socio-economic backgrounds. In the Nordic countries, there was growing interest and activity related to industrial democracy which sought to give workers greater influence over decisions which affected them. There were similar concerns in France and Germany, which led to legal and workplace reforms. However, there was also a backlash against Social Democratic and Labour-led governments in the United Kingdom as well as in some of the Nordic countries.

4 The best of British experience (1970–1973)

We arrived in London in the summer of 1970. Gwen obtained work as a Physiotherapist at a major London hospital and I asked Keith Jackson at BEA if I could obtain a temporary job in the airline before the University term began at the end of summer. I was appointed as a job analyst as part of a team which was conducting job evaluation in the airline. This served two purposes: first, I earned a reasonable salary for a couple of months before taking up my scholarship which paid a lower amount; second, it provided me with an orientation to the airline and enabled me to look around for a group of employees to study for my research project.

At the end of my stint as a job analyst, the manager of my department, Bob Horwood, hosted a small farewell at a local hotel after work. In his short speech, he said 'When I heard that we would have an Australian working for us, I expected some uncouth sort of chap. But Lansbury, you turned out to be quite couth!' Several years later, after I completed my PhD and published a book based on my research, Bob Horwood wrote a generous review in an academic journal. By then, he had become a member of the British Airways Board. By this time, I had returned to 'uncouth' Australia!

When I commenced my research in the airline, I looked for a group of professional employees who would be suitable subjects for my study. One possibility was to examine relations between the pilots and management, but this had already been done by a previous doctoral candidate from LSE, who also happened to be an Australian (Blain, 1972). However, I discovered a group of technical specialists in the Management Services Division who nicely fitted my needs. This was a recently created department which was mainly concerned with introducing and operating information technology (IT) systems within the airline. There were other technical specialists within the Division which provided various consulting services to the airline. The key groups were systems analysts, operations researchers, productivity services and human factors/psychologists. There were also numerous computer programmers. This was during the early stages of computerisation of operations in airlines as well as other industries, so IT was a new and exciting field.

After renting an apartment in the suburbs of London for the first couple of months, we were fortunate to be admitted to an international student residence in the heart of Bloomsbury, called William Goodenough House (WGH). It was near the University of London administrative buildings and a pleasant short walk to LSE. The residence was managed by the Dominion Student Trust and was mainly for postgraduate students who came from one of the former British dominions, which included a wide range of countries from the United States to the Sudan! WGH was mainly for single female postgraduates but also had a number of apartments for married students and included families.

Opposite WGH, on the other side of Mecklenburgh Square, was London House which was for single, male postgraduates. Many facilities, including the use of the large enclosed garden in the middle of the Square, were available to the residents of both Houses. Now there is a unified organisation called Goodenough College. The facilities included a well-stocked library, where students worked on their research as well as dining rooms and sporting facilities such as tennis and squash courts. There were also cultural activities and special events such as the BBC hosting a quiz show 'Any Questions?'. It was an idyllic place to live as a postgraduate student and we made many friends during our three years residence, many of whom have remained life-long friends. Our son, Owen, was born in June 1973 and began his life at WGH and has been able to obtain a British passport!

While I was studying the new technical specialists who were introducing IT to BEA, Gwen changed occupations from physiotherapy to computer programming. Her initial training and work experience were undertaken at the London Stock Exchange. Then she became a programming teacher for a company which trained programmers from client companies. Gwen also enrolled in a Diploma of Sociology which was offered on a part-time basis by the University of London.

I commenced my doctoral studies at the LSE initially with Ray Loveridge as my supervisor. He was enthusiastic about my topic and loaned me a monograph by Archie Kleingartner on professional employees and unionisation, which was based on his PhD at the University of Wisconsin-Madison. Kleingartner's monograph provided me with an excellent review of the literature and a strong justification for research in this area. However, soon after I arrived, Ray Loveridge was appointed to the newly established London Business School (LBS) and I had to decide whether to remain at LSE or move with Loveridge to the LBS. Given the long history and prestige of the LSE, which was a major centre for industrial relations research, it was not a difficult decision to remain at LSE. However, I had to find a new supervisor and was most fortunate that Keith Thurley kindly accepted me as his research student.

During the early 1970s, industrial relations was a 'hot topic' in the United Kingdom. The Wilson Labour government had been defeated by the Conservatives led by Edward Heath. Widespread strikes by trade unions had been a major contributor to loss of support for the Wilson government. A Royal Commission on Industrial Relations, appointed by Labour and led by Lord Donovan, had concluded that major reform was needed. The Heath government introduced a controversial Industrial Relations Act which was criticised by Labour and the unions as borrowing heavily from US laws which would strip workplace rights from workers and their unions.

Massive industrial action by the National Union of Mineworkers, in particular, contributed to the defeat of the Heath Conservative government. However, industrial unrest continued under the Callaghan Labour government and ushered in 'the winter of discontent' which was followed by the election of the Thatcher Conservative government. Ultimately, the unions paid a significant price for their continuing industrial disruption and would result in Labour being kept out of government for more than a decade. However, it was against this background of high levels of public interest in industrial relations that I undertook my doctoral research in British airlines.

Inside British European Airways: the rise of the technical specialists

My decision to study the role of management services in BEA was based on my interest in the emergence of new technical specialist and professional occupations related to the application of IT and other techniques to improve efficiency in the airline. Like many other organisations in both the private and public sectors, BEA was undergoing major changes as the result of computerisation. Within the airline, the introduction of computer technology was affecting everything from ticketing to the scheduling of flights.

Although IT was the dominant group, other smaller specialists were involved in assisting the airline's operations through the application of advanced mathematical techniques to predict and compare the outcomes of alternative decisions, as well as the use of ergonomics, work measurement and method study. My topic was of interest to BEA because the IT and other management services staff were regarded as difficult to manage because they did not fit easily with the bureaucratic structure of the airline, yet they were likely to become increasingly important in the future.

My project was undertaken during a period when there was a growing interest in the emergence of new professional and technical services and speculation on what impact these might have not only on organisations but for society as a whole. J.K. Galbraith (1967) warned against the rise of 'technostructure', a new 'power elite', that was becoming 'the guiding intelligence or brains of the enterprise' and responsible for major corporate decision-making. Other research at this time focused on potential role conflict between the technical specialist's orientation to 'cosmopolitan' values and the manager's focus of the 'local' needs of the organisation (Delbecq and Elfner, 1970).

There were emerging studies of IT personnel which highlighted differences between those who were primarily concerned with the development of techniques in contrast with others more orientated to the application of IT to the needs of the organisation (Sheldrake, 1971). I was also influenced by the 'socio-technical systems' school of thought developed by researchers at the Tavistock Institute of Human Relations in the United Kingdom who emphasised the need to appreciate the interaction between the social and technical aspects of work and organisational life.

My research project was conducted in two phases. During the first phase, approximately 70 management services staff were interviewed for about 90 minutes using a structured set of questions covering five broad areas: their current job, attitudes to the role of management services in the airline, previous career history and future aspirations, interests outside of work, attitudes to professional associations and trade unions and other issues. A questionnaire was constructed mainly on the basis of a content analysis of the interviews and, after pre-testing, was distributed to all 346 staff in Management Services. A response rate of approximately 70 per cent was achieved.

In phase two, one year later, follow up interviews were conducted with all of the initial interviewees, who still remained with the airline, in order to ascertain whether their attitudes had substantially changed. Feedback was also obtained on the results of the larger questionnaire survey. Views of management services staff to the anticipated merger of British European Airways (BEA) and British Overseas Airways Corporation (BOAC) were also examined. One of the first functions to be merged was the management services department of each airline.

Research outcomes

Three hypotheses drove my research. First, that management services as a new and expanding part of the technostructure in the airline would encroach on management functions. Second, that the relationships between management services staff and line managers would be characterised by conflict due to strong interdependence between them. Third, that the professional and technical orientations of management services staff would be incompatible with the bureaucratic practices of the airline. Hence, a major problem facing the airline management was how to effectively integrate the management services personnel with the rest of the organisation. The results of the research only partly supported these hypotheses but they did lead to some other significant findings.

Rather than subverting line management in the airline, the role of management services and the introduction of computerisation tended to strengthen managerial authority. The main conflicts experienced by management services staff were not so much with line managers but were between various specialist groups sharing a common task environment. This arose mainly as a consequence of the process of occupational specialisation whereby newer groups, such as systems analysts, sought to extend their sphere of operations to cover areas or activities of less technically competent groups, such as programmers. Operations researchers tended to be the most expansionist of the technical specialists and became increasingly influential. It is interesting to note that currently, former operations researchers are chief executives of airlines, such as Alan Joyce at Qantas Airways.

An important finding of the research was that the various specialist groups comprising management services differed considerably in their role conceptions and career orientations. Three categories were identified: careerists, functionaries and academics. 'Careerists' expected to remain in their present specialist field

48   *The best of British experience*

but to move beyond the airline to other organisations where their skills were in demand. They were found predominantly in IT areas. 'Functionaries' expected to progress within the airline but to use their specialist skills as a stepping-stone to more senior roles in line management. They were drawn mainly from productivity services. 'Academics' expected to deepen their specialist expertise either within the airline or elsewhere, such as research in a university. They were strongly represented in operations research. While individuals would not necessarily remain in these roles, and could change career orientations, these categories represent various role conceptions which can help to shape an individual's attitude to work, relationships with others and disposition towards an employer.

It was fortuitous that during my research, the merger of BEA with BOAC to form British Airways was announced and one of the first decisions confronting the newly formed British Airways Board was which IT system would be chosen for the new airline. BOAC relied on IBM as the single supplier for its IT system while BEA used a variety of suppliers including ICL, UNIVAC and DEC. The Board decided to unify the reservations systems of the two airlines on IBM equipment as recommended by BOAC. This was a controversial decision, opposed by many BEA staff and resulted in a one-day strike by 160 BEA computer staff who complained about 'the failure of management to keep (us) informed of their future with the new airline'.

The Board announced that it would invest $14 million in new IBM equipment to provide central facilities for the whole of the new airline and would offer BEA staff either redundancy or retraining. Commenting on what it called 'the shotgun wedding of airline computers', *The New Scientist* noted that 'rationalisation of computer systems, in the wake of the airline merger, has shown that change can be as brutal to the technologists as anyone else'.

My doctoral research project was funded by BEA in collaboration with the Air Transport and Travel Industry Training Board. I was fortunate to receive cooperation of management services staff in both BEA and BOAC. The results of the research were conveyed to the 'research partners' through a series of seminars as well as written reports and articles in the *Training Board Research Bulletin*. A number of research papers appeared in academic journals in the United Kingdom, and a book based on the thesis was published (Lansbury, 1978b). In a review of the book in *The British Journal of Industrial Relations*, Horwood generously described it as 'definitive' and 'a genuine portent for the future development of organisations and society' (Horwood, 1981). The type of applied research which I undertook was seen as useful by airlines and the Industry Training Board because it dealt with issues of current and future importance. During subsequent years, IT and related employees are even more significant in organisations now than they were when I conducted my research in the airlines.

I was fortunate in my choice of topic for doctoral research. I have continued to pursue an interest in the impact of technological changes on work and careers in a variety of industries. The opportunity to work in a research department within a large enterprise provided me with valuable insights into organisational dynamics and change. As an 'insider' in the airline, I was able to gain access to information and people which would have been difficult for an 'outside' researcher. I continued to be involved in international airline studies, through my involvement in a global airline research project initiated by MIT as well as engagement with Qantas in Australia in various teaching and consulting projects. The area of my doctoral research continues to be topical with the important role played by IT and technical specialists introducing change in organisations.

Keith Thurley: my supervisor at the London School of Economics

Keith Thurley was a pioneer in several fields of research, including the role of first line management or supervisors in industry, not just in the United Kingdom but also in Japan and various European countries. He was one of the first academics who studied Japanese enterprises at the 'shopfloor level' as well as the transfer of Japanese management systems to the West as Japanese companies began operations in other parts of the world. Thurley had a variety of early lifetime experiences which equipped him admirably for his later academic career. Born in 1932, he experienced both the latter part of the Great Depression and the Second World War during his school years.

After completing secondary school, Keith Thurley had a brief stint in the British civil service and then enrolled for a Bachelor of Economics and Diploma in Personnel Administration at the London School of Economics. During 1953–1954, he undertook compulsory national service in the British Army in Japan. During his days off, Thurley was a volunteer worker in a shanty town near Tokyo where 800 families shared one tap. There he would meet a Japanese volunteer, Fusae Kobayashi (Elizabeth), whom he would later marry and bring to the United Kingdom. After national service, Thurley worked for four years as Assistant Labour Officer at Courtaulds in Coventry, which gave him valuable industrial experience and aroused his interest in the role of the supervisor in industry.

Keith Thurley returned to LSE in the late 1950s, on secondment from Courtaulds, to work on a research project on supervisors in British industry. This resulted in an influential publication which challenged conventional views about supervisory roles and training (Thurley and Hamblin, 1963). Thurley argued that supervisors needed to be viewed in the wider organisational and societal context. He later extended his research to other countries and co-authored an influential book with Hans Widernius from Sweden in 1973: *Supervision: A Reappraisal*. In 1989, again Thurley co-authored *Towards European Management*, again with Widernius, extending their research to managers across Europe. Thurley's interest in Japan continued with comparative studies of Japanese and British electrical engineers. In 1985, Thurley co-authored *Japan's Emerging Multinationals* (Takamiya and Thurley, 1985).

When I met Keith Thurley in 1970, he was a Senior Lecturer in Industrial Sociology attached to the Department of Industrial Relations but also involved in teaching the Diploma of Personnel Administration. He was very active in the development of the field of Human Resource Management (HRM), but

50 *The best of British experience*

always from an analytical and often critical perspective. He was concerned that HRM needed to develop a stronger research base. In 1980, he was appointed to a new professorship at LSE with a focus on HRM. Thurley was instrumental in integrating the teaching and research in both industrial relations and HRM at LSE. He also saw the need to bring the study of management and industrial relations together and co-edited *Industrial Relations and Management Strategy* with Stephen Wood in 1983. Sadly, Keith Thurley died at the age of 60 in 1992 just as many of his contributions were being recognised and he was publishing important new comparative research on Japanese and British management and organisational behaviour.

Keith Thurley's academic supervisory style was unobtrusive, and he acted more as a 'sounding board' for ideas than suggesting how one should proceed. In retrospect, I realise how much I was influenced not only by his ideas but also by his approach to supervision of research. In my first year as a doctoral student, I took Thurley's graduate class in Industrial Sociology and continued to broaden my understanding of the subject. Just as I was completing my doctoral thesis, in 1973, Thurley was co-editing a special issue of the *British Journal of Industrial Relations* on the theme of industrial sociology and industrial relations. He invited me to submit a substantial 'research note' on my thesis entitled 'Professionalism and Unionisation Among Management Services Specialists' (Lansbury, 1974). This provided me with my first publication in a major journal and gave me a 'jump start' to publish other papers from my doctoral research.

My first research grant in Australia was stimulated by Thurley's work and resulted in a jointly authored book, with Peter Gilmour, entitled *Marginal Manager: The Changing Role of Supervisors in Australia* (Gilmour and Lansbury, 1984).

When the foundation Chair of Industrial Relations at LSE became vacant on the retirement of Ben Roberts, in 1984, Thurley contacted me at MIT, where I was on study leave, and invited me to apply. I was selected to be the short list of applicants and flown from Boston to London for an interview. When I failed to gain the position, Thurley explained that the selection committee felt that my research was too much like his, and they were seeking someone in a different specialisation. But I regarded this as a compliment and was grateful to have been considered for the position.

The Fabian Society and Swedish Social Democracy

During our time in the United Kingdom, Gwen and I joined the British Fabian Society. It was founded in 1884 to advance the principles of democratic socialism by reform rather than revolution. Among its founders were Beatrice Webb and her husband Sidney as well as writers such as George Bernard Shaw and H.G. Wells. Sidney Webb also co-founded the London School of Economics in 1895, using a bequest left to the Fabian Society. We attended meetings and conferences of the Fabian Society where we met various Labour politicians, policy makers, academics and journalists. The Wilson Labour government had lost the 1970 General Election to the Conservative Party, led by Edward Heath, just before we arrived in London. The Fabian Society was an interesting venue for discussions about reshaping Labor policy for the next election.

I joined the youth committee of the Fabians which published its own series of policy-related 'Young Fabian Pamphlets' and conducted seminars and conferences aimed at encouraging younger members to generate new ideas for the Labour Party. I organised a one-day conference on the controversial Industrial Relations Bill which had been introduced by the Conservatives. Guest speakers from the union movement, universities and the Labour Party addressed issues arising from the Industrial Relations Bill. I recall receiving an unexpected phone call at home from prominent British Labour politician and former senior Minister Tony Crosland, seeking further information about the event before he accepted my invitation to speak at the conference. It was exciting to meet some of the great names in the Labour Party from the past as well some of the future leaders.

I met a fellow Australian, Jim Kennan, who was active in the Fabians and who authored a Young Fabian Pamphlet entitled 'Australian Labour: A Time of Challenge' just before the Whitlam Labor government was elected in 1972. Kennan was working in London as a teacher and would later return to Australia to become a barrister and be elected as a Labor MP, rising to Deputy Premier of Victoria and leader of the parliamentary Labor Party in Opposition. With Kennan's encouragement, I wrote a Young Fabian Pamphlet on *Swedish Social Democracy* (Lansbury, 1972). This was partly based on the lectures I gave at the University of Melbourne in 1969 but also covered the Swedish general election of 1970 when Olof Palme, then only 41 years of age, was elected leader of the Social Democrats and won a narrow victory.

My pamphlet on Swedish Social Democracy, at approximately 25,000 words, was my longest publication to date. Somewhat ambitiously, I attempted not only to provide a critique of various economic and social policies of the Social Democratic Party in recent decades but also to recommend what the British Labour Party could learn from the Swedish experience. Although I raised a number of problems facing the Swedish Social Democrats, I reached the conclusion that 'the ability of the Social Democrats to hold power for three decades and to maintain a constant programme of reform in welfare, education and the economy is not equalled elsewhere in Europe'. Not all Labour-oriented commentators were enthusiastic about the 'Swedish model'. In 1971, Anthony Howard, editor of *The New Statesman*, wrote an article entitled 'Sweden: the Fading Dream' in which he concluded that in Sweden he had seen the future (of Tony Crosland's projection of socialism in Britain) and 'it does not work'!

To my surprise, *The Times* (6 March 1972) featured my Fabian publication in an article entitled 'Off Key Notes in Swedish Rhapsody'. It claimed that

> not so long ago British commentators with an interest in Scandinavia were forever being asked to talk on such themes as 'Sweden: a model for Europe'.... Now a more discriminating view of Sweden is coming into fashion, not the least among British socialists. A good example of this is a Young

Fabian Pamphlet on Swedish Social Democracy (which) avoids giving the impression of a visitor returned from the promised land. Sweden too, it is appreciated, has her problems.

The main focus of the article in *The Times* was on 'middle class' opposition to Olof Palme's policies aimed at greater 'equalisation' as well as 'anxiety about Sweden joining the Common Market because of the possible conflict between full membership of the EEC and their own tradition of political neutrality'.

The most unexpected outcome of the pamphlet on Sweden, however, was a letter I received from Dame Margaret Cole, a well-known author, political activist and an early Fabian socialist, now aged in her mid-80s. Dame Margaret wrote telling me that she had also authored a publication for the Fabians about the Swedish Social Democrats after they gained government in the early 1930s. She invited my wife, Gwen, and myself to afternoon tea in her London flat where she revealed that she had lived at 45 Mecklenburgh Square during the First World War: the same address of the student accommodation where we now resided. She also told us: 'I remember standing on the balcony watching the German zeppelins on their bombing raids over London'.

Learning that I was studying at the LSE, she told us that she had worked with Sidney Webb (the founder of LSE) and his equally famous wife, Beatrice, at the Fabian Research Bureau in the early 1900s. But, she declared: 'I fell out with Beatrice because she suspected me of having an affair with Sidney. But if you knew Sidney, that is the last thing you would want to do!' Dame Margaret asked me if I was related to the Labour Party leader of the 1930s, George Lansbury. Margaret had worked alongside George in the Peace movement and the Labour Party. Alas I was not. Her brother Raymond Postgate married Daisy, one of George's daughters. Margaret married G.D.H. Cole, a famous Oxford historian and political thinker. She was later elected as a Labour representative on the London City Council. Unfortunately, I was not directly related to George, unlike his great nephew, Malcolm Turnbull who later became Liberal Prime Minister of Australia. Dame Margaret died a few years after our meeting at the age of 87.

Foreign correspondent for *The Nation*

During our period in London, I became a regular correspondent for *The Nation*, which was the fortnightly precursor of *The National Times*. It was like an Australian version of the British *New Statesman* and gave me an opportunity to practice as an amateur journalist. There were plenty of topical issues to write about, including debate on whether the United Kingdom should join the European Economic Community, trade union opposition to the Heath government's proposed industrial relations reforms, growing unrest in Eastern Europe and rising racial tensions in the United Kingdom. Of my 28 articles, which *The Nation* published between 1970 and 1973, just over half were about Britain while the rest concerned issues in European countries, many of which we visited.

My first article was entitled 'Remembering Dubcek' after we made a trip to Czechoslovakia and Eastern Europe. The last was on 'Willy Brandt's Ostpolitik' after we visited Germany. The copy editor at *The Nation* made my articles sound more interesting with titles such as 'Think Tank Warfare', 'Franco, Priests and Workers', 'Histadrut: Mr Hawke's Model' and 'Jenkins: a British Whitlam'. I wrote several articles on Sweden, where Olof Palme appeared to be taking the country in a more radical direction. I was surprised when the First Secretary of the Swedish Embassy in Canberra took me to task, in a letter to the editor of *The Nation*, for implying that the Social Democrats were in coalition with the Swedish Communist Party (which they were not) although the minority Swedish government were relying on the 17 votes of Communist members of the Riksdag (parliament) to get some of their legislation passed.

5 Monash University in the Whitlam and Fraser eras (1974–1980)

In 1972, the election of the Labor government in Australia, led by Gough Whitlam, was a momentous event. It was the first federal Labor government since 1949. We were anxious to return to Australia and participate in the reforms which Whitlam promised to introduce. Indeed, the 'Whitlam years' (1973–1976) presaged major economic, social and political reform activities. However, I needed to finish my PhD thesis and find a job. Gwen was also expecting our first child. I had completed two years of my scholarship and had one year left. I began to apply for lectureships at a number of Australian universities in Sociology, which was a fast-growing field at the time, but I was unsuccessful. I received an offer from the University of New South Wales which had advertised a lectureship in Industrial Relations but they insisted that I come immediately and I was not prepared to leave London until I had completed my PhD. Then two positions were advertised at Monash University in Melbourne: one in Sociology and the other in Administrative Studies. I applied for both. I was more interested in the first position but was offered the second. This turned out to be fortuitous as I joined a small but expanding department which would ultimately become the Graduate School of Management. Furthermore, the department was in the Faculty of Economics and Politics which was large, well-resourced and had many prominent academics in a wide range of fields.

During the 1960s, when I was an undergraduate at Melbourne University, the recently established Monash University was regarded as progressive and exciting with new approaches to higher education. Monash also gained the reputation as a 'radical campus' as it was the site of large 'teach-ins' on the war in Vietnam where speakers, often drawn from the Monash faculty and students, expressed strong opposition to Australia's involvement in the war. Monash students also joined their overseas counterparts in demanding greater rights for students in the design of curricula and a voice in university governance. As a student, I often visited Monash as it was close to my parents' home and I was keen to be involved with some of the student activities. Despite rivalry between the 'establishment' Melbourne University and the more unconventional Monash, there were close relations between student associations. I contributed to joint publications of the two student newspapers and became friends with a number of Monash students. As previously mentioned, I was a member of the ad hoc 'Melbash' intervarsity debating team which nearly reached the grand final of the national debating championships in Adelaide.

By the end of 1973, when I joined the academic staff at Monash, the more radical student activities had ceased but there was considerable excitement surrounding the new Whitlam Labor government. Some Monash academics had been appointed to key roles in the government and were involved with introducing reforms in a wide range of fields, including industrial relations. My first published article in *The Journal of Industrial Relations*, 'Performance against Promise: the Labor Government and Industrial Relations' (Lansbury, 1974), gave a positive assessment of the Whitlam government's achievements. But by the time it was published, the Whitlam government had been dismissed by the Governor-General, in highly controversial circumstances, and Labor lost the subsequent federal election. The Whitlam government was criticised for introducing too many reforms too quickly in its brief period in office. However, the government had the misfortune to be engulfed in the global oil crisis which resulted in a record inflation rate of 20–25 per cent and interest rates that rose to around 18 per cent. Rapidly rising prices and wages led the Whitlam government to introduce a policy of wage indexation in 1975. However, by the time this policy had an effect, the Liberal National Party Coalition was in power. It is worth noting that the indexation system remained in place until 1981, followed by an attempted 'wage freeze' by the Coalition government and the election of a Labor government led by former national union leader, Bob Hawke, in 1983.

Teaching and research at Monash

In the Department of Administrative Studies, I was assigned to teach Organisational Behaviour and Human Resource Management mainly in the Master's degree programme. This was designed along the lines of a Master of Business Administration (MBA) but was called a Master of Administration (MAdmin). This nomenclature was mainly to distinguish the Master's degree at Monash from the one offered at the longer-established MBA programme at Melbourne University. I found it stimulating to teach the Masters' students as they were from a wide range of backgrounds from business, the public sector, educational institutions, trade unions and professional bodies. However, the Department of Administrative Studies had only a small core academic staff and relied on specialists from across the broader Faculty as well as adjunct staff to teach a wide range of subjects.

Industrial relations was taught by staff in the Department of Economics, principally by Di Yerbury who was a Senior Lecturer and had a PhD in Labour Law. I attended the course by Yerbury. She was a brilliant teacher and invited notable union and employer representatives as guest speakers. Yerbury's course was a great learning experience for me and she asked me to give some guest lectures. Halfway through my first year at Monash, in 1974, Yerbury was appointed by the Federal Minister for Labour, Clyde Cameron, to become the First Assistant Secretary, heading the Wages Division of the Department of Labour. This was a key role as wage indexation was just being introduced, the Labour government was concerned about wage and price inflation, and National Wage Cases were important in terms of implementing government policy.

Di Yerbury not only oversaw the federal government's submissions to the annual national wage case but also was involved in negotiations with unions and employers 'behind the scenes'. Through her generosity, I gained insight into the dynamics of the wage determination system and met a number of the key union, employer and government representatives. She later became a Foundation Professor at the AGSM at UNSW and subsequently, Vice-Chancellor of Macquarie University.

Monash had several eminent economists who were interested in labour issues. Allan Fels had just returned from Cambridge where he had been a post-doctoral fellow having completed his PhD at Duke University in the United States. Allan had published a book on the operation of the British Prices and Incomes Board and would later preside over similar bodies in Australia, culminating in his role as the foundation head of the Australian Competition and Consumer Commission (ACCC). During his academic career, Fels was head of the Graduate School of Management at Monash and Dean of the Australian and New Zealand School of Government (ANZOG). He held a number of other roles including Chair of the Australian National Mental Health Commission. During my time at Monash, Allan had yet to occupy many of these roles, taught Labour Economics and was a generous colleague. I sought his advice on a number of occasions, including my decision to move to Sydney, and he always made time to give thoughtful consideration to my concerns.

Towards the end of my period at Monash, I was a commentator on industrial relations at a major Economics 'Summit' which was organised by Allan Fels. The keynote speaker was Sir Richard Kirby, former President of the federal Industrial Relations Commission. It was well known that Sir Richard and Bob Hawke were both keen punters. They would sometimes suspend proceedings of the national wage cases so that they could retire to Sir Richard's chambers to listen to a major horse race in which they both had a betting interest. Fels asked me to meet Sir Richard at the airport when he arrived from Sydney and drive him to Monash. Sir Richard gave an excellent speech to a packed audience at Monash and I followed his presentations with some comments on the state of the labour market and the problem of youth unemployment.

About 20 years later, I attended a dinner at Women's College at the University of Sydney where Sir Richard was the guest speaker. He was over 80 years of age but gave a witty and interesting speech. I joined a small group to have coffee with Sir Richard after the dinner. As soon as he saw me, he came over and said: 'I remember you from Monash when you talked about youth unemployment and I have often thought about that conference and our interesting discussion'. I thought it was extraordinary that he could recall our meeting but it exemplified why Sir Richard Kirby was such an admired person.

Bill Howard was another influential colleague at Monash who taught both labour economics and industrial relations. Howard left school at an early age and joined the Federal Department of Labour, gaining a degree in Commerce from the University of Melbourne through part-time study. Howard's exceptional academic results earned him a postgraduate scholarship to Cornell University in the United States where he gained a PhD. Howard was a 'contrarian' in many ways, expressing views which were often against the mainstream of academic thought and public policy. He was a strong advocate of collective bargaining of the type which he had witnessed in the United States. He was a critic of the arbitration system which he considered rendered the unions dependent on the tribunal. He particularly admired the mining unions in Broken Hill which eschewed the arbitration system and gained collective agreements with the employers through exercising their bargaining power.

Howard had an idiosyncratic teaching style and provoked debate with his students in his class. Many found it difficult to work out whether he was taking a 'right'- or 'left'-wing perspective as he would often put contrary positions in order to create an argument. Some of Howard's academic papers, particularly on union theory, are still prescribed reading and provoke debate. Sadly, he suffered from dementia after he retired. I recall phoning him to inquire how he was faring. He apologised for his difficulty in holding a conversation but said 'I am chuffed that you called me'. I learned a great deal from Bill Howard, and he left a valuable legacy for those of us who were fortunate to be his students and colleagues.

The Dean of the Faculty of Economics and Politics was Donald Cochrane, whom Bill Howard irreverently called 'Genghis Khan' and 'the Ayatollah'. Cochrane was the foundation Dean when Monash began as a new university in 1961 and remained in that role until he retired in 1981. As Howard's nickname implied, Cochrane was a powerful and intimidating Dean who created a well-funded and large Faculty based on the Cambridge model where he had gained his PhD. The Economics department was large and gained a reputation as one of the best in Australia. The Politics Department was also very lively with prominent scholars in various specialist fields.

However, Cochrane appeared to personally decide all appointments and promotions in the Faculty. He disdained Management as a field of scholarship, and the Department of Administrative Studies remained small and did not award MBA degrees until after Cochrane retired. Nevertheless, the Whitlam government invited Cochrane to chair an Inquiry into labour market training which led to the establishment of the innovative National Employment and Training Scheme. He was also the inaugural chair of the Australian Trade Union Training Scheme. During his time, Cochrane was possibly the most influential Dean of Economics in the country and was respected by both sides of politics, unions and business.

Expanding horizons at Monash

I had many interesting students while at Monash. Ed Davis was my first postgraduate research student who became a life-long friend. Davis arrived at

Monash from Cambridge where he had completed an honours degree in political economy and been a school teacher in the United Kingdom. At Monash, Davis tutored in Economics and enrolled in a Master's degree by research. Davis chose to study internal decision-making within one of Australia's largest and most influential left-wing unions: the Australian Manufacturing Workers Union (AMWU). The union's origin was as a craft union, representing skilled workers in the metal trades, but it gradually expanded by mergers with a range of smaller unions in the manufacturing sector.

During the period when Ed Davis undertook his research, the union's leadership comprised several high-profile members of the Communist Party of Australia and left-wing members of the Australian Labor Party (ALP). Davis won the confidence of the leaders of the Victorian Branch of the union and was able to undertake detailed interviews and observe executive meetings. Davis later extended his study to several other unions for his PhD. His research gave me an opportunity to get to know the leadership of the AMWU, as well as other unions, and enabled me to conduct subsequent research, often in collaboration with Davis. We became life-long friends and co-authors of numerous publications based on our joint research. Davis later became a Professor of Management and Dean of the School of Economics and Business at Macquarie University.

Several of my colleagues in the Faculty of Economics and Politics were active in the Monash staff association, which was affiliated with the national body which later became the National Tertiary Education Union (NTEU). The governing body at Monash, known as the University Council, had several staff and student positions which were filled by election. I was elected to the Council with the support of the staff association and sought to represent the views and interests of academic staff. By this stage, the Whitlam government had been replaced by the Liberal National Party coalition, led by Malcolm Fraser, student fees were reimposed and the expansion of university funding was curtailed by the new government. There were lunchtime meetings between the staff and student representatives before each monthly Council meeting to discuss issues of common interest. I used to sit next to a quietly-spoken Law student by the name of Peter Costello who adopted a low profile in these meetings. I assumed he was a left-leaning student and was surprised when he later emerged as a prominent lawyer representing the employers in a landmark case against the unions, became a Member of Parliament and finally was the Treasurer and potential heir-apparent to Prime Minister John Howard in a long-serving Coalition government.

During my first two years at Monash, I was engaged in publishing papers from my doctoral thesis in key British and Australian journals as well as gaining a contract from a university publisher to rewrite my PhD thesis as a book. I also began to explore issues in Australian industrial relations which I had touched on in my doctoral thesis. These included the emerging importance of professional and white-collar workers in organisations as well as unions and professional associations which represented their interests. I also sought to improve my knowledge of the workings of the Australian industrial relations system in terms of wage determination and dispute settlement. My first major international paper on this subject, entitled 'The Return to Arbitration: Recent Trends in Dispute Settlement and Wages Policy in Australia', was published in the *International Labour Review* (Lansbury, 1978 a). This paper would later be cited as an example of how my writings helped to explain and interpret developments in Australia to a wider international audience (Wailes, 2011). In truth, I was just beginning to understand idiosyncratic aspects of the Australian industrial relations system!

I was assigned to teach courses in Organisation Behaviour and found there were few books or academic journals which used Australian examples. I was fortunate to meet a fellow member of the Department of Administrative Studies, Peter Gilmour, whose office was opposite mine and who shared my concern about the lack of Australian teaching materials. Gilmour's background was in Operations Management and Logistics, which is sometimes referred to as Management Science. We shared an interest in examining organisation and management issues from a multi-disciplinary perspective. Gilmour had been a champion Australian swimmer, specialising in the Butterfly stoke, and narrowly missed selection in the Australian Olympic team. However, he won a sporting scholarship to study at Cornell University in the United States, where he continued his swimming, and then undertook a PhD at Michigan State University. We discussed our complementary approaches to teaching management subjects and decided to propose a book to a publisher which would take an 'integrated' approach, combining insights from behavioural and management sciences. Not only did Longman Cheshire accept our proposal for one book but also agreed to our proposal that we become joint editors for a new Australian Management Series. This led to additional publications by ourselves as well as by a wide range of authors whom we invited to contribute to the series.

Getting to know the 'Players' in industrial relations

Industrial relations is an applied field of knowledge, and part of its appeal to me has always been meeting and learning from people who were actively involved not only in day-to-day activities but also the more strategic aspects of this field. When I began teaching at Monash, I invited union and employer representatives to speak to my class and engage in discussions with the students, a number of whom pursued later careers in industrial relations. Three industrial relations practitioners who stand out in my memory of that period are Bill Kelty, who became the Secretary of the ACTU, Laurie Carmichael, a leading official with the AMWU, and Ian Macphee, former employers' association leader and later Minister for Employment and Industrial Relations in the Coalition government led by Prime Minister Malcolm Fraser.

Bill Kelty

One of my first guest speakers from the union movement was Bill Kelty, who later became Secretary of the ACTU and one of the most influential figures in Australian industrial relations. I had invited a friend, Bruce Hartnett, who worked for a white-collar union, to be a guest speaker at one of my morning classes. Our students were mostly part-time and classes began at 8.00 am. Bruce contacted me the night before and said he was unable to attend but that he had asked a young research officer at the Storemen and Packers' Union (SPU), Bill Kelty, to replace him. I arrived early at the classroom and saw someone sitting there who I assumed was an undergraduate student. When I inquired if he was in the wrong room, I received a gruff reply that he was my guest speaker. The class was then treated to a forceful presentation by Bill Kelty on the future agenda of the union movement. The SPU was regarded as a militant union and was pioneering new demands such as superannuation for its members. Bill Kelty and Simon Crean, who later led the ACTU as Secretary and President, respectively, were both in their first jobs as research officers for the SPU, which later became the National Union of Workers.

During the next few decades, I interacted with Bill Kelty on numerous occasions. However, he could be quite acerbic. I recall a rather puzzling interchange I had with him in the early 1980s when we were both at an industrial relations conference in the Blue Mountains. He was critical of some mistakes which he said were in a book written by me. 'Which book was that Bill?', I inquired. He told me the title and I recognised it as having been written by some of my colleagues. When I told him this, his response was: 'Well you academics need to check your facts more carefully'.

As Secretary of the ACTU from 1983 to 2000, Kelty was one of the key architects of the Accord on Prices and Incomes between the trade union movement and the Hawke/Keating Labor governments and one of its most effective advocates. Kelty was so deeply involved with government policy during this period that he was known as an 'honorary member of Cabinet'. He was a Board member of the Reserve Bank of Australia between 1987 and 1996. After Kelty retired from the ACTU, he did not seek a political career but joined the Board of Linfox, a private company owned by his friend Lindsay Fox. He has been a Commissioner of the Australian Football League (AFL) since 1998.

Laurie Carmichael

During the period of the Whitlam government, the Minister for Industrial Relations was a former union leader, Clyde Cameron. He was a strong proponent of education and training for union officials and shop steward and established the Trade Union Training Authority (TUTA). I was interested in contributing to union education programmes and became an occasional guest presenter for both TUTA and individual union programmes. The Amalgamated Metal Workers' Union (AMWU) had some of the longest established and developed education programmes. Laurie Carmichael, an Assistant National Secretary of the AMWU, was active in promoting training for his union's members. One day, I received an invitation from Max Odgen, the Education Officer for the AMWU, to join Carmichael and himself at a union education programme. I was very keen to do so as I had not met Carmichael but knew his reputation as a fiery and powerful speaker.

I was invited to make a presentation on piecework and bonus systems to a workshop for shop stewards from the International Harvester plant in Geelong. I knew very little about this subject but I was asked to provide a simple explanation about different systems and how they worked. I gave my presentation and was followed by Carmichael who told the shop stewards: 'Now that you have been told about bonus systems, I am going to explain to you why our union policy is to reject these systems as exploitation'. I had not been advocating bonus systems but simply outlining how they were generally constructed. I complained to Carmichael that I thought I had been 'set up' and felt rather foolish. He replied that it was nothing personal and I had done a good job explaining the different systems, but his role was to instruct the shop stewards that it was union policy not to have anything to do with bonus systems. At lunch, I was approached by the chief shop steward and expected to face further criticisms of bonus systems. But instead he asked me if I could send him a copy of my presentation. I responded that Laurie had warned them off having anything to do with bonus systems. He replied: 'Laurie's a great bloke but our members working here all depend on getting a good bonus and we need to know how we can work the system to our advantage!'

In later years, when I moved to Sydney, I would often invite Laurie Carmichael to come and speak to my classes. He was an impressive speaker willing to challenge the students and expose them to a union perspective. Towards the end of his career, he was recruited by Bill Kelty to the ACTU and was greatly honoured by the trade union movement when he died in his 90s.

Ian Macphee

Ian Macphee was Minister for Productivity from 1976 to 1979 in the Coalition government led by Malcolm Fraser. His background was in industrial relations as he had been an advocate for employers and Director of the Chamber of Manufacturers in Victoria. He was regarded as a moderate in the Liberal Party and took a constructive approach to industrial relations. I met him early in his period as Minister and discovered that he had an interest in worker participation in management. We discussed some of the Nordic countries' experiences in this field. I also chaired a debate, hosted by the Institute of Directors, where Macphee debated the merits of corporate social responsibility against John Elliott, a businessman on the conservative right-wing of the Liberal Party.

I had been at Monash for a couple of years and was having some difficulties with my head of Department, Professor Keith Collins, who expressed some concerns about some of my research topics. Collins had become an academic late in his career, which had been spent mostly in the Navy where he been a high-ranking officer. He called me into his office one day and told me that, after some hesitation, he was recommending me for tenure but suggested that

I should focus my energies on research which was more closely aligned with mainstream management.

Soon after my difficult discussion with Collins, I received a call from Macphee's office saying that the Minister would be visiting Monash for some other purpose but wished to meet me. Macphee arrived with several of his ministerial staff and must have gone to the Departmental office and asked for me because he arrived at my door with Professor Collins. Realising that my room was too small to accommodate everyone, Macphee asked Collins if we could use his office for our meeting. I was not sure if this was going to make things even more difficult in my relationship with Collins but it seemed to increase my credibility. I was appointed to the research committee of the Productivity Promotion Council of Australia, which was in Macphee's portfolio, which may have been more in keeping with a management school's priorities.

Macphee was promoted to a Cabinet position as Minister for Employment from 1982 to 1983. He proved to be a moderating influence on the Fraser government and defended the role of compulsory arbitration and the industrial relations system. He resisted pressure from within conservative elements of the Cabinet, including the Treasurer John Howard, for more radical industrial relations reforms. However, when Howard became Leader of the Opposition, Macphee was dropped from his shadow portfolio and lost pre-selection to David Kemp, who was aligned with the right-wing of the Liberal Party. After retirement from parliament, Macphee served on the Board of CARE Australia, a humanitarian aid organisation, chaired by former Prime Minister Malcolm Fraser.

Publish or perish? The research imperative

During my early years at Monash, I was aware that it was important to produce academic publications but there was not the emphasis on aiming for the top international journals as there is today. I thought that publishing books would result in a higher profile, and I was keen to become a book author. I was also interested in a wide range of issues, and, having spent three years focusing on a single topic for my PhD, I wanted to expand my horizons. However, Jim Stern, a visiting professor from the University of Wisconsin (UW)-Madison, who was spending a six-month sabbatical at Monash, took me aside one day and told me that in order to build an academic career, I needed to focus on one or two topics in which I could become an expert and that I should be aiming to publish my research in the appropriate academic journals.

I did not realise that publishing a textbook was regarded as a low order priority in academia and that I should be pursuing research grants in my specialist field rather than following a random series of topics which interested me. Nevertheless, during my first five years at Monash, I published four books: one was a revision of my doctoral thesis, one was a textbook and two were on topical issues of the day. While I would not advise an early career researcher these days to follow my example, a couple of the books contributed debate in the media on current issues. I gained valuable early experience attempting to explain why issues such as improving the quality of work life (QWL), worker participation in management and reforming vocational education and training were important for Australian society.

Organisations: An Australian Perspective

Peter Gilmour and I published a short textbook, *Organisations: An Australian Perspective*, in 1976. It was quite successful and was revised and republished in four editions, the last of which was in 1991. It was probably somewhat audacious of Peter and I to publish a textbook when we each had only been teaching for a couple of years in the management field. Nevertheless, we sought to bring a new approach to the subject and to incorporate examples from Australian experience. We began with an introductory section which placed Australian organisations in a broader social, economic and political context. We then examined theories of organisation in terms of organisations as social systems and in terms of change and development. The third section of the book focused on individual and group behaviour in organisations and discussed the concept of worker participation in management, which was a somewhat radical idea at the time. The penultimate section comprised chapters on the impact of technological change on organisations, which was emerging as an important issue. Finally, we examined possible future scenarios for organisations from individual and environmental perspectives.

We were fortunate that there were few other Australian textbooks in this field at the time. In an introduction to the book, the Monash Dean, Donald Cochrane, wrote that University teachers in Australia had been 'only too ready to adapt, without too much questioning, texts designed for use in other countries'. He commended the book for urging that 'managers (should) adapt to new social attitudes, accommodate new approaches to work, respond to new approaches to learning, react to fluctuating economic conditions, adjust to changing economic policies of governments and be ready to introduce new technological processes'. The book was revised in 1983 and 1991 with the addition of a stronger emphasis on psychological dimensions, with Robert Spillane as co-author, and was retitled *Organisational Behaviour: The Australian Context*. Somewhat to our surprise and satisfaction, our publisher informed us that our book had found a niche in accounting courses where students were urged to gain a greater understanding of the social and behavioural aspects of organisations in which their practices were being applied.

Marginal Manager: The Changing Role of Supervisors in Australia

One of the Whitlam Labor government's key areas of reform was the education system. Although education is principally the responsibility of state governments, there is a history of the federal government providing grants and other forms of funding for education. One of the major initiatives by the Whitlam government was to end fees for most university courses in order to provide greater access to those who qualified for entrance to university but found the fees prohibitive. The Labor government also sought to upgrade the quality and status of technical and further education below university level. It established a Technical and Further Education Commission (TAFEC) with funds to transform this sector. Included in the reforms were research funds to undertake specific projects.

Peter Gilmour and I were interested in educational reform not only from an academic perspective but also because our children were entering the educational system and we were concerned about their future. We successfully applied for one of the first research grants issued by TAFEC in order to investigate the way in which supervisory and first-line management education was being delivered by Technical and Further Education (TAFE). We also sought to explore how students responded to these courses and applied what they learned in practice. Our research approach was strongly influenced by the work of my former PhD supervisor, Keith Thurley, who had published research on supervisors in the United Kingdom, Europe and Japan. The project resulted in a report and recommendations to TAFE as well as several academic papers and a book: *Marginal Manager: The Changing Role of Supervisors in Australia* (Gilmour and Lansbury, 1984).

Our research project on supervisors and first line managers involved an Australia-wide survey of students undertaking courses in TAFE colleges, a review of the curricula in each state and recommendations on how these courses could be modernised to better meet the needs of both students and the organisations in which they were employed. Following Keith Thurley's example, we argued that supervisors needed to play a key role in organisational change and become facilitators of workplace reform. The research grant provided us with the opportunity to visit a wide range of organisations in various industries around Australia, including manufacturing, mining and services, investigating the changing role of supervisors. We also drew on the example of the Volvo company, which I visited in Sweden, where workplace reforms provided workers with greater control over the organisation of their work. While this did not mean that supervisors became redundant, it did require them to play a different role and assist workers to become more self-managing.

Based on our survey and case study research, we concluded that supervisors could be a force for either reaction or reform as organisations continued to change. We proposed four alternative roles for supervisors in the future. First, they could continue in their role as a 'sub-manager' with a rather limited role and little prospect of promotion to a managerial level. Nevertheless, they would provide valuable assistance to line managers in terms of allocating employees to jobs, scheduling activities and assisting with recruitment, selection, training and assessment. Second, they could become first line managers along the lines of the German concept of 'meister' with a higher level of formal qualifications and a greater degree of authority. In Australia, this would require enlarging the scope of the supervisory role and responsibilities. Third, they could have their role redefined as a technical specialist, particularly where they are supervising the work of highly trained employees. A typical example was a research and development team undertaking complex tasks in which the supervisor played an integrative role. Finally, the supervisor could perform more of a facilitator role in semi-autonomous work groups, where the workers take more responsibility in allocating work between them, and are accountable for their own quality control and decision-making. This has been more typical of work organisation in Nordic countries where the supervisor assists and guides rather than controls the work of other employees.

In his introduction to our book, eminent US scholar George Strauss from the University of California-Berkeley, who undertook pioneering work in this field, noted that one of the driving forces behind the need for change in the supervisor's role were advances in technology which were impacting on organisations. According to Strauss, 'this is especially the case in companies engaging with various forms of job redesign, group technology and quality of work life experiments that the authors describe. All of these vastly change the first line manager's job... (which now is) to provide advice and win consensus rather than to give orders'. Strauss noted that a key finding from the research reported in our book was that the role of the supervisor will differ according to such factors as the nature of the work, the size of the organisation and the skills and attitudes of the workers involved. Strauss concluded that our study demonstrated that management needed to give much more thought to the roles they expect the first line manager or supervisor to play now and in the future. Strauss later was a visiting professor at Sydney University and became a valued mentor to me and other colleagues in the Department of Industrial Relations.

Although our study was conducted many decades ago, there has been relatively little subsequent research on the role of the supervisor, even though much has changed in terms of the technologies used by workers and organisations. The use of teams is much more prevalent than in former times and employees generally have higher formal qualifications than previously. With the decline of large manufacturing organisations, particularly in Australia, and the expansion of smaller but more complex high tech companies, supervisors require greater technical knowledge as well as more effective 'soft skills' when dealing with employees. The typical Australian workplace is now more likely to be in the service sector where the emphasis is not on production of goods but on interaction with clients and the public. Greater emphasis on transparency in managerial activity and workplace behaviour, particularly where there are concerns about discrimination or violation of employee rights, means that supervisors' behaviours as well as their effectiveness are under greater scrutiny than previously. The conclusions from our study still appear to be relevant to challenges faced by supervisors and their employing organisations.

Ticket to Nowhere? Education, Training and Work in Australia

At about the same time that Peter Gilmour and I obtained a grant from TAFEC to examine supervisory education in TAFE, I received an invitation from John Helmer to co-author a book on education, training and work in Australia.

Helmer had been a classmate of mine in Political Science at the University of Melbourne, gained a PhD at Harvard and subsequently pursued a diverse career in academia as well as an independent writer and journalist. Helmer persuaded Penguin Books in Australia to commission a series of books on new ideas for public policy. Helmer had read an opinion piece I had written on the need for greater emphasis on vocational education. Peter Gilmour had been undertaking a postgraduate qualification in teaching and was also interested in educational reform. We accepted John's offer and produced a book called *Ticket to Nowhere: Education, Training and Work in Australia*, published by Penguin in 1978. The title of the book was suggested by Helmer who was inspired by a book with a similar title: *Education and Jobs: The Great Training Robbery* by Ivar Berg, published by Penguin in 1973, which focused the need for training and educational reform in the United States.

The summary on the back cover of our book posed the question: 'Does the Australian education system allow people to achieve their full potential? Or does it offer a ticket to nowhere? Peter Gilmour and Russell Lansbury focus on professional, managers, women, migrants and the unemployed to see what tickets they get. They show that the gross inequalities of the system enable the advantaged to continue to move into well-paid, secure and stimulating work, while the disadvantaged are relegated to low-paid, boring jobs with little hope of security or advancement'. While this description rather oversimplified our argument, it did provide an accurate summary of the book.

We suggested various ways of how to reform the education system to achieve greater equality of opportunity including raising the standards of teaching in schools serving lower socio-economic regions in order to 'narrow the gap' between the most and least privileged schools. We also argued that equality of opportunity could only be achieved by reforms which addressed both the education system and the labour market, which are highly interdependent. In relation to higher education, while university reforms were needed, the upgrading and better resourcing of technical and further education should be the highest priority. We argued that 'active labour market' policies were needed to ensure that those who had lost their jobs or found it difficult to gain employment could be assisted. We advocated the adoption of some aspects of the Nordic approach (also found in some parts of North America) where students are given opportunities to spend a period of time in a 'folk high school' or 'community college' where they can 'try out' various skills and interests before they enter a skilled trade, technical specialism or profession. We concluded that education systems should be sufficiently flexible to enable individuals to make changes in their work situation and learn new skills at any stage of their working life.

We began research for the book during the period of the Whitlam Labor government when there was enthusiasm for educational reforms at all levels. The federal government assumed responsibility for funding higher education, which had hitherto been a matter for individual states. University fees were abolished and there followed a significant increase in the number of women, many with young children, who entered tertiary education. There was a major expansion of

Institutes of Technology and Colleges of Advanced Education which were intended to emphasise more vocationally oriented courses. TAFE remained a state responsibility but was given a boost of federal funds. However, there remained many challenges in terms of raising the status of institutions below the level of universities. The percentage of non-completion rates of apprenticeships and other trade-related courses also remained high and in need of attention. By the time the book was published in 1978, the federal Labor Party was in opposition, and the incoming Liberal National Party Coalition government had reimposed university fees and abandoned many of the Labor-initiated reforms.

The book gained favourable publicity and achieved a high number of sales, mainly due to being made required reading in a number of TAFE level courses. During the course of writing the book, I was interviewed on ABC radio during a visit to Sydney. In the ABC studio at the same time was Jack Mundey, the leader of the Builders Labourers Federation in NSW. He was being interviewed about the 'green bans' which were being placed by his union to protect the built and natural environment against inappropriate development. I was very pleased to meet Jack Mundey and had a chat with him after our respective interviews. I noticed that he had a black eye and asked him how this had occurred. 'I was jogging in a park near my home the other day when a big bloke came up beside me and belted me', he said. I was concerned and asked him if he had reported it to the police. 'Nah', said Jack. 'Anyway they haven't killed me yet'! Fortunately, Jack Mundey lived until 2020. He became a major figure in the conservation movement and an elected member of the Sydney City Council among many other achievements.

A symposium on the book was held at La Trobe University in Melbourne which attracted some notable participants from business, education and trade unions who discussed issues raised in our book. Senator John Button, who was the shadow Minister for Education in the federal Labor Party, expressed interest in some of the policy proposals. He later invited me to join his staff as a policy adviser but said to me: 'Education will never be a vote winner and I intend to move to a more important portfolio involving industry development where your proposals would be very relevant to improving the skills of the workforce'.

John Button became a reforming Minister for Industry in the Hawke Labor government and developed what became known as 'Button Plans' to reform the automotive and steel industries in order to make them more efficient. This involved rationalisation of the industries and upgrading of technology, with retraining of the workforce. However, this did not occur until the election of the Labor government in 1983, led by Bob Hawke, and valuable time was lost in reforming both education and industry during the Liberal National Coalition government led by Malcolm Fraser between 1975 and 1983.

Performance Appraisal: Managing Human Resources

In 1974, soon after I joined Monash University, the Whitlam government announced a Royal Commission on Australian Government Administration headed by the legendary Dr H.C. (Nugget) Coombs, former Governor of the Reserve Bank and one of the last 'Mandarins' who had served at the highest levels of the Commonwealth Public Service since the 1940s. Two of the four commissioners had been professors at Monash: Enid Campbell from the Law School and Joe Isaac from Economics. By the time it reported in 1976, the Whitlam government was out of office, and most of the Commission's recommendations were not implemented. Yet many of its ideas did eventually filter through and had an impact on the public service. Coombs was highly respected on both sides of politics even though many of his ideas challenged the status quo.

The Coombs Report was critical of the Australian Public Service as 'excessively hierarchical, excessively rigid and inflexible and excessively resistant to organisational change'. Among its most controversial recommendations were the enactment of anti-discrimination legislation and the enhancing of equal employment opportunity. The Coombs Report also recommended the establishment of a separately defined senior executive category and statutory expression of the merit principle for promotion. Many of these recommendations were subsequently introduced, but not until many years later.

Professor Joe Isaac left Monash University to take up a Deputy President role on the Australian Industrial Relations Commission in 1994 and soon after was appointed to a part-time Commissioner's role on the Coombs Royal Commission, with responsibility for overseeing research. The Coombs Commission engaged academics and consultants for specific research tasks. I was invited to undertake a minor project investigating performance appraisal systems and their use within the Australian Public Service. During 1975, I undertook a survey of performance appraisal systems across the APS and a sample of large private-sector organisations. In the course of this research, I also visited a number of organisations and interviewed managers and staff to gain insight into how the appraisal systems operated, the attitudes of employees and their perceived effectiveness by managers, employees and unions.

These days, the term 'performance management' has replaced 'appraisal' and perhaps reflects a more 'managerialist' approach. This contrasts with my recommendations which were to have a 'two way' approach in which employees could also provide feedback to management on their performance. This has been partly achieved through the so-called '360 degrees' approach in which performance of an individual can be viewed from the perspective of a wider range of managers, colleagues and subordinates. I also argued for the emphasis in performance appraisal to be placed more on the personal and career development of employees rather than using it simply as a method of assessment for the purposes of paying a bonus or determining promotion. Certainly, the prevalence of performance appraisal systems and their use for multiple purposes has become greater since my research was undertaken for the Royal Commission.

Following the submission of my report, about 20 representatives from the departments in the Australian Public Service as well as from a similar number of private-sector organisations which I had surveyed came to Monash University for a one-day seminar to review and comment on my findings. To my surprise about 50 participants attended and lively discussion occurred about different approaches to performance appraisal. Interest was expressed in having a longer and more structured follow-up at which academic research would be discussed alongside examples drawn from organisations in the private and public sector. Thus began a series of two- to three-day seminars which continued for almost a decade. In the course of these seminars, I gathered papers from the international literature and identified a number of organisations which were practising innovative approaches to this subject. In 1981, I edited a book entitled *Performance Appraisal: Managing Human Resources* which was published by Macmillan in several editions. It included both theoretical chapters as well as case studies from organisations in Australia and around the world, including North America, United Kingdom and Israel.

In the preface to the book, I noted that one factor which had been a major influence in the design of appraisal in the United States was 'equal opportunity legislation'. A number of federal court decisions in the United States had argued that appraisal systems must meet various criteria such as being essential to the 'safe and efficient conduct of business', that no other method can be used to achieve the same necessary business purpose that would be less discriminatory in its effects and that an organisation which uses an appraisal system must demonstrate that it is 'valid', namely, that it is job related and accurately measures significant aspects of job performance. I argued that Australia was likely to follow the US example as laws were passed to prevent discrimination and provide equal opportunities for all employees.

I predicted that unions would become more interested in these matters, particularly in the public sector and among white-collar and service-sector workers. I thought that unions would seek to become more involved in the design and introduction of new appraisal systems and handling problems arising out of their application. This has proved to be more applicable to the public sector where unions remain strong and influential than in the private services sector where managerial prerogative is more dominant.

Later, I was invited by the head of the Public Service Board in New South Wales to chair the Executive Performance Management Advisory Committee (EPMAC), which met for several years and comprised several heads of Departments and Authorities. The role of the EPMAC committee was to review all public service organisations in NSW to ensure that they had effective systems of appraisal to monitor the performance of senior management. With the assistance of external consultants, criteria were developed for performance management systems to which individual organisations had to adhere. This meant that individual organisations had flexibility in designing systems providing they met certain agreed principles. Once the systems were reviewed and approved by EPMAC, organisations were permitted to proceed. There was also follow-up a year or so later to ensure that the systems were working effectively. A major strength of the overall system was that it was applied across the entire state public service and that EPMAC provided oversight. A weakness was that it was only required to be applied to the performance of senior management and did not necessarily permeate the rest of the organisation. The experience of chairing EPMAC gave me the opportunity to implement some of my ideas in practice.

Improving the Quality of Work Life

One of the first graduate students I met at Monash was Geoffrey Prideaux, a senior public servant in the federal Department of Labour, who was also enrolled in a Master's degree in Administration at Monash University. We established a friendship and research partnership which resulted in several projects and publications which lasted well beyond my period at Monash. Prideaux later became a senior academic, completing a PhD at Boston University and heading the School of Management at the Royal Melbourne Institute of Technology University. Prideaux and I wrote a book on *Improving the Quality of Working Life* which was published in 1978. There was increasing interest in this subject in North America and Europe where Centres and Institutes dedicated to QWL were established. When Prideaux and I wrote our book, interest in this field was only just emerging in Australia. Our book was divided into two: the first section argued that the QWL needed improvement in Australia. The second half of the book set out 'actions for change' and included examples of how work and organisational structures could be redesigned; safety and health improved in the workplace, working time could be varied and new approaches to management adopted which would create a better life at work.

Kenneth Walker, an eminent Australian social scientist who had headed the International Institute for Labour Studies at the International Labour Organisation, noted, in his foreword to our book, that the OECD, ILO, European Union and World Health Organization all had urged their member countries to improve the quality of working lives of their citizens. Walker argued that the industrial relations system in Australia had the potential to both foster as well as hinder improvements in the quality of life at work. On the positive side, Australian workers (then) were well represented by trade unions, aided by arbitral tribunals, which could facilitate their voices being heard. However, Walker criticised Australian unions for failing to offer their members technical and educational services which could improve their ability to have meaningful dialogue and negotiations over issues relating to their QWL. He also argued that the dominance of the arbitration system tended to focus the attention of the parties on what could be obtained from the tribunals rather than how they could improve their daily relationship.

Sabbatical leave in France and the United States

From mid-1977 to early 1978, I was granted my first sabbatical leave of six months. The first part was spent in France at the European Institute of Business Administration (INSEAD) at Fontainebleau. The second was at the Industrial

Relations Research Institute at the UW-Madison, United States. I was interested to work with Kenneth Walker whom I had met during my doctoral studies at the LSE when he was at the ILO in Geneva. Walker's initial education at the University of Western Australia (UWA) had combined Psychology and Economics and he obtained a PhD at Harvard on industrial relations under the supervision of John T. Dunlop. After a period as Professor of Psychology at UWA he joined the ILO and became Deputy Director General in charge of the International Institute for Labour Studies, which was a quasi 'think tank'. While at the Institute, Walker had initiated research into industrial democracy and became a leader international figure in this field.

In correspondence with Walker, after he moved from the ILO to INSEAD, I discovered that the French government had established an inquiry into industrial democracy ('autogestion') under a prominent French Deputy, Pierre Sudreau. With Walker's support, I obtained a French government grant to investigate how the Sudreau Report was received and its recommendations applied in France. I was able to discuss the ideas in the Report with the author and gain insight into the debate in France through interviews with the protagonists, for and against the proposals. Eventually, there were legislative reforms in France to establish a form of works councils which have provided a means of participation in decision-making at the enterprise level for French workers. The experience enabled me to gain a deeper understanding of the variety of perspectives on industrial democracy in Europe.

The second half of my sabbatical at the UW-Madison was a life and career-enhancing experience. While at Monash, I was fortunate to meet two US visiting professors: Jim Stern and Morris Weisz. Both had been invited to Monash by Joe Isaac before he moved to the Australian Industrial Relations Commission. Jim Stern was a Professor of Economics and former Director of the Industrial Relations Research Institute (IRRI) at UW-Madison. After graduating from university as an engineer, Stern served in the US Navy during WW2 and then worked in Paris for the US-funded Marshall Plan to revive European economies after the war. After returning to the United States, he gained a PhD in Economics from University of California-Berkeley. Stern then joined the United Auto Workers' Union (UAW) during its halcyon days in the 1950s and worked directly for Walter Reuther, the union President. Most of Stern's subsequent academic career was at UW-Madison where he specialised in public sector collective bargaining and became an active arbitrator. Morris Weisz came as a visitor to Monash after retiring from the OECD where he was a senior official, having built a career in the US Department of Labor at the international level serving as a US Labor Attache in several countries. Weisz had begun his working life with the clothing workers union in New York. He also went to UW-Wisconsin as a visiting scholar after he was at Monash.

Jim Stern invited me to be a visiting scholar at the Institute for Industrial Relations Research at UW-Madison, with my family, for three months in 1977–1978. While at the Institute, I was fortunate to meet many of the legendary industrial relations academics who were nearing retirement. They included

Jack Barbash, Everett Kassalow and Solomon Levine. Younger faculty members included Dick Miller and Donald Schwab. Morris Weisz was also at the Institute and knew many of the older generation academics who, like himself, had been active in the labour movement during their earlier career. I was surprised how willing many of the older academics were to spend time discussing industrial relations with me. I also met several PhD students from a range of countries with whom I would continue to have contact in later years. In December, I attended the annual Industrial Relations Research Association (IRRA) in New York and met many other academics from throughout the United States.

It was also my good fortune to be visiting UW-Madison at the same time as a group of eminent Swedish academics, including Nobel Prize winning economist Gunnar Myrdal and his equally famous wife Alva Myrdal. Both had served as ministers in previous Social Democratic governments in Sweden and were founders of the Swedish welfare state. The Myrdals, aged in their mid-70s, were visiting scholars in the Institute of Poverty at UW-Madison where they gave several seminars. I had heard Alva Myrdal deliver an address at the University of Lund in 1967 when she was a prominent member of the Swedish government. Alva Myrdal had held senior positions at UNESCO and was an active participant in UN disarmament conferences. She was awarded the Nobel Peace Prize in 1982. Gunnar Myrdal was an economist and sociologist who was awarded the Nobel Prize for Economics in 1974. He held many academic positions as well as working with the UN. It was a great privilege to meet the Myrdals and attend seminars given by them in Madison.

I was also fortunate to meet two other prominent Swedes, Walter Korpi and Rudolf Meidner, who were visiting UW-Madison during 1977 and were experts in my areas of interest. Walter Korpi was the Director of the Institute of Social Research at the University of Stockholm. He had worked as a researcher at the Swedish Metal Workers Union and urged the Social Democratic government to do more to strengthen the welfare state and active labour market policies. Rudolf Meidner had been a prominent economist with the Swedish Trade Union Confederation (LO) and had been a student of Gunnar Myrdal at Stockholm University. Meidner was the co-author of the so-called 'Rehn-Meidner model' of economic growth and wage policy with Gosta Rehn when they worked together at the LO. Their model had a strong influence on the Swedish Social Democratic governments from the 1950s to the 1970s as it advocated economic growth combined with egalitarian wage policies and a strong welfare state.

The Swedish Social Democrats had lost the national election in 1976. One of the factors which was believed to have contributed to this loss was a proposal by Meidner to establish a wage earners' fund. If enacted, all companies over a certain size would be required to use up to 20 per cent of their profits to issue new shares to workers. The aim of the fund was to enable workers, through their unions, to eventually gain greater decision-making influence in private-sector companies. Hence, the proposal was regarded as a step towards economic democracy. The Social Democrats finally regained government in 1981 and enacted a modified version of the fund in 1983, but this was dismantled by a Conservative government in 1991.

Meidner was in the process of writing a book on his proposals while he was in Madison and I had the opportunity to attend a series of seminars which portended publication of his 1978 book *Employee Investment Funds: An Approach to Collective Capital Formation*. Meidner argued that his proposal was not only aimed at giving workers greater economic democracy but also to prevent a flight of capital from Sweden and ensure greater domestic investment in Swedish industry. But he worried that his wage earner proposal had been portrayed as too radical and had assisted conservative parties to win the election.

The months that I spent at UW-Madison in 1977–1978 made a deep impression on me. Not only did I learn more about Swedish social democracy but I also gained an appreciation of the way in which US universities emphasised collaboration between local and international academic researchers. I retained life-long associations with people I met in Madison, several of whom later came to Sydney as visiting scholars and on Fulbright fellowships. The Industrial Relations Research Institute became a model for research centres which I would help to establish at Macquarie and Sydney universities. I am greatly indebted to Jim Stern who had facilitated my visit to Madison and allowed me to accompany him to arbitration sessions which he conducted between union and employer representatives in Wisconsin. The Madison visit laid the foundation for a Fulbright Fellowship which I gained to attend Harvard and MIT in 1984.

Advocating industrial democracy in Australia

Unfortunately, the advocates of improving the QWL during the late 1970s and early 1980s failed to convince employers, unions and governments that this should be a priority and relatively little progress ensued. A similar fate was experienced by those who took a more radical approach to change at the workplace through 'industrial' or 'workplace democracy'. The concept of industrial democracy can be traced back to the late nineteenth century in England, when Sidney and Beatrice Webb published a book with this name (Webb and Webb, 1897). However, industrial democracy has taken different forms and meanings over the past century or more. The Webbs described industrial democracy as a pre-condition for democratic socialism. The Fabian tradition was continued by G.D.H. Cole who argued that genuine political democracy could only be achieved when industry was organised on a participatory basis and employees became self-governing in the workplace. In the United States, early writings by John R. Commons and Selig Perlman stressed the importance of first establishing union control in the workplace (Lansbury, 1980).

The revival of interest in the concept of industrial democracy from the 1960s onwards came mainly from Europe where it was associated with employee participation in various aspects of decision-making within the enterprise. However, examples during this period varied considerably from co-determination and works councils in West Germany to so-called 'self management' in the then Yugoslavia. Fred Emery, an Australian psychologist, based at the Tavistock Institute of Human Relations in the United Kingdom, in collaboration with Eric Trist, distinguished between direct or participatory democracy at the workplace level, with indirect or representational democracy, which generally involves the election of representatives to decision-making bodies within the enterprise. Emery favoured the former which found expression in 'self-managing groups' within the Norwegian off-shore oil industry and other sectors which he investigated with Einar Thorsrud. After returning to Australia in the late 1960s, Emery was engaged in a number of experiments with self-managing groups in organisations but few survived in their original form.

During the 1970s, there was considerable debate about introducing industrial democracy or a milder form of employee participation in management within Australia. The trade union movement was divided as some union leaders were apprehensive about works councils or similar bodies displacing unions in the workplace, while managers feared losing their authority if they had to share decision-making with others in the workplace. Nevertheless, the Labor government of South Australia, under the leadership of Premier Don Dunstan, established a Unit for Industrial Democracy in the Premier's Department to undertake research and collaborate with employers and unions in fostering various forms of worker participation.

Olle and Ruth Hammarstrom played an important role in the South Australian Unit when they came from Sweden in 1976 for 18 months on an exchange programme between the Australian and Swedish Labour ministries. They were both very active in informing unions and employers in Australia about the Swedish experience with democracy in the workplace. After returning to Sweden, Olle became Research Director at one of Sweden's largest white-collar unions, while Ruth became Human Resource Director at Folksam, a major cooperative insurance company. Both retained strong connections with Australia and hosted many visitors to Sweden. They returned to Australia in 1990 to spend a year as visiting researchers in the Department of Industrial Relations at the University of Sydney. Sadly, Ruth died in a tragic ferry disaster in the Baltic in 1994 when returning to Sweden from Estonia where she had been involved in assisting the Estonians to introduce cooperatives. Olle and his family remain our close friends.

In 1980, I published a book entitled *Democracy in the Workplace* which I hoped would stimulate an informed debate on this subject. The book included both local and international research which had been published in various journals but had not been brought together in one collection. I also gathered case studies of employee and union-management cooperation and asked people who had been involved in such activities to write chapters for the book. The book created interest and was reviewed favourably in academic journals and some newspapers. However, there was no ground-swell of support among employers or unions for these examples of employee participation to be replicated. Nevertheless, following the election of the Hawke Labor government in 1983, there was considerable government support for union-employer cooperation.

By 1986, there were enough new examples of employee participation and involvement to justify a new edition of the book, which I jointly edited with Ed Davis, entitled *Democracy and Control in the Workplace*. The addition of the word 'control' in the title was recognition of the fact that there was a growing debate about whether changes at the workplace to grant workers a greater voice would lead to 'worker control'. Conversely, there was a view that by collaborating with management, workers were ceding greater control to management.

The Hawke Labor government discussed the option of commissioning a 'Green Paper on Employee Participation'. There was considerable discussion between employers and unions which resulted in a degree of consensus and joint expressions of support for some forms of employee participation in management. An important report was published by the ACTU in 1986, entitled *Australia Reconstructed*, following a high-level union delegation to Europe, with a particular focus on Germany and Sweden. The report supported the general concept of industrial democracy but focused more on recommendations for restructuring the Australian economy and providing unions with a more active role in policy making. It also recommended that merging unions into larger entities would strengthen their bargaining power. It was this latter recommendation which gained the most support from the unions and was eventually enacted.

However, action to achieve industrial democracy did not have support from business organisations. This was partly because the Business Council of Australia seized the agenda by arguing strongly for a shift to enterprise bargaining as a key industrial relations reform. The BCA and other employer organisations eventually convinced the Hawke government to support enterprise bargaining and the unions agreed, albeit with a different conception of how a decentralised system would work. The latter part of the 1980s and early 1990s saw industrial democracy fade from the industrial relations agenda as the new enterprise bargaining system consumed the attention of the government, unions and employers. The Hawke government eventually released a *Discussion Paper on Employee Participation*, but this contained no concrete proposals for reform and the issue disappeared as a matter of public policy.

Life beyond Monash University

After the overseas sabbatical, we returned to live in Melbourne for a further three years. However, the experience in Europe and the United States stimulated my desire for new challenges and would ultimately lead to our move to Sydney. Nevertheless, Melbourne offered a number of opportunities outside of university life. Not only did we have family but also many friends from our younger days in Melbourne. With two other families, we purchased some land near Acheron, two hours from Melbourne, on which we built an inexpensive pre-fabricated house as a weekend 'retreat'. We agisted a horse from a farmer so that Gwen could teach our children to ride. We had many enjoyable holidays there. One of our partners, Jim Kennan, went into politics and became Deputy Premier and later the parliamentary leader of the ALP in Victoria. John Howie, our other partner, became a prominent Labor lawyer.

Monash University is in an outer suburban area of Melbourne which, in the early 1970s, offered affordable housing. We purchased a house within walking and cycling distance from the campus. Our daughter Nina was born in June 1975 and we became a family of four. Living close to the campus on a housing estate with other young families, many of whom were attached to Monash, was a very congenial place to bring up our children. We were also close to our extended family. Gwen undertook studies for a BA in Sociology and Geography and then later upgraded her Physiotherapy degree to a Bachelor of Applied Science. We took advantage of childcare and pre-school activities on campus for both of our children. We also were foundation members of a new branch of the ALP based on our local residential area which incorporated Monash University. We named it the 'Notting Hill Branch', after the local hotel near the university, and many of the members were staff and students at Monash University.

Gwen and I became active not only in our local ALP branch but also in the Victorian Fabian Society which held discussion meetings, ran an annual lecture series, published pamphlets and books and sought to influence ALP policy from a social democratic perspective. With the support of local branch members, I was elected to the Victorian ALP Policy Committee on Industrial Relations and gained a taste of how policy decisions are made. I met some impressive union officials on the industrial relations policy committee, including Simon Crean and Bill Kelty. However, my attempts to persuade the committee to adopt a policy on industrial democracy failed as some saw this as a threat to the union monopoly of worker representation. This changed in time and both the ACTU and the ALP later developed comprehensive policies on industrial democracy, although these were not enacted. I discovered that the unions regarded industrial relations policy as their exclusive domain. I recall telling a prominent union leader how pleased I was to have been elected to the industrial relations policy committee. 'Why are you wasting your time?' he asked me. 'The unions set the industrial relations policies for the ALP, not the policy committee!'

There were also lessons I learned about factional politics, which I should have known from my studies in Political Science. Our new Notting Hill branch invited speakers from all factions to address us. We wished to remain independent and not bound to a particular faction, but we came under strong pressure from both the Left and Right to join them. This was important in terms of being part of a voting bloc at the Party conference and in pre-selection ballots for candidates to stand in state and federal elections. With a federal election coming up, our federal electoral assembly met and chose a member of the Notting Hill Branch to stand for the seat of Bruce which was regarded as a 'safe' Liberal seat. A few months before the election, I was contacted by a senior member of the ALP who invited me to stand as the candidate for Bruce. 'You won't win', he told me, 'but if you stand and do well, we will find you a more winnable seat next time'. I responded that I was not interested in being a politician and that a candidate had already been pre-selected by the usual procedures. 'Don't worry', he replied, 'We can de-select her and declare you as the candidate'. I protested that this was unconstitutional but was told: 'It's not personal, just politics'! Needless to say, I did not stand for election but our candidate lost!

I continued to play a minor role in ALP politics as I was determined to contribute to the defeat of the Coalition government, led by Malcolm Fraser. Professor Mal Logan, who would later become the Vice-Chancellor of Monash, had been a senior public servant during the Whitlam Labor government. He was an adviser to Bill Hayden who had succeeded Gough Whitlam as federal Labor leader. At the invitation of Hayden, Logan assembled a group of academics to draft a series of policy documents on various topics which could provide Hayden with ideas for policy reforms. I was asked to draft the industrial relations policy paper and joined with others in discussion with Logan, which proved to be a more interesting experience than being on the ALP policy committee! Just before the 1983 election, Hayden was replaced by Bob Hawke as he was regarded as a more likely candidate to defeat Malcolm Fraser. After Hawke's election as Labor PM, new policies were introduced, some of which may have been derived from the documents we prepared for Bill Hayden. However, the centre piece of the industrial relations reforms was the Accord on Incomes and Prices, which was heavily influenced by union leaders, and was not among my policy proposals. But the Accord provided the foundation for significant social and economic reform by the Hawke and Keating Labor governments from 1983 to 1996.

Experiences of organisational consulting

My experience of organisations beyond school and universities was very limited, apart from my doctoral research at British Airways, when I arrived back in Australia to teach in the Management Department at Monash University. However, my friend Peter Clark was already active in this field and would later become a leading consultant to organisations in Australia and internationally. I had met Clark when we were undergraduates at Melbourne University where we were both active in student associations. Peter Clark and I arrived in London around the same time, and he enrolled in a PhD at the London Business School while I was at LSE. We also returned to academic jobs in Melbourne in the same year and continued our friendship and collaboration to this day.

Peter Clark had already gained experience as a consultant after completing an MBA at Melbourne University and working in the United Kingdom. Clark has an insightful mind and provided me with crucial assistance while I was struggling with my doctoral thesis and trying to make sense of the data I had collected. During the seven years I spent at Monash, and later in Sydney, I collaborated with Clark on consulting projects in a range of organisations in the public and private sectors. These experiences greatly enhanced my understanding of problems faced by managers and employees in the workplace. The projects I undertook with Clark also enabled me to gain a greater insight into 'action research' which Keith Thurley at LSE and others at the Tavistock Institute in London advocated. The term was first coined by Kurt Lewin in the United States in the 1940s and 1950s but came into vogue in the 1960s and 1970s. Simply put, action research can be defined as achieving organisational change through the simultaneous process of taking action and doing research, linked together by critical reflection. We engaged in this process in most of our projects. As academics, we sought to link what we did in our consulting roles with our understanding of organisational theory. I used examples from our engagement with various organisations in subsequent publications.

One of the organisations for which Peter Clark and I consulted was a major multinational company in the glass industry. Initially we were approached by the HR Director at head office who sought our assistance at one of the company's major plants which was regarded as performing below its potential. A previous investigation had identified problems with first-line managers as a major contributing factor. Our discussions with managers and employees revealed that there were deeper problems arising from rapid changes in the industry. During the next 12 months, we held separate consultations with people at different levels and functions in order to identify issues of importance to them. This included several residential workshops away from the plant with representatives from all levels in the organisation. Through this means, critical issues were identified, and task forces were established to find long-term solutions.

As a result of our consultations with management, union representatives and the workforce, the company adopted a collaborative approach to meet the ongoing social and technological changes facing the industry. The project attracted attention from the head office of the company in the United Kingdom and led to us undertaking work in other plants. Peter Clark left academia and established a successful consulting business with the glass company as one of his long-term clients. I continued to collaborate with Peter Clark but focussed my attention on research rather than consulting.

6 Transition to Sydney
The Hawke/Keating era begins (1981–1986)

Although Monash had provided me with wonderful opportunities, I was interested in research being undertaken elsewhere, particularly at the University of New South Wales (UNSW) in Sydney where I began to collaborate with Bill Ford and Dexter Dunphy in the Department of Organisational Behaviour. Furthermore, when Di Yerbury left the Federal Department of Labour and returned to academia, she assumed a foundation Chair and Professorship at the newly established Australian Graduate School of Management (AGSM) at UNSW. Hence, when approached about an appointment in the Management School at Macquarie University in Sydney, I was very interested. However, I was also invited to apply for a professorship in Management at the recently established Deakin University which was based in Geelong near Melbourne. I applied and was offered both positions, but Macquarie University only offered an Associate Professorship compared with the full professorship at Deakin.

However, Sydney proved to be a more attractive proposition especially after my family and I visited Sydney during a lovely sunny week in the middle of winter from cold and wet Melbourne. We were also given a very warm welcome by the head of the Management School at Macquarie, Bruce McKern and his colleagues, particularly Robert Spillane who had encouraged and supported my application for the position. It was also a bonus that my close colleague from Monash, Peter Gilmour was offered and accepted a parallel position to mine by Macquarie University.

Leaving Melbourne imposed hardship on Gwen who gave up some good working opportunities when we moved to Sydney. Owen had just completed his first couple of years at primary school, and Nina was about to begin at the same school. We also would be leaving behind my widowed mother, Gwen's parents and many friends. However, we chose to live at Clareville Beach on the northern beaches of Sydney, and the children settled happily into school. Our house overlooked Pittwater and Gwen stated that she had 'now found the place I wish to live for the rest of my life'. This proposition was tested a couple of years later when I was invited by the acting Vice-Chancellor at the University of Melbourne to apply for a professorial chair and director's position at the Melbourne Business School. Gwen told me that I would have to move back to Melbourne by myself if I was offered the job. I never applied and we have remained happily in Sydney ever since. After completing a Master's degree in Community Health at UNSW and having undertaken various health research projects, Gwen was appointed to a lectureship in Physiotherapy at the University of Sydney.

Macquarie University was established in 1964. The university is located on a beautiful green campus in the northern suburbs of Sydney and, at that time, was only about 40 minutes drive from our home at Clareville. It now has a major 'high tech' industrial park and has seen exponential growth in student numbers to over 40,000. In 1981, the Management School had only a small number of full-time academic staff. Since then, the Graduate School of Management has grown substantially. Its MBA and related programmes are highly ranked both in Australia and overseas, particularly in Asia where it offers degrees.

The Management School was led by Bruce McKern who, along with Donald Gibson, had taken a Doctoral degree in Management from Harvard and modelled the MBA programme on the 'Harvard case study method'. I learned to write case studies using data gained from organisations based in Sydney, but often with international operations, such as Qantas Airways. The MBA was the main programme, and students took this part-time while working. Most of the students had at least five years work experience and were in junior management roles. There was also an Advanced Management Program which was conducted full-time over four weeks in summer when the participants lived on campus in student housing. The teaching programme was intensive, using didactic learning methods as well as having numerous guest speakers from industry. The programme had been going for ten years when I joined the School and was very well supported by major private-sector companies and government instrumentalities which paid substantial course fees to enable their employees to participate. There were also 'refresher' programmes lasting a few days to a week on various topics during the year. Together with Robert Spillane, I conducted short programmes on Human Resource Management and Industrial Relations each year when I was at Macquarie. The School also had a high-powered advisory board, chaired by the CEO of IBM and included CEOs from major companies in banking, oil and gas, mining, retail and manufacturing companies as well as the public service and unions.

Soon after my arrival at Macquarie, I was asked to teach industrial relations in the advanced management programme. I thought that one way to make my sessions more interesting would be to take the class of about 30 participants to view a case before the NSW Industrial Commission. The registrar at the Commission suggested I ask Justice Macken if he would be willing to have my class attend his court and then discuss the case with him afterwards. When I met the Judge, he told me that he had a case coming up which might interest the class, so the visit was arranged. At first, it seemed a simple case of a waitress and her lawyer bringing a case of unfair dismissal against her employer. But as Justice Macken probed her employer's lawyer more deeply, it transpired that the 'late night supper club', where the waitress had worked, was one of many 'entertainment venues' owned by Abe Saffron who, at that time, was a major crime figure in NSW. Saffron's lawyer was reluctant to describe the duties of the 'waitress' and what she was paid, but the Judge decided that a significant termination payment was justified. After the hearing, Judge Macken met the class and explained the intricacies of applying labour law to cases involving businesses owned by Abe Saffron. The next day the sensational details of the case were in the newspapers and my students saw industrial relations as a much more interesting subject than they had anticipated!

Teaching and research at Macquarie University

At Macquarie, I was required to teach across a wide range of units including Organisational Behaviour, Organisational Design and Development, Human Resource Management and Industrial Relations. Robert Spillane led the teaching in the units dealing with organisational issues to which he applied his background and expertise in Psychology. Together, we initiated a number of intensive programmes, building on the annual Advanced Management Program, which were aimed at providing a 'refresher' as well as an introduction to current thinking and application of concepts in organisational psychology and HR as well as industrial relations in organisations.

I encountered some difficulties in my first year at Macquarie when I was invited to teach a unit called 'Management and Society' to the MBA students. I decided to focus on some current social and economic issues facing Australia. During 1981–1983, there was a recession and rising unemployment, so I asked the students to address the issue of how government and the wider community should respond to the looming job losses. A group of students complained that this was not a relevant issue for MBA students who were taking the degree in order to be more effective business managers and not to solve the problems of society. I realised that I was failing to convince them about the importance of this issue for management. I invited Laurie Carmichael, a leading trade union leader, to speak to the class. He challenged the students to consider the social responsibility of management and drew on his personal experience as a young person attempting to enter the workforce during the latter period of the Great Depression. He succeeded in getting the message across to most of the class although some remained unconvinced. However, at the end of the year, I was approached by a student who told me that he and others in the class had lost their jobs during the year and felt demoralised. However, after undertaking the assignment and listening to Carmichael, he realised that becoming unemployed was not his fault but the consequence of larger economic forces. I felt that the teaching the unit had not been in vain.

Robert Spillane and I co-authored *Organisational Behaviour: The Australian Context* (revised and published in 1983) which included chapters on 'Motivation and Group Behaviour', 'Action Approaches to Organisational Behaviour' and on topical issues such as 'Occupational Stress and Work Effectiveness', 'Job Design' and 'Democracy in the Workplace'. Our general approach in the book was to take a more critical stance towards current management and organisational practices, arguing that:

> In Australia we are yet to develop the consciousness of the need to change our system of industrial relations, redesign our systems of work and organisation and upgrade the skills of our nation's labour force in order to survive the massive changes between now and the end of the twentieth century (which at that stage looked a long way off!).

Like its predecessors, the book went through several reprints until we revised it again in 1991. This revision was about 50 pages longer but while this edition did not include new chapters, there were some changes in emphasis reflected in chapters such as 'Occupational Stress and Health Management', reflecting a broader approach to well-being at work, 'Employee Participation and Industrial Democracy' and integrating 'Technological Change, Management and Industrial Relations'. These changes reflected some of the key reforms introduced by the Hawke Labor government, elected in 1983, during their first eight years in office. The book ended with a section entitled: 'Management's Crisis of Legitimacy' in which we argued that: 'Managers are rightly blamed for poor productivity and profits (as well as) being incompetent and inefficient... They consistently fail to allow employees to accept responsibility and authority for their job, work group and plant or office community'. We hoped that our book might stir managers out of their complacency.

During most of my years at Macquarie Graduate School of Management, the Hawke Labor government had industrial relations as well as economic and social reform at the heart of its agenda. This made it easier to persuade my colleagues and the head of the Management School that a unit of study in Industrial Relations should be compulsory in the first year of the MBA. It was also fortuitous that in 1982, the year after I joined Macquarie, *Industrial Relations: An Australian Introduction*, which I had co-authored with John Hill and Bill Howard, was published. This was not strictly a textbook but a series of essays which we had written on various topics. We rather boldly stated in the preface that 'rather than replicating detailed descriptions provided elsewhere of the various parties, institutions and processes involved in Australian industrial relations, this book seeks to provide some analysis of the operations of these'. Furthermore, we noted that 'the three authors developed a "team teaching" approach to industrial relations at Monash University, and this book reflects many long hours of discussion about the subject'. This latter statement was true, and I missed the camaraderie that I had at Monash when we shared teaching of the subject.

At Macquarie, I continued to pursue my interest in the concept of industrial democracy. In 1980, I edited *Democracy in the Workplace*, which I revised in 1986, with Ed Davis, as *Democracy and Control in the Workplace*. During the early 1980s, there was considerable optimism that the 'time was right' for progress to be made in industrial democracy, particularly after the Hawke Labor government was elected. Under the Accord between the trade unions and the Labor government, there were a number of initiatives to improve the working lives as a 'trade-off' for workers and their unions exercising wage restraint. These included increasing the 'social wage' through improvements in education and health care which would be shared by all Australians. At a National Economic Summit, sponsored by the government soon after its election, emphasis was given to improving cooperation between employers, unions and the government.

Macquarie management mission to China in 1982

Bruce McKern was one of the first Business School professors in Australia to seek closer academic contacts with management specialists in China. He invited Professor Sun Yao Jun from the Chinese Academy of Social Sciences (CASS) to visit Macquarie University in February 1981 to learn about Australian management education and attend the Macquarie Advanced Management Program. As a result of the relationship, which McKern established with Sun, an invitation was extended to pay a return visit as guest of the CASS in May 1982. I was fortunate to join the 'mission' which was funded by the Australia-China Council. It had recently been established by the Australian Department of Foreign Affairs to promote mutual understanding and foster people-to-people relations between Australia and China. Our role was to give some lectures, meet with academic researchers in management and strengthen relations with the Chinese Academy. My wife, Gwen, also accompanied us.

It was a very interesting time to visit China. The country was still recovering from the Cultural Revolution, which had ended only six years before. Deng Xiaoping had succeeded Mao in 1978 and would transform China during the next ten years as he opened the Chinese economy to Western influence. During our visit, the traditional 'Mao suit' was still worn in all cities except Shanghai but there was considerable interest in learning about Western management practices. Bruce McKern gave lectures on Western financial management and attracted much greater attention than my lectures on organisation theory! Many of the academics and government officials we met had spent much of the previous decade undertaking 're-education' and doing hard manual labour in rural areas. They were uncertain about the future and wondered how long Deng would be able to continue his market economy reforms, which began in 1980.

We travelled extensively in China by various forms of transport including steam trains, planes and hair-raising trips by car in chaotic traffic. We visited Beijing, Shanghai, Suzhou, Chengdu and climbed Mt Emei in Sichuan, the highest of the four sacred Buddhist mountains in China (now a UNESCO world heritage site). We also visited the site of the terracotta warriors outside Xian, which had only been discovered in 1974 and was still in the early stages of excavation. We felt very privileged as there were few Western tourists, and we were accompanied everywhere by Professor Sun who was deeply interested and well informed about Chinese history.

However, the most personal memories of the visit are the encounters and discussions we had with Chinese academic colleagues, many of whom were trying to make up for the years they had lost during the Cultural Revolution. We noticed that some of the younger students who attended our lectures (via an interpreter) seemed to be bored and paid little attention compared with the older academics. We asked if our lectures were inadequate but were told that many of the students had missed most of their secondary education due to the Cultural Revolution. They were now uncertain what to believe as the old economic orthodoxy was being phased out, but the new economic system was yet to be fully revealed. Looking back on this period, after many subsequent visits, it is difficult to comprehend the magnitude of changes which have occurred since the early 1980s.

At one of the universities in Shanghai, we met the Dean of the Economics Faculty who spoke excellent English. We learned that he had graduated from MIT in the 1930s. He had suffered greatly during the Cultural Revolution, and he also expressed uncertainty about the future of China. We discovered that the Dean was greatly admired by his colleagues. We assumed that this was related to his resilience during the difficulties of the previous decade. But we were told that his fame was due to having been the 'Foxtrot dancing champion' in Boston in the 1930s! We later witnessed the renewed popularity of Western-style ballroom dancing, particularly among older Chinese.

We managed to undertake a minor research project during our visit to China, with the assistance of Dr Ng Sek-hong at the University of Hong Kong. Ng and I had been PhD students at the London School of Economics with the same supervisor. Ng was well informed about workplace relations in Chinese factories and suggested that we make inquiries about the role of the workers' congresses in state-owned enterprises we visited.

The workers' congresses were introduced during the 1940s following the Communist victory in China as the official mechanism for elected workers' representatives to participate in decision-making and management at the enterprise level. We sought information about the role of workers' congresses in several of the companies we visited. Not surprisingly, we discovered that the influence of the congress varied according to the willingness of management to engage with the workers' representatives. They did not appear to be very effective as a means of giving workers greater influence (Lansbury and Ng, 1987). However, with the rise of worker militancy in some areas of China in recent years, the state has shown some interest in reviving the workers' congress as a channel for workers to express their views to management (Zhu and Chan, 2005).

The visit to China in 1982 remains a very strong memory, and it has been interesting to follow the changing attitudes of the Chinese government towards worker representation in management of both state-owned, private and foreign-owned companies. There did appear to be some progress towards collective bargaining and the possibility of independent worker organisations being allowed to operate outside the official All-China Federation of Trade

Unions (ACFTU). However, as President Xi Jinping has tightened his grip on power, prospects of a more liberal approach to employment relations and free trade unions have become less likely in the near future.

The Labour-Management Studies Foundation at Macquarie University

Soon after arriving at Macquarie, I sought to establish something similar to what I had observed at McGill University in Montreal, Canada, which had an Industrial Relations Centre located in the Business School. The Centre had the support of both employers and unions and conducted seminars and conferences which were attended by a wide range of practitioners and academics. The McGill Centre had also established a database holding all the major collective bargaining agreements in Canada which they coded and made available to their member organisations as well as students wanting to undertake research on collective agreements. With the support of the Director of the Management School, Bruce McKern, I approached the key union peak councils and gained the support of the Labor Council of NSW as well as the ACTU. Large companies were also approached and asked for donations to establish the Centre. Eventually, sufficient funds were obtained to begin some activities, and a board was established which was chaired by Cliff Dolan, President of the ACTU, and on which sat several CEOs as well as other union officials and representatives of Macquarie University.

The proposal to establish the Foundation created some unexpected controversy. Opposition was expressed by some academic staff in Law and Social Sciences on the grounds that any programme involving industrial relations should not be located in the Management School as it would be subject to undue influence by employers, even though we proposed to have both union and employer representatives on the board of the Foundation. The proposal for a new Foundation had to be approved by the University Council. In response to objections raised by several opponents to the Foundation on the Council, the head of the Management School, Bruce McKern and I were required by the Vice Chancellor to consult with those who were opposed to the venture.

Our attempts to convince our opponents to support our proposal were unsuccessful, so we embarked on discussions with members of the University Council to persuade them that programmes initiated by the Foundation would not be biased as unions, and employers would have equal representation on the board. Two of the key Council members we had to convince were Mary Gaudron, the Solicitor-General of NSW who would later become a Justice of the High Court, and Elizabeth Evatt, who was Chief Justice of the Family Court. Both questioned us closely about the proposal, and once we had their support, we knew that we had succeeded. We also invited representatives from other schools in the university to be members of the board. Finally, the Foundation was approved by the Council, and we commenced programmes.

86 Transition to Sydney

The accord on wages and prices

Our initial activity in 1984 was a two-day conference on the Accord. We invited national leaders of the peak employer bodies and unions to participate as well as the Federal Minister of Industrial Relations to speak at the conference dinner. As this was one of the first events to assess the Accord, after its first year of operation, the conference drew over 200 participants and was a great success. The main opponents of the Foundation attended, and some chaired sessions during the conference. This was the first of several annual conferences held by the Foundation which covered topics such as industrial relations reform, superannuation, skills training and employee participation in management. Other activities included a public lecture series held at the NSW Industrial Relations Commission as well as various seminars addressed by academics and practitioners.

The Hancock Report on industrial relations reform

One of the most important conferences held by the Labour-Management Studies Foundation considered the Hancock Report. This Report was by a Committee of Review of Industrial Relations Law and Systems chaired by Professor Keith Hancock, then Vice-Chancellor of Flinders University of South Australia. This was one of the first conferences to discuss the Report. It featured all four members of the Committee: Keith Hancock, who chaired the Review, George Polites, who represented the employers and Charlie Fitzgibbon, who represented the unions.

The Report recommended maintaining the fundamental architecture of the federal system of conciliation and arbitration with some modest improvements in its functioning. There was a general consensus that the system was not in need of fundamental reform although there were some minor criticisms and reservations. Don Rawson from the Australian National University, for example, argued that 'we should be moving away from the immensely complex and self-defeating legal structures – to a system which involves more voluntarism and less compulsion, more flexibility and less rigidity'. Rawson recommended that there should be less regulation, less law, fewer judges, recognition, not registration of parties and a tripartite industrial relations tribunal instead of just employers and unions.

In retrospect, the Hancock Report reflected the prevailing consensus, exemplified by the Accord, that a centralised system of industrial relations had served the Australian economy very well. While the Report recommended some minor reforms, Hancock noted that the committee had concluded 'that conciliation and arbitration should remain an important component of the industrial relations system'. Yet there were some 'straws in the wind' reflected in comments by Geoff Allen, Executive Director of the Business Council of Australia (BCA) when he said 'the real business concern with Hancock is its tendency to further centralise at a time when we should be going in the other direction'. In fact, in the next few years, the BCA would lead a campaign to reform the system by introducing enterprise-level bargaining and reduce the powers of the federal tribunal over wage determination. It was later joined by the ACTU which argued for greater emphasis on workplace bargaining and a reduction in the arbitration system. Initially, the Industrial Relations Commission was sceptical on the grounds that the employer bodies and unions had different conception of what enterprise bargaining entailed. However, in 1991, the Commission supported a shift to a decentralised system, and the Industrial Relations Reform Act 1993 extended the scope of enterprise bargaining in law.

Superannuation reform

The next conference was on Superannuation. This also attracted a large number of participants from industry and trade unions. The conference followed a historic decision by the Federal Commission in 1986 to conciliate between the unions and employers on the introduction of superannuation. Agreement had been reached between the ACTU and the federal government on superannuation reform, and this would gradually flow through the industrial relations system. The Labor government subsequently legislated on the issue making superannuation payment compulsory and becoming a key feature of the Australian industrial relations system.

At the conference in July 1986, there was vigorous debate between employers and unions on the merits of superannuation and how it should be regulated. The late Bryan Noakes, then Director General of the Confederation of Australian Industry (CAI), accused the Commission of having 'invited unions to use their industrial muscle to force employers into superannuation against their will'. Geoff Allen, then Executive Director of the BCA, singled out for criticism 'Accord politics and government complicity in union tactics', which he argued had 'seriously corrupted the development of optimum and orderly superannuation arrangements'. However, other employers such as Tim Beamish of the Victorian Road Transport Association claimed that his industry had negotiated a satisfactory agreement with the unions in accordance with prevailing conditions. Several union leaders echoed these sentiments and indicated that they had already reached agreement with key employers in their industry. Gary Weaven of the ACTU claimed that the unions' superannuation campaign was consistent with the Accord reached with the federal government and would proceed accordingly. Justice Macken of the NSW Industrial Relations Commission argued that the establishment of industry-wide superannuation schemes under appropriate administration would have a positive influence on both unions and employers.

Vocational training and labour market programmes

Two other conferences convened by the Labour-Management Studies Foundation marked significant developments in industrial relations in the 1980s. In 1985, the Hawke Labor government released the report by a Committee of Inquiry into Labour Market Programs, chaired by Peter Kirby, which became known as the Kirby Report. It was one of many inquiries made into deficiencies in arrangements for training, re-training and recurrent education in Australia in recent decades. However, during the 1980s, there was a sharp increase in unemployment, the length of unemployment and the level of youth unemployment. The principal recommendations of the Kirby Report aimed at increasing the participation of young people in secondary and post-secondary education, the development of a new training system for young people combining education and work and wage subsidies to improve access to work for those facing significant disadvantage in the labour market. However, the main initiative suggested by the Kirby Report was a new traineeship system which would broaden the range of structured training arrangements outside the traditional apprenticeship system which focuses on traditional trades. The traineeship system would be aimed mainly at 16 to 17 year olds but could eventually be open to mature-aged people and those seeking to return to the workforce.

The conference heard from speakers from the education sector, employers and trade unions who all embraced the recommendations of the Kirby Report although there were the predictable concerns about funding. Don Anderson from the University of Melbourne warned that

> the traineeship idea is likely to be seen as just another program for the least capable of school students unless great care is taken. It needs to be presented on a par with apprenticeships and higher education as a legitimate and worthy path from school to adult vocations.

Dr Peter Scherer from the Bureau of Labour Market Research argued that for the new traineeship system to be successful, it needed to be regarded as a new system and not just another government programme. He quoted from the Report that 'labour market programs and similar interventions should be seen as an integral part of an overall economic policy rather than operating at the margin'.

With hindsight it can be seen that traineeships did become an accepted system of skills development and accreditation alongside traditional apprenticeship. However, there remain major problems with attracting and retaining young people in these schemes. Attrition and non-completion rates remain high, and there is concern that many traineeships in industries such as hospitality do not provide high-quality education. Furthermore, while the proportion of young people entering university has grown significantly in the decades since the Kirby Report, the proportion of young people entering apprenticeships and traineeships has not expanded to the same extent and continue to have lower status and earnings potential.

Employee participation and industrial democracy

Finally, another important conference hosted by the Labour-Management Studies Foundation in 1986 was on 'Implementing Employee Participation and Industrial Democracy'. This coincided with the launch of *Democracy and Control in the Workplace* and included a number of case studies from industry. A key case study was presented by John Siddons, chairman of a leading tool manufacturer and Senator with the Australian Democrats. He explained that Siddons Industries had been restructured into a cellular organisation which provided workers with greater control over their work. They also introduced a works council as well as profit sharing and an employee share ownership scheme. In addition to an emphasis on research and development, to create technically advanced products, the workplace reforms at Siddons Industries had assisted the company to survive intense international competition.

Another example of employee participation was Lend Lease, a leading construction firm which had an employee share ownership scheme from its inception which meant that employees were the largest group of shareholders, owning approximately 26 per cent of the company. The Ford Motor Company was represented at the conference and described their employee involvement scheme at its Melbourne and Sydney assembly plants. Both the head of the main vehicle building industry union and the manager responsible for the implementation of the programme joined the discussion. George Campbell, then head of the AMWU which represented skilled maintenance workers at Ford, warned that workers and their unions needed to be involved in key decisions related to technological change which was impacting on the auto and other manufacturing industries.

A major discussion topic at the conference was the role of government policy. The conference was opened by Bob Carr, who later became the Labor Premier of NSW. He urged employers and unions to adopt industrial democracy practices like the Germans and Swedes but argued that the federal government needed to take the lead with appropriate policies and incentives. The conference was held prior to the federal government releasing its long-anticipated 'Green Paper on Industrial Democracy'. Eventually, as noted above, this was downgraded to a 'Discussion Paper' and the Hawke government lost interest in pursuing the issue. In retrospect, had the government passed legislation at that time to provide some minimal requirements for consultation on matters such as workplace changes and the introduction of technologies, it could have provided a basis for some form of industrial democracy. There were examples at the time in European countries such as Sweden and France where legislation was passed to establish rights of workers to participate in decisions which affected them at work, but this was not the case in Australia.

Cliff Dolan: the foundation chair

Cliff Dolan was an excellent chair of the Labour-Management Studies Foundation board. Prior to becoming Bob Hawke's successor as President of the ACTU, from 1980 to 1985, he was Deputy President and had been Federal Secretary of the influential Electrical Trades Union. He was widely respected by all parties in industrial relations: unions, employers and government officials. Cliff Dolan was most helpful in facilitating contact with a wide range of people involved in industrial relations. He also had a wry sense of humour. He once gave us an amusing account of a private dinner which he attended with Bob Hawke at the invitation of Malcolm Fraser at the Prime Minister's Lodge in the late 1970s. It seems that Fraser was seeking Hawke's support for some industrial relations reforms. The alcohol was flowing freely at the dinner until Fraser turned to his butler and asked: 'Did Whitlam (his predecessor) buy this wine?' The butler answered: 'Yes sir, I believe this was in Mr Whitlam's collection'. A furious Fraser responded: 'Then get rid of it. I am not going to drink any of Whitlam's…'. Thereupon, Mrs Fraser appeared and declared: 'You've had enough to drink Malcolm. It's time you went to bed and the rest of you can go home!' And the dinner party ended. In 1983, Bob Hawke defeated Malcolm Fraser in a federal election and succeeded him as Prime Minister. Hawke declared that he would abstain from alcohol for the period he was Prime Minister.

After I moved from Macquarie to Sydney University, my friend and colleague Ed Davis replaced me in the Graduate School of Management and continued the activities of the Labour-Management Studies Foundation. Ed focused attention on the issue of equality for women in the workplace. In collaboration with Valerie Pratt, the distinguished foundation Director of the Affirmative Action Agency, Ed, conducted annual conferences and published in a series *Making the Link*.

Senior Fulbright Scholar at the Sloan School of Management, MIT, and Harvard University

In 1984, I was granted six months study leave. I gained a grant from the German government Academic Exchange Program (the DAAD scheme) to visit the Institute of Sociology at the University of Bochum in Germany in order to conduct a study of how works councils dealt with issues related to technological change in the automobile assembly industry. Professor Friedrich Fuerstenburg invited me to be a visitor at the University of Bochum and generously organised visits to German auto plants.

I began with a month in Germany and then was joined by my Gwen, Owen and Nina for a month's holiday in Europe and the United States. I was fortunate that Gwen was willing to allow me to spend five months away from home while she looked after our children while also completing a Master's degree in Community Health. It was not an easy time for her, and I am greatly indebted to her generosity in giving me this time to spend on research.

I was also awarded a Senior Fulbright Scholarship to spend three months at the Harvard Trade Union Program and with the Industrial Relations group at the Sloan School of Management at MIT in Boston. I was fortunate in each case to have senior academics in each institution support my application and host my visit. At Harvard, John Dunlop chaired the Trade Union Program while Bob McKersie headed the Industrial Relations group at MIT.

It was a formative experience being a visitor at these two great universities. Unfortunately, the Harvard Trade Union Program was in recess but I did have discussions with the Acting Director, Jim Medoff, who was at the Kennedy School of Government and had just published an influential book with Richard Freeman entitled *What Unions Do* (Freeman and Medoff, 1984). This book argued that unions played a valuable social and economic role. The data cited in the book demonstrated that the higher wages earned by union members were justified by the fact that they achieved higher productivity than non-union workers. They also showed that unions provided an important voice for workers when they channelled worker discontent into improving workplace conditions. This book provided a counterargument to those who accused unions of performing a monopoly function and raising wages above competitive levels. However, the unionisation rate among workers in that period was much higher than it is today, and the incentive to join unions has declined as unions are less able to provide benefits than they did in the mid-1980s.

Despite not being able to participate in activities of the Trade Union Program, I was able to attend many events at Harvard including lectures and seminars at the Harvard Business School. Later, in 2002, the Harvard Trade Union Program was restructured and renamed the Labor and Worklife Program. A new director, Eileen Bernard from Canada who had both a union and academic background, focused on a wider range of issues relating to work and employment and involved a wider range of instructors from various universities. It is now housed in the Harvard Law School and is led by Sharon Block, a former senior official in the US Department of Labor. Many Australian trade union officials, as well as others from the United States and around the world, continue to attend courses provided by the Program.

I was fortunate to be at MIT when Tom Kochan, Harry Katz and Bob McKersie were writing their seminal book *The Transformation of American Industrial Relations* (Kochan et al., 1986). I was welcomed as a visiting scholar and invited to the regular seminars as well as joining in informal discussions of the book as each chapter was completed. I was impressed that the authors of the book would expose their ideas to the scrutiny of academic colleagues and graduate students while the book was in development. However, I realised that this was the hallmark of the way in which colleagues in the industrial relations group at MIT were willing to have their work in progress scrutinised. As a result of this process, the arguments in the book were tested and developed making the final work much more robust.

The key argument in the book was that the 'New Deal' era, which shaped industrial relations during the Roosevelt era and continued from the 1950s to the end of the 1970s, was now coming to an end. The decline of unionisation and the rise of corporate power in the United States meant that employers were assuming a dominant role and bypassing unions in order to deal directly with their employees. The thesis of the book was contested by those who believed that no fundamental transformation had occurred but simply incremental change accompanied by other economic and social developments (Chelius and Dworkin, 1990). John Dunlop, who was the 'elder statesman' of industrial relations and labour economics at Harvard, argued that the recession of the early 1980s had created simply a temporary setback and that the system of US industrial relations had not fundamentally changed. The book also introduced the concept of 'strategic choice' and developed an industrial relations matrix that differentiated between three levels of decision-making about industrial relations activity within the enterprise.

In hindsight, the transformation was well underway not only in the United States but also in other advanced industrialised countries where union membership and union influence were in significant decline. In a retrospective symposium in *The Industrial and Labor Relations Review*, in 2017, several contributors were invited to assess the long-term impact of the book, 30 years after its publication. My contribution argued that the book not only provided an authoritative account of changes which were occurring in the United States but also stimulated research in other countries where industrial relations was undergoing fundamental change (Lansbury, 2016a).

During the early 1990s, Kochan and others embarked on a global project incorporating both developed and emerging economies. In a number of publications, it was revealed that most countries were experiencing intense pressures to adapt their traditional industrial relations practices in response to increased global competition and changing technologies. Yet there was considerable variation in the pace of change and the degree to which individual industrial relations systems were able to adapt through minor incremental adjustments as opposed to fundamental transformations.

The period I spent at MIT had long-lasting influence on me. I was fortunate to meet academics such as Tom Kochan, Harry Katz, Bob McKersie and Joel Cutcher Gershenfeld who became life-long friends and collaborators. I also began working on the first edition of *International and Comparative Industrial Relations* which I co-edited with Greg Bamber, then at Durham University in the United Kingdom, who had been a fellow doctoral student with me at LSE. My family and I stayed briefly with the Bamber family on our way to the United States, and we scoped out the contents of the book and began to contact potential contributors to write country chapters. I was able to discuss ideas for the book with colleagues at MIT and also incorporate new concepts which were being developed by scholars at the Centre for European Studies at Harvard whose seminars I attended. I was invited to give seminars at the University of Wisconsin (UW)-Madison and McGill University in Montreal. I also received an unexpected invitation from Keith Thurley, my former PhD supervisor at LSE, to come to London and be interviewed for the chair of Industrial Relations at LSE which had become vacant on the retirement of the foundation Professor Ben Roberts.

Keith Thurley had recently been appointed to a second Chair in the Department of Industrial Relations where he was to focus on Human Resource Management. He told me that a short list of candidates had been drawn up for the Chair of Industrial Relations but that the selection committee was divided between two candidates. Keith Thurley told me: 'You might be someone who would be acceptable to the committee and slip between the other two'. He added that he had been permitted to invite me to be on the 'short list' even though I had not applied. I flew to London and was interviewed by members of the Department as well as the selection committee. In the end, the successful candidate was an eminent labour economist, David Metcalf, who went on to a stellar career. Thurley explained to me that I was regarded as acceptable for the appointment but that the committee thought 'you were too like me and they wanted someone who would bring different skills and interests to the Department'. I told Keith Thurley that I regarded this as a compliment and that I realised how much I had followed his example in comparative research and focusing on the changing role of management. I also received an invitation to give a seminar at the UW-Madison and later discovered that I was under consideration as a potential appointment to a position in comparative industrial relations, which ultimately went to the eminent German sociologist Wolfgang Streeck. Having sought neither of the positions at LSE nor UW-Madison, it boosted my confidence to know that others had considered me a worthy candidate.

Technological change and co-determination in the German auto industry

My work in Germany and funding from the DAAD was arranged by Friedrich Fuerstenberg, Professor of Sociology at the University of Bochum. I came to know Friedrich through the International Labour and Employment Relations Association (ILERA), of which he later became President, and shared an interest in industrial democracy and the automotive industry. Before taking up a professorship, Friedrich had pursued a career in Daimler Benz where he became director of training. His early publications focused on the operation of works councils in Germany and comparisons with joint consultative committees in Britain. Friedrich arranged for me to visit a variety of automobile assembly plants in Germany owned by Daimler Benz, Volkswagen (VW) and Ford so that I could compare how works councils in each plant dealt with issues of technological change. I was joined by one of Friedrich's former PhD students who kindly assisted with interviews in German. Greg Bamber from Durham University in the United Kingdom also joined in the visits and we later co-authored a publication based on our fieldwork (see Bamber and Lansbury, 1986).

The experience of interviewing works councillors, union representatives and managers in each of the plants was most interesting and revealed a diversity of approaches between the different automobile companies. Under section 90 of the Works Constitution Act 1972, management is obliged to keep the works council informed about the process of technological innovation. However, the process may extend over a long period of time, and works councils complain that they are often not informed earlier enough for them to make a meaningful intervention. During the early 1980s, when our project was undertaken, there was a period of declining economic growth and rising unemployment in Germany. Unions and works councils were concerned about preserving jobs and feared that increasing automation could cost jobs in the industry. At VW, for example, the works council was pressing the company to implement a policy of preserving jobs during the downturn when production in the early 1980s fell by almost 10 per cent. Concern about unemployment was a major factor driving the unions' campaign to reduce working hours so that jobs could be preserved.

Even though the works councils all operated under the same legislation, which gave them identical rights to information and consultation, the extent of their influence appeared to vary according to the strength of the union membership and organisation. Most of the workers in the plants were members of the German metalworkers union (IG Metall), but the influence of the union on the works councils varied from highly significant, in the case of VW, to less significant in Daimler Benz. In the large VW plant in Wolfsberg, the works council appeared to have extensive influence over decisions about technological change as well as other matters, while this was less the case in relation to the works council at the Sindelfingen plant. The Ford Motor Company produced fewer vehicles than VW or Daimler Benz but was still a high volume manufacturer in 1984. During our visit, the works council at Ford's Cologne plant was in conflict with the company over the introduction of quality circles, partly as a consequence of recent lay-offs in response to a three-year decline in sales.

While relations between the companies, works councils and unions appeared to be very functional at the time of our visits, a few months later, there was a bitter dispute throughout the auto manufacturing and other industries over reducing the basic working week from 40 to 35 hours. The outcome of this dispute was a compromise of 38.5 hours per week from 1985. However, negotiations were permitted at the plant level over how the reduced hours would be achieved. This represented a decentralisation of collective bargaining and an increase in the role of works councillors in negotiating the application of reduced working hours at the plant level.

The opportunity to undertake fieldwork in Germany gave me a deeper insight into how the German system of workplace relations functioned in practice. It was also an interesting time to be examining technological change as this was emerging as a major issue in many countries. During the 1980s, the German economy was experiencing significant structural changes which were impacting on industrial relations. The union strategies were focused on protecting their members against the loss of jobs, deskilling and increased workload and stress in the face of new technologies in the workplace. Many employers were seeking to develop and utilise new technology in order to increase productivity and competitiveness, while also providing a more humane form of job design. The German government initiated a programme for the 'humanisation of worklife' administered by the Federal Ministry for Research and Technology, involving both unions and employers, which was directed at encouraging technological change as well as employment stabilisation and the maintenance of skills and qualifications. A growing number of collective agreements contained provisions related to the introduction of technology, thereby rendering Germany a leader in integrating technological change and industrial relations.

Technology, Work and Industrial Relations in Australia

My appreciation of the importance of technological change for Work and Industrial Relations began in the early 1980s when governments in a number of countries began to issue reports on the implications of economic and social implications of the 'post-industrial revolution'. In this 'new economy', the majority of the population would no longer be engaged in producing raw materials, finished products and directly related services such as retailing, storage and transport. As noted by the then Australian Minister for Science and Technology Barry Jones, the labour market was undergoing 'a fundamental change from physical production work towards mental work, although large numbers were still employed in providing quasi-domestic services', such as care of children and the elderly. He further argued that there was a shift from *necessary* work, providing food, water, shelter, fuel, etc., towards *discretionary* work, or things we *choose* to have, such as information, entertainment and tourism. Jones wrote these words in the foreword to a book I co-edited with Ed Davis and published in 1984 entitled *Technology, Work and Industrial Relations*, which followed his path-breaking book *Sleepers Wake! Technology and the Future of Work*, published in 1982, and has been revised and republished many times.

Technological change and the future of work is once again at the forefront of public discourse and invites the question what can we learn from past analyses of these issues?

In 1980, the Fraser Coalition government released the report of the Committee of Inquiry into Technological Change in Australia (CITCA), headed by Rupert Myers, Vice-Chancellor of the UNSW, which it had commissioned in 1978. One of the key recommendations of the Report was that the government sponsor a test case before the Australian Industrial Relations Commission to set minimum standards to be observed by enterprises on the notification, provision of information and consultation when technological change it to occur. The Fraser government declined to support this recommendation on the grounds that these matters did not lend themselves to effective legislation or award provision. However, the Hawke Labor government subsequently supported the ACTU mounting such a test case and introduced legislative amendments to implement other recommendations such as a national Occupational Health and Safety Commission to address the impact of technological changes on workers' health.

Technology, Work and Industrial Relations included chapters by representatives of employers' organisations and unions about issues raised by technological change for management and the workforce in Australian organisations. We also invited case studies on a range of industries including banking, insurance, retail, the media and public instrumentalities. Other chapters focussed on the impact of technological change on organisations and jobs, women's employment, occupational health and safety as well as the adequacy of laws on job protection and redundancy resulting from new technology. In the concluding chapters, Bill Ford drew attention to the failure of Australia to develop the appropriate 'balance of skills' in the workforce which will be needed to cope with new technology. He compared Australia unfavourably with Japan and certain European countries, such as Germany and Sweden, where greater emphasis has been given by governments and employers to equipping their workforce with appropriate skills for the future (Ford, 1984).

Sol Encel continued this theme in the final chapter in which he focused on the 'ambiguity' of technological change in that 'it destroys jobs but also creates them. It fragments skills but generates new ones. It increases power at the centre but also puts new resources at the disposal of many people'. Encel's recommendations emphasised the importance of education and training in equipping the workforce for the 'third industrial revolution' in which science, technology and production have become interlinked and which the main job growth will be in the tertiary or service sector. However, Encel's concern was that the technical and further education systems in Australia were not adequate to meet this challenge (Encel, 1984). This continues to be the case in 2020 as we enter the 'fourth industrial revolution'.

Technological change in retail distribution

In 1983, there was an opportunity to undertake a research project on technological change in retail distribution centres when a major food chain, Woolworths Limited, decided to establish the Theo Kelly Foundation, in honour of its founder, at Macquarie University. The Foundation funded teaching and research in the food industry. There was industrial disputation, during this time, at Woolworths and other companies. Automation was being introduced into warehouses, workers were fearful about the future of their jobs and unions were making various demands on their behalf. Greg Bamber, who was visiting from Durham University, and I investigated two of Woolworths distribution centres: one in Sydney where there were major problems in making the transition to automation and another in Brisbane where the process had been successful. We visited each centre and interviewed workers, management and union representatives. We subsequently wrote academic papers and a case study which are still relevant to current issues related to the introduction of technological change in workplaces, even though the types of technology have changed (see Bamber and Lansbury, 1988).

Woolworths was one of the pioneers in modernising its warehouses by introducing high-bay automated storage and retrieval systems. They utilised information technology which, at that time, was novel in the context of food warehousing. While the distribution centres were not completely automated, they were highly computerised. When the new Woolworths distribution centre opened in Sydney, it was regarded as one of the most sophisticated computerised handling system in operation. Yet during its first two years of operation, the centre was plagued with equipment failures, workers' complaints and stoppages. The senior management at Woolworths' headquarters in Sydney pronounced the new distribution centre as a 'disaster'. By contrast, an identical distribution centre owned by Woolworths in Brisbane had made a successful transition to using automated systems.

In response to the continuing crisis at the Distribution Centre in Sydney, with supermarket shelves becoming empty, the CEO of Woolworths decided to hire Linfox to solve the problem. Linfox was predominantly a transport company, owned by Lindsay Fox, which provided the trucks to take goods from Woolworths' distribution centres to supermarkets. Fox saw this as an opportunity to enter the distribution centre segment of the retail food industry and took personal charge of the project. He decided that the key reason for failure in Sydney was due to industrial relations. Fox met with the workers, their shop stewards and union officials and negotiated an agreement which involved retraining for workers on the new computerised equipment, increased pay for productivity improvements resulting from automation and new work practices, and a paid redundancy scheme for those who did not wish to work with the new system. Within a year, the Sydney Distribution Centre had achieved similar success to its counterpart in Brisbane and Linfox moved on to Coles and other companies to assist them with their transition to automation.

In our analysis, the Woolworths case confirmed the importance of viewing the distribution centre as a 'socio-technical system', revealed in earlier work by Emery and Trist at the Tavistock Institute. They noted that while the technical system tends to put 'limits on the type of work organisation possible... A work organisation has social and technical properties of its own that are independent of technology' (Emery and Trist, 1969). In the Woolworths case, the transition to an automation meant that the work organisation needed to change, but this was initially met with resistance by the workers in Sydney. The necessary changes were achieved by Lindsay Fox through negotiation with the workers and their union. These changes included training for workers to acquire extra skills, redundancy arrangements for those workers who did not wish to continue working under the new arrangements and incentives for workers to adopt new working arrangements in order to achieve productivity improvements. The Woolworths case study reinforced the importance of management negotiating change with the workforce as well as demonstrating that technology alone does not determine the outcomes of change (Bamber and Lansbury, 1991).

International and comparative industrial relations

In 1986, I was the rapporteur on technological change at the World Congress of the International Industrial Relations Association (IIRA), held in Hamburg in 1986. This involved selecting papers on the theme of technological change and its impact on industrial relations and human resources in various countries. Papers presented at the congress were revised and published in a co-authored book with Greg Bamber, entitled *New Technology: International Perspectives on Human Resources and Industrial Relations* (Bamber and Lansbury, 1989). The book was published in 1989 but republished by Routledge in 2014 in its 'Revival' series, designed to retain significant books from its 'back list' in print.

The book focused on international comparisons of unions, employers and governments in various countries as they responded to technological change.

Contributors were drawn from Europe, North America and Australia with the key themes being the impact of technological change on workers and organisations in relation to skills, labour markets, gender and industrial relations. A common thread between different countries was the extent to which collective bargaining, employee participation and human resource management processes had been successful in assisting with the adaptation to new technologies. Where industrial relations were traditionally adversarial, as in most English-speaking countries, unions were more likely to resist technological change compared with those in countries such as Germany and Scandinavia where there was a stronger tradition of social partnership.

One interesting initiative discussed in the book was the concept of 'model technology agreements' at an industry level between unions and employers, an example of which was developed by the International Federation of Commercial, Clerical, Professional and Technical Employees (FIET). A more recent example, taking a similar approach, are International Framework Agreements (IFAs) negotiated between some global union federations and multinational enterprises. The IFAs are a means of voluntary regulation of labour standards across national boundaries and often incorporate core ILO standards.

While IFAs deal with broader issues than technological change, they seek to achieve cooperation between unions and employers on issues of common interest which extend beyond the boundaries of one country. However, even in Europe where conditions for the development of transnational collective bargaining over issues such as technological change appear to be most favourable, the weakening of multi-employer bargaining at the national level is undermining the opportunities for cross-border agreements (Marginson, 2015).

During my study leave in the United States, I began work on the first edition of *International and Comparative Industrial Relations: A Study of Developed Market Economies* with Greg Bamber. The concept of the book emerged during Greg's study leave as a visiting scholar at Macquarie University. We developed a proposal which we submitted to Allen and Unwin in Australia which was publishing a series of industrial relations books in collaboration with the Industrial Relations Research Centre at the UNSW, under the general editorship of John Niland. The book focused on countries in the OECD and divided them into three groups: English-speaking countries, Continental European countries and Japan (as the only representative of Asia). We began with an introductory chapter entitled 'Studying International and Comparative Industrial Relations' in which we provided a rationale for a book on this subject, examined the emergence of an international dimension of industrial relations based on the growth of multinational enterprises and international organisations of unions, employers and governmental bodies. We analysed theoretical approaches to comparative industrial relations from systems theory, convergence versus divergence, political economy and strategic choice. We concluded by making a distinction between Type 1 countries whose industrial relations tended to be adversarial and Type 2 countries which tended to pursue a 'social partnership' approach. This typology was a simple formulation of a more sophisticated approach which would later be proposed by Hall and Soskice as 'liberal market economies' and 'coordinated market economies' (Bamber and Lansbury, 1987).

Almost 30 years later, in 2016, the sixth edition of *International and Comparative Employment Relations: National Regulation, Global Changes* was published. The most surprising feature of the book is that it has survived so long. Several features of the 2016 edition are in contrast to the first edition in 1987. The title has changed. Employment relations has replaced industrial relations in the title and is explained as follows: 'We adopt the term *employment relations* to encompass both IR and HRM. Where they are appropriate, however, the terms IR and HRM are used in this book'. While this might seem to be simply a semantic point, it underlines the fact that human resource management has emerged as a far more significant topic during the past three decades. In the 1987 edition of the book, HRM received only two references in the index compared with 11 references in the 2016 edition. It is interesting that the main reference to HRM in 1987 was in the chapter on the United States where it was noted: 'Modern personnel practice is oriented to human resources management, the notion that the labour factor in production is valuable, worth investing in, and worth preserving' (Wheeler, 1987). By 2016, HRM was defined more broadly as 'the effective overall management of an organisation's workforce in order to contribute to the achievement of desired objectives and goals' (Nankervis et al., 2011).

Several other features distinguish the sixth edition compared with the first edition of the book. Three additional countries were added, all of which were from Asia: China, India and South Korea. There were also two additional co-editors: Chris F. Wright and Nick Wailes, both of whom had been students and academic staff in Work and Organisational Studies (formerly the Department of Industrial Relations) at the University of Sydney. In his foreword to the sixth edition, the late Willy Brown of Cambridge University noted the substantial changes which had occurred in industrial relations since the first edition in 1987:

> Back in the 1980s, unions played a dominant role in employment relations in developed economies. But by the 2010s, their role in market sectors has withered to become, at least In some countries, almost insignificant. The driving forces behind these changes have been international- in trade, in ownership, in finance and in technology. It is only by placing national developments within this international context that we can understand them and their implications for employment standards.
>
> (Brown, 2016: vii)

The 2016 edition also began with an introductory chapter which emphasised the impact of globalisation on employment relations at both the local and international levels. In the 1987 edition the terms global and globalisation were not even mentioned in the subject index. The introductory chapter examined the 'varieties of capitalism' approach, which has been very influential in discussions of international and comparative employment relations. Two additional categories were added to liberal and coordinated market economies in relation to the countries covered in the book: European developed economies, Asian developed economies and Asian emerging economies. In the concluding chapter, it was argued that while examining the national institutional context within which employers and unions operate is still important, there are other factors such as multinational enterprise companies and international institutions such as the EU and ILO which shape employment relations patterns. The chapter concluded with the *raison d'etre* for both the book and the continuing relevance of the field of study: 'students of employment relations need to go beyond simple models to examine the complex political, economic and social factors that influence work and how it is regulated in a rapidly changing international economy' (Wright et al., 2016: 361).

Plate 1 Graduation at the University of Melbourne with Freda and Gwen in 1969.

Plate 2 At the ILO in Geneva with Gwen for the World Congress of the International Industrial Relations Research Association (IIRA) in 1970.

Plate 3 Hiking on Hinchinbrook Island in Queensland with Nina, Gwen and Owen in 1992.

Plate 4 At Government House with Gwen, Nina and Owen for the Order of Australia ceremony in 2009.

Plate 5 In Tiananmen Square Beijing with Gwen and Sun Yao Jun in from the Chinese Academy of Social Sciences 1982.

Plate 6 Arriving in Moscow on the Trans-Mongolian train with Gwen in 2004.

Plate 7 Cycling with Gwen from Vietnam to Laos in 2014.

Plate 8 At Macquarie University Graduate School of Management with Ed Davis in 1989.

Plate 9 In Boston with Tom Kochan from the Sloan School of Management, MIT, in 1994.

Plate 10 At the University of Sydney with Olle and Ruth Hammarstrom visiting scholars from Sweden in 1991.

Plate 11 With Marian Baird, Ron Callus and Keri Chikarovski, Minister for Industrial Relations at a function for the Australian Centre for Industrial Relations and Teaching (ACIRRT) at the Mitchell Library, 1993.

Plate 12 With Ron Callus, Justice Lance Wright, President of the Industrial Relations Commission of NSW and High Court Justice Michael Kirby who delivered the Laffer lecture at the University of Sydney in 2002.

Plate 13 Guest speakers at an International Forum on 'Employment Relations in a Global Context' University of Sydney in 2011. From the left: Willy Brown, Ged Carney, Russell Lansbury, Janice Bellace, Chang-Hee Lee, Tayo Fashoyin, Peter Anderson, Ron McCallum, Rae Cooper, Tom Kochan, Marian Baird, John Buchanan, Peter Auer and Mia Ronnmar.

Plate 14 With Graham Worrall, my former history teacher and Alan Johnston, a fellow student, at a Melbourne Boys High School reunion, 2011.

Plate 15 Receiving an honorary Doctor of Letters from the Vice-Chancellor Professor Di Yerbury at Macquarie University in 2005.

Plate 16 Janice Bellace receiving an honorary Doctor of Economics at the University of Sydney, with Chris Wright and Marian Baird in 2017.

Plate 17 Colleagues in Work and Organisational Studies at the University of Sydney. From the left: Marian Baird, Alex Veen, Anya Johnson, Stephen Clibborn, Bradon Ellem, Rae Cooper, Chris Wright and Rawya Mansour in 2020.

7 New horizons at the University of Sydney (1987–1999)

It was a great privilege to be appointed to the Chair of Industrial Relations at the University of Sydney in 1987. When I applied for the position, the department had been without a professor for several years, and there had been considerable debate as to whether it should be closed and the academic staff re-absorbed into the Department of Economics. Fortunately, the Dean, Stephen Salsbury, decided to retain a separate Department of Industrial Relations and appoint a professor in the discipline who could help to further develop research and teaching in the field.

The Department of Industrial Relations was created within the Faculty of Economics in 1976 although subjects in Industrial Relations had been taught at the University of Sydney since 1953. Kingsley Laffer began teaching the subject and laid the groundwork for establishment of a separate department, although this only occurred after his retirement. He also initiated the formation of the Industrial Relations Society in Australia and became the founding editor of *The Journal of Industrial Relations*, under the auspices of the Industrial Relations Society. Laffer was a visionary who achieved his goal of Industrial Relations becoming an accepted field of study at the University of Sydney and elsewhere. Laffer worked tirelessly to achieve his objective, not only within the University of Sydney but also by persuading employers, unions, arbitral authorities and government officials to support his endeavours in the broader field of promoting industrial relations scholarship and research.

Kingsley Laffer encountered considerable resistance from within the Department of Economics at the University of Sydney where incumbent Professors Simkin and Hogan insisted that Industrial Relations should remain within Economics and be denied separate departmental status. Indeed, Laffer only succeeded in establishing the Department of Industrial Relations after he persuaded the Vice-Chancellor Bruce Williams, an eminent economist, to overrule opposition by the then Dean of the Faculty of Economics, Syd Butlin.

The Department of Industrial Relations had a difficult birth and an unsettled early period of development. From 1976 to 1978, Bert Turner, who was the Montague Burton Professor of Industrial Relations at Cambridge University, was appointed as a visiting professor. He was succeeded by John Corina, an eminent labour economist from Oxford University, who remained for only four years before returning to the United Kingdom. The Dean, Stephen Salsbury, then took over as acting head of the Department and invited George Strauss from the University of California-Berkeley to become a visiting professor and assist him to determine whether the department should continue. Fortunately, George Strauss supported the continuation of the Industrial Relations Department and played a key role in the selection of a new professor. He became a valued mentor to me and to other members of the Department, welcoming us as visitors to Berkeley.

I was approached by the Deputy Dean of the Faculty of Economics, Murray Wells, who encouraged me to apply for the position and I was very pleased to be appointed. I was impressed with the existing staff in the Department of Industrial Relations. Colleagues who were invaluable in assisting with rebuilding the Department included Ron Callus, Keith Whitfield, Greg Patmore and Richard Morris. The Dean permitted the appointment of several new staff, and we were fortunate that Suzanne Jamieson, Robin Kramar, Mark Bray and Jim Kitay joined and provided valuable expertise in Labour Law, Human Resource Management and Industrial Relations. While several of these colleagues later left to take up professorships at other universities, the combination of new and established staff enabled the Department to provide a wider array of courses and attract an increasing number of students.

One of the factors inhibiting the growth of students studying Industrial Relations at Sydney University was that, unlike some other departments in the Faculty such as Government and International Relations, we were excluded from accepting students from the Arts Faculty. In 1990, the Dean of Arts reluctantly gave us permission to accept 40 students per year from Arts to enrol in Industrial Relations. However, the demand by Arts students to take Industrial Relations grew strongly each year and we were permitted gradually to increase enrolments. Suzanne Jamieson was a highly successful lecturer in the first year introductory unit in Industrial Relations as well as Labour Law. Soon two streams of the entry level unit were being offered and attracting many hundreds of students. The fourth year honours year also expanded and proved popular among students from both the Economics and Arts Faculties.

The 'Golden Age' of industrial relations?

Success in attracting students into our courses was partly the product of a 'golden age', from the mid-1980s to mid-1990s, during the period of the Hawke Labor government. The Accord between the unions and the Federal government became the centrepiece of national economic policy. Our courses were regarded by students not only as academically interesting but also having a practical and professional value. We began to broaden our course offerings to encompass emerging fields such as Human Resource Management, Employment Law, Organisational Behaviour and Management. We also provided an 'industrial relations practice' unit, as part of the undergraduate degree, which enabled senior-level students to gain a placement during the university vacations with an employer in the private or public sector as well as with a union or employer association and the Industrial Relations Commission. This unit expanded as the result of increasing student demand and became an important component of the undergraduate programme. Some students gained job offers on graduation with organisations where they had undertaken 'Industrial Relations Practice'. It also provided the Department with excellent contact with practitioners and assisted access to guest speakers and research contacts. Some of these organisations also offered academic prizes and scholarships to students who achieved the best results in units offered by the Department.

During the early 1990s, in addition to the expansion of students taking our undergraduate units in Industrial Relations, we embarked on establishing innovative postgraduate programmes. These comprised: Graduate Certificates for those students without a first degree but relevant work experience, Graduate Diplomas for those who wished to take only a one-year programme and a combined Master's degree in Industrial Relations and Human Resource Management. Two new combined degrees with other Faculties also proved to be popular. A Master of Law and Labour Relations was offered in conjunction with the Law School and could be taken by students without an undergraduate degree in Law. A Master of Coaching and Human Resources was also developed in collaboration with the Department of Psychology. The PhD programme, which had been in abeyance until a new professor was appointed, also expanded in the 1990s. These new degree programmes expanded the number of students taking Industrial Relations and related subjects.

For over 20 years, the Faculty of Economics was led by Stephen Salsbury as Dean, except for occasional periods when Accounting Professor Murray Wells, temporarily replaced him. Salsbury was an American-born economic historian with a PhD from Harvard. He was politically conservative and had a photograph of himself with former US Republican Party leader, Newt Gingrich, at the entrance to his office. Yet he was a consistent supporter of the Department of Industrial Relations and mentored Greg Patmore whose PhD thesis he had supervised and whom he appointed as Associate Dean replacing long-term incumbent Murray Wells. Another colleague from our Department, Jim Kitay, followed Greg Patmore in that role. Salsbury permitted staff numbers in Industrial Relations gradually to be increased, and he supported our new programmes and degrees.

Peter Wolnizer was selected as Dean in 1999 to replace Stephen Salsbury and continued in this role for the next decade. Wolnizer had been the Dean of a combined Faculty of Business and Law at Deakin University during the 1990s. He gained his PhD from the University of Sydney and was a Senior Lecturer in Accounting before his appointment to the Chair of Accounting at Deakin. Wolnizer sought to modernise the Faculty of Economics at Sydney. Soon after his appointment, he split the Faculty into a School of Business and a School of Economics and Political Science. Departments were replaced by Disciplines and reported to the heads of their respective schools. I was offered the inaugural Head of the new Business School but declined and chose the alternative option of Associate Dean for Research, a position I held from 2000 until 2008, just prior to my retirement.

At the suggestion of Greg Patmore, and after discussion with the staff, the Department of Industrial Relations was renamed the Work and Organisational Studies (WOS) Discipline. The rationale for this change of name was to reflect the fact that the subject offerings of the Department were now much more diverse. Although Industrial Relations remained a key area, other fields such as Human Resource Management and Organisational Studies were becoming more important. It was also decided that WOS should be attached to the Business School where we would play a prominent role in offering subjects, such as Management, which related to people and organisational issues.

Workplace industrial relations research in Australia

Soon after my appointment as Professor of Industrial Relations at the University of Sydney, Ron Callus suggested that we should establish a research centre which would focus on key issues of importance, particularly workplace industrial relations. Ron Callus' suggestion was fortuitous because soon after I was invited to a meeting with the Chancellor Sir Herman Black. He had been a member of the Faculty of Economics for many years before becoming Chancellor and still took a keen interest in the activities of the Faculty including delivering some undergraduate lectures. Sir Herman asked me if I had any initiatives in mind. I responded that I would like to establish an industrial relations research centre, and he offered me a 'one off' grant of $2,000 to get the centre started. Sir Herman said he wanted to meet me again in one year's time to see what we had achieved in terms of raising other funds and undertaking research.

A few months later, Ron Callus and I established the *Centre of Industrial Relations Research at the University of Sydney* (CIRRUS). We invited a number of employer and union representatives to join our advisory board. Sir John Moore, who had recently retired as the President of the federal Industrial Relations Commission agreed to chair the board. Our first activity was a conference on *Industrial Relations in the Workplace*. We subsequently applied for a grant from the Australian Research Council (ARC) to begin research on this topic, in conjunction with colleagues at several other Australian universities. About this time, the federal government announced a programme of Key Centres for Research and Teaching in specific fields. Although Industrial Relations was not mentioned as a field of interest, we applied and were told that our application had merit. Encouraged by this response, Ron Callus and I travelled to Canberra to meet the head of the ARC, Professor Don Aitkin, and put the case that Industrial Relations should be included in the next round of applications. Aitkin suggested that we add 'teaching' to the title of our proposal. The following year, we re-applied and were successful. Monash University was also offered a centre in the same field. *The Australian Centre for Industrial Relations Research and Teaching* (ACIRRT) was established in 1989 with Ron Callus as Deputy Director and me as Director. CIRRUS was absorbed into ACIRRT and Sir John Moore agreed to be Chair of the new Centre.

Ron Callus was keen to lobby the Federal government to fund a major survey of workplace industrial relations in Australia similar to that which had recently been conducted in the United Kingdom. We again visited Canberra and spoke with Dr Roy Green in the office of the Minister for Industrial Relations, Ralph Willis. Others were also urging the federal government to take this initiative, including Emeritus Professor Joe Isaac, and eventually, the decision was made to fund the first Australian Workplace Industrial Relations Survey (AWIRS). Ron Callus was appointed as Director of the AWIRS project and relocated to Canberra for over two years, having obtained leave without pay from the University of Sydney. A number of academics, including Joe Isaac and myself, received invitations to be on the advisory board for AWIRS. The survey was a revelation about Australian workplace industrial relations, which had been neglected by previous research. Traditionally, the focus of research was on the structures and processes of industrial relations beyond the workplace, such as the arbitration system. One of the key findings of the AWIRS project was that only in a minority of workplaces could unions be classified as 'active bargainers' in which there was an active union presence and formal procedures and structures to handle industrial relations (Callus et al., 1991).

In a 'companion volume' to the AWIRS publication, a collection of case studies was produced from an ARC grant which enabled researchers from a variety of universities to investigate the dynamics of industrial relations at the enterprise level in various industries (Lansbury and Macdonald, 1992). The project was the successful outcome of the initiative taken by the recently formed ACIRRT, in conjunction with colleagues at the University of Melbourne, to supplement the results of AWIRS with more detailed analysis of specific workplaces. The general picture of industrial relations in Australia which emerged from the case studies was one of cautious pragmatism on the part of both unions and management. In contrast to the criticism by the Business Council of Australia (BCA) of union structures and arbitration processes as barriers to change, the case studies revealed that when management actively sought to involve workers and their local union representatives more effective change was achieved. Management rarely encountered strong resistance when they clearly explained their strategy and the likely outcomes for the workforce. *Workplace Industrial Relations: Case Studies* (Lansbury and Macdonald, 1992) is a positive example of academics joining forces in a collaborative project. The book not only sought to advance knowledge in our field by undertaking original research on a neglected issue but it also sought to influence public policy about industrial relations. Evidence presented by the findings of both AWIRS and the workplace case studies revealed the weakness of union and management bargaining structures at the enterprise level and raised doubts about the viability of moving too quickly to enterprise bargaining systems without adequate preparation.

The Australian Centre for Industrial Relations Research and Teaching (ACIRRT)

During its first two years of operation, ACIRRT focused on its core objective of improving the quality of research and teaching in industrial relations. A survey of all higher education institutions, including universities and Colleges of Technical and Further Education, was undertaken in collaboration with the Federal Department of Industrial Relations to ascertain what courses were being offered by which institutions and needs perceived by teachers and students for improvements in industrial relations education. A conference on teaching industrial relations was held with both local and international speakers from the United Kingdom, United States and New Zealand. Other conferences were held on specific topics such as Labour History, Comparative Industrial Relations, Economic Restructuring and Industrial Relations, Occupational Health and Safety and Swedish Experience of Managing Innovation and Change. A Summer School for Trade Union officials was also conducted on the theme of 'Organising Strategies for the 1990s', co-sponsored by the Labor Council of NSW, and with the Federal Minister for Industrial Relations, as the keynote speaker. The Centre also inaugurated the Kingsley Laffer Library in the presence of the Vice-Chancellor, the Federal Minister for Education and Kingsley Laffer himself.

On returning from the AWIRS project in Canberra, Ron Callus became Director of ACIRRT and I continued as Head the Department of Industrial Relations. Although Key Centres were potentially funded for up to nine years by the ARC, they had to demonstrate that they were performing successfully in order to continue receiving funding. There was also a strong expectation by the Federal Department of Education that Centres would become financially independent. ACIRRT was remarkably successful under the leadership of Ron Callus and later under John Buchanan. After achieving the maximum of nine years funding from the ARC from 1989 to 1998, ACIRRT became financially independent, with minimum levels of financial support from the University of Sydney, and continued until 2018. Ron Callus continued as Director of ACIRRT from 1991 to 2005, when he retired and was replaced by John Buchanan, who had been Deputy Director during Ron's tenure.

During its most productive period, ACIRRT had approximately 25 staff and was undertaking a wide range of applied and policy research projects for Federal and State governments, unions and employers and gained research grants from the ARC, ILO and the National Centre for Vocational Education Research. ACIRRT published two major books and numerous reports as well as papers in academic journals and books and had its own series of Working Papers and Research Reports. It also established the first database of enterprise agreements, known as the Agreements Database and Monitor (ADAM). It became the most authoritative source of information on enterprise agreements until the Federal Department of Industrial Relations decided to establish their own database and make it freely available to the public. Many students and young researchers received invaluable training during their employment in ACIRRT and went on to complete higher degrees and work for universities, unions, employers, government and non-government organisations.

John Buchanan was director from 2005 to 2018 and changed the name of ACIRRT to the Workplace Research Centre (WRC). However, as Liberal National Coalition governments became predominant at both the Federal level and in NSW, and industrial relations became less of a priority issue, it became more difficult to obtain funds for applied research and in 2018 the WRC closed its operations. However, industrial relations research continued to be undertaken by staff and PhD students in WOS.

Workplace reform in Australia: 'designing the future' 1991

A period of optimism for workplace reform in Australian continued from the late 1980s into the mid-1990s. The Hawke Labor government established a path-breaking Accord with the trade union movement following its election in 1983. This was followed by a successful 'summit' which brought together employers, unions and other representative bodies to achieve consensus on economic and social goals for Australia. There appeared to be broad support emerging for workplace reform which would not only have benefits for employers and the workforce but also for Australian society as a whole.

In 1991, an innovative and ambitious conference was convened by an independent organisation, *Workplace Australia*, to 'help people develop visions for the future and a better understanding of what can be achieved'. The conference was attended by over 700 participants from a wide range of Australian workplaces and industries. They collaborated in discussions about workplace reform and learned from each other's experiences. A unique aspect of the conference was on-site workshops held prior to the conference and follow-up activities afterwards. The conference also attracted approximately 120 overseas participants who shared their experiences and learned from workplace reforms being undertaken in Australia.

The conference was the initiative of Neil Watson (my friend from Political Philosophy days at Melbourne University) who used the 'search conference' concept which he developed at Australia Frontier. An inspiration for the conference was Fred Emery, a pioneer of theory and practice of workplace democracy, whose work was celebrated and honoured at the event. Watson gained the support of major employers and unions as well as sponsorship from a wide range of sources. The President of Ford Australia and head of the Australian Manufacturing Council, Bill Dix, was the conference chair. Keynote speakers included Bob Hawke, Prime Minister of Australia, and Senator Peter Cook, Federal Minister for Industrial Relations.

At the end of the conference, a recommendation was issued by *Workplace Australia*, on behalf of the participants, which called upon the union movement and employer organisations 'to develop jointly a charter for workplace reform and strategy for its implementation'. It also requested that the Australian government and Opposition 'give implementation of this charter bipartisan support'. Following the conference, a new organisation was formed called *Workplace Australia: the National Centre for Productivity and Working Life*, headed by Neil Watson and Kate Nash. It conducted follow-up conferences in Australia and New Zealand and assisted organisations to implement workplace reforms. However, following the defeat of the Keating Labor government in 1996, the momentum for collaboration between employers and unions to undertake workplace reform dissipated.

Engaging with practitioners and policy makers in industrial relations

Soon after I arrived at the University of Sydney, we established an Advisory Board to build closer relations with trade unions, employers, governments and the industrial relations tribunals. The Board also assisted us with advice on how our programmes could be more relevant to industrial relations practitioners and assisted us to promote our courses in the wider community. Sir John Moore, former President of the Australian Industrial Relations Commission, accepted our invitation to chair the Board. Others who served on the board included Anna Booth, then National Secretary of the Clothing and Allied Trades Union, Sue Bussell, Executive Manager of Industrial Relations for Qantas Airways and Heather Ridout who became Chief Executive of the Australian Industry Group (AiG) and Michael Easson, Secretary of Unions NSW.

In 1993, an annual Kingsley Laffer Memorial Lecture was established to commemorate the founder of Industrial Relations as a field of teaching and research at the University of Sydney. Laffer lecturers included Prime Ministers, Bob Hawke and Julia Gillard, Justice Michael Kirby, High Court of Australia as well as prominent union, employer and community leaders such as Dr Iain Ross, President of the Fair Work Commission, Sharon Burrow, Secretary of the ACTU, Jennifer Westacott, CEO of the BCA, Professor Tim Soutphommasane, Australian Human Rights Commission and Dame Quentin Bryce, former Sex Discrimination Commissioner and later Governor General of Australia and the Reverend Tim Costello, Chief Advocate for World Vision Australia. International academics included Professors Tom Kochan from MIT, David Weil from Brandeis University and Chris Howell from Oberlin College in the United States.

Many industrial relations practitioners, policy makers and political leaders have been associated with the Department of Industrial Relations and its successor, WOS. They have served as Honorary Professors, as members of the Advisory Board and as visiting lectures. Some are listed below with anecdotes to illustrate that industrial relations can have its lighter side.

Bob Hawke

Bob Hawke dominated the industrial relations arena for decades, serving as President of the ACTU from 1969 to 1980 and as Prime Minister from 1983 to 1991.

He was a Rhodes Scholar at Oxford and commenced a PhD at ANU before joining the ACTU as a research officer. He modernised the trade union movement and presided over important economic reforms. Through the Accord on wages and prices, he forged a broad consensus between the union movement, employers and government. However, tensions over leadership succession in the government led to the replacement of Hawke as Prime Minister by Paul Keating in December 1991.

My colleague Greg Patmore suggested that we invite Bob Hawke to become an Honorary Professor in Industrial Relations at the University of Sydney after he lost the Prime Ministership. He accepted our invitation, delivered the inaugural Laffer lecture and served as an Honorary Professor for six years from 1992 to 1998. He was generous with his time with both staff and students and delivered a number of lectures and seminars.

Bob Hawke was a great raconteur, which was on display when the Vice-Chancellor of the University of Sydney held a small dinner party to welcome Hawke as an Honorary Professor. On that occasion, Hawke told entertaining stories about his meetings with various world leaders, including dinner at the White House with President Ronald Reagan. According to Bob Hawke, Reagan amused his guests with an endless stream of anecdotes. Towards the end of the evening, Hawke asked Reagan: 'Ron, can I ask you what you are doing about the problems of the US economy?' Reagan replied: 'Oh the economy is a very complex issue, Bob, so that's why I have booked you in for golf with (Secretary of State) George Shultz tomorrow morning. George knows all about the economy and can answer all your questions'.

During the VC's dinner, someone asked Bob Hawke if he was writing a book, now that he had retired from politics. 'Yes', replied Hawke, 'it will be a bestseller because I have an excellent co-author, Professor Roy Higgins'. The questioner then asked: 'What is Professor Higgins' area of expertise?' Hawke replied: 'Horse racing- he was one of Australia's leading jockeys'. 'So what is the book about?' the questioner continued. 'Betting', replied Hawke, 'We have a perfect system and it will make the punters very rich!' I doubt if the book ever appeared but Bob Hawke had a reputation as an avid fan of sports, particularly horse racing. However, he did publish *The Hawke Memoirs* (Hawke, 1994).

In a tribute to Hawke after his death in 2019, Ron Callus and I wrote:

> Bob Hawke was one of a kind and a giant in the world of industrial relations. His skills, intellect and innovative approach to bringing about change was right for the time. We are yet to see a leader of his calibre to emerge and take on the challenge of the new order.
>
> (Callus and Lansbury, 2019)

John Howard

In 1992, John Howard was the Shadow Minister for Industrial Relations, having lost the leadership of the Liberal Party in 1989. The student association in our

Department at the University of Sydney asked me to chair a debate on the future of industrial relations between John Howard and Martin Ferguson, then President of the ACTU. Both were graduates of the University of Sydney. Unfortunately, Martin Ferguson was not able to attend, and his brother Laurie, who was a member of the federal parliament, took his place. John Howard demonstrated his formidable debating skills and command of detail and easily outclassed his opponent.

After the debate, I invited both speakers and the students who had organised the event to afternoon tea. Ferguson declined but Howard accepted and engaged in lively discussion with the students. He was asked why he had accepted the relatively lower status shadow portfolio of Industrial Relations when he had held the more senior position of Treasurer in the previous Coalition government. Howard's answer was emphatic: 'Because by reforming industrial relations you can change Australia'. He was also asked if he would challenge John Hewson, then Liberal leader, if Labor won the next election. Howard responded that he expected Dr Hewson to win the election and be the next Prime Minister. But he did ask the students how they felt John Hewson was performing as Liberal Party leader, and it seemed that Howard was looking beyond the next election. In fact, Hewson lost the 'unlosable' election, and Howard won back the leadership and became the second longest serving Australian Prime Minister from 1996 to 2007.

Bert Evans

When Bert Evans retired in 1996, after leading the AiG and its predecessor the Metal Trades Industry Association (MTIA) for 17 years, Prime Minister John Howard commented that 'his career and achievements ... provided a salient example of what can be achieved with a constructive approach to industrial relations'. This was an accurate statement about Evans who was regarded by many as the 'employers' version of Bob Hawke' because of his popularity and ability to resolve disputes as a tough but fair negotiator. However, an amusing and heartfelt tribute was delivered by former Labor Prime Minister, Paul Keating at a retirement dinner for Bert Evans at Taronga Park Zoo. Keating noted that, like himself, Evans had grown up in the working-class suburb of Bankstown where their fathers had played billiards together at the Bankstown Workers Club. Keating's father cited Bert Evans as an example whom Paul should follow because 'that young man has a big future'. 'And look at Bert' declared Keating, 'he ended up heading Australia's most important employers' organisation and I am just a washed-up Prime Minister!' Another former Prime Minister, Bob Hawke, also spoke that evening about the strong personal and professional association he had forged with Bert Evans during the Accord years when he helped Hawke and Keating gain employer support for their economic and industrial relations reforms.

Bert Evans followed Bob Hawke as the second Laffer lecturer in 1994. The AiG provided valuable support to both the Department of Industrial Relations and ACIRRT, our research centre. Ron Callus, Director of ACIRRT, told me an amusing story about Bert Evans' attitude to research. The AiG had commissioned ACIRRT to undertake a research project but the results were contrary to what he had hoped. Evans asked Callus: 'Can't you do some more research and come up with the results that I want?' However, he reluctantly accepted the outcome and continued to support the work of the Centre. After his retirement, the AiG established the Bert Evans Scholarship to encourage undergraduate students to undertake the final honours' year in Industrial Relations at the University of Sydney. The last activity in which I was involved with Bert Evans was a conference *Thirty Years After the Accord*. It brought together some of the key figures in the Accord years, including Bob Hawke and Bill Kelty, with current leaders of unions and employers to discuss what could be learned from this period. Evans remained a strong supporter of a collaborative approach to building Australia's economic and social future. Needless to say, Bert Evans was not a supporter of the divisive reforms introduced by the Howard government, and the AiG was marginalised by the government in favour of other employer groups who were in stronger agreement with their approach.

Heather Ridout

As the first woman to head a major employers' association, the AiG, Heather Ridout was a 'trail blazer' for other women who have subsequently attained leadership roles in the field of Industrial Relations. Ridout joined the MTIA after completing a degree in Economics from the University of Sydney and eventually led the enlarged AiG, as Chief Executive, through the global financial crisis and other difficult periods. After her retirement from AiG, Ridout chaired Australian Super (a $170 billion superannuation fund) and served 12 years on its board of directors.

Ridout took a courageous decision prior to the federal election of 2007 when most of the other employer associations, headed by the Australian Chamber of Commerce and Industry (ACCI), established a 'fighting fund' to support the conservative Liberal and National Parties. Ridout announced that AiG would not join the other employer bodies because AiG was not a 'political organisation' and would seek to work constructively with whichever political parties won the election and became government. It was significant that the head of ACCI, who initiated the employers' 'fighting fund', subsequently became a Liberal Party candidate and won a seat in federal parliament. It was a difficult decision by Ridout to refuse to join in solidarity with the other employer associations in supporting the conservative parties in the election as many of her members would have been Liberal Party members. But it exemplified Ridout's principled approach to leadership.

After the 2007 election, which was won by the ALP, the AiG became the main employer organisation to which the Labor government turned for advice. Ridout was also appointed to a number of advisory bodies by the government to the chagrin of other employer organisations. However, Ridout steadfastly maintained that the AiG was not a partisan body and collaborated with governments of all political persuasions.

Heather Ridout served on the Advisory Board of both the Department of Industrial Relations and ACIRRT at the University of Sydney and was of great assistance to us when we successfully applied to the ARC to become a Key Centre of research and teaching in Industrial Relations. In her Kingsley Laffer memorial lecture in 2004, Ridout spoke about the concept of 'fairness' and how it should be integral to all Industrial Relations systems. She also assisted us as an opening speaker at the World Congress of the International Labour and Employment Relations Association (ILERA) for which AiG was a key sponsor.

Anna Booth

Anna Booth graduated from the University of Sydney with a Bachelor of Economics, with honours, having specialised in Industrial Relations. During her illustrious career in industrial relations, Booth led a major national union, became a Vice President of the ACTU, established a consulting practice specialising in dispute prevention and resolution and served as Deputy President of the Fair Work Commission.

When Ron Callus and I decided to establish a research centre in Industrial Relations, we invited Anna Booth to be an inaugural member of the advisory board. Anna became a key supporter and assisted us with our successful application to the ARC to become a Key Centre for research and teaching. She continued as a member of the ACIRRT advisory board and participated in many of our early activities. In recent years, she has been Chair of the Advisory Board of the WOS Discipline which succeeded the Department of Industrial Relations.

Booth initiated an innovative programme in the Commission called *New Approaches: Cooperative and Productive Workplaces*. Under this programme, Commission members train and facilitate employers and employee representatives, including unions in the interest-based approach to negotiating enterprise agreements, organisational change and resolution of disputes. It is Booth's intention that this programme will expand the scope for unions and their members to influence how workers' experience their own workplaces.

Sue Bussell

As Executive Manager for Industrial Relations at Qantas Airways, Sue Bussell had one of the most significant roles in Australian Industrial Relations and was one of the most senior women in the aviation industry. She began her career as a flight attendant with Qantas Airways and became Federal Vice President of the overseas branch of the Australian Flight Attendants Association. She later moved to the Australian Postal and Telecommunications Union as Federal Industrial Officer, consolidating her early career in the trade union movement. She was subsequently appointed by the Victorian government as a Commissioner of the Victorian Industrial Relations Commission.

Her career in industrial relations management began at Ansett Australia and then continued at Qantas where she served in various functions. Being in charge of industrial relations at Qantas was not an easy role. Bussell spoke of her early experience of negotiating with the Pilots Union whose senior officials did not take kindly to sitting opposite a 'former hostie' representing Qantas management!

My association with Sue Bussell began 30 years ago when she was in her early management roles at Qantas. She became involved with industrial relations education at the University of Sydney as an occasional lecturer and member of the advisory board of the Department of Industrial Relations and its successor, the Discipline of WOS. She was instrumental in establishing and maintaining the Qantas scholarship for final honours students in Industrial Relations at the University of Sydney and delivered the annual Kingsley Laffer Memorial lecture at the University of Sydney in 2010. She received an Order of Australia (AM) for her services to industrial relations.

Iain Ross

In 2012, Iain Ross was appointed President of the Fair Work Commission (as it is now known) and as a Judge of the Federal Court of Australia. Ross has also held other senior legal and administrative appointments. He has degrees in Economics and Law as well as a PhD in Law from the University of Sydney where he is an Adjunct Professor in both Law and Industrial Relations. He has played a key role in the teaching and research activities of the WOS Discipline.

Iain Ross is unique among presidents of the Commission, past and present, in holding a PhD in Industrial Law. For his doctoral thesis, Ross examined the impact of legal architecture, conciliator style and other factors on the settlement of unfair dismissal claims in the industrial relations court of Australia. He found that the outcome of conciliation, whether or not the claim was settled, was determined by the context of the dispute and the conciliation process.

My first meeting with Iain Ross was in the late 1980s when I had recently joined the University of Sydney, and he was Legal Officer with the ACTU. Ross came to see me to discuss education and research matters related to trade unions. He later became Assistant Secretary to Bill Kelty at the ACTU and represented the trade union movement on a number of key bodies, including the National Labour Consultative Council and the National Occupational Health and Safety Commission. He was seconded to the office of the then Treasurer (and later Prime Minister) as a consultant on microeconomic reform.

In the early 1990s, I was conducting research at a large auto components plant in Sydney when I discovered that Iain Ross had achieved an agreement between the unions and management, after years of industrial conflict. The industrial relations manager told me that until the intervention by Ross, on behalf of the ACTU, the plant was on the verge of closing down. Recently, I was invited by Ross to present a lecture at a seminar hosted by the Fair Work Commission. I sent him draft of my lecture and received a number of detailed suggestions and the latest research findings on the subject. These anecdotes illustrate Iain Ross's effectiveness 'behind the scenes', whether settling an industrial dispute or keeping my research up to date!

All of the people I have mentioned above exemplify the generosity and support which I received during my career at the University of Sydney and contributed to the success of our academic programmes, which continued well after I retired as a full-time member of staff.

The Swedish Centre for Worklife Research

In 1990, I was granted six-months study leave and was awarded a Visiting Fellowship at the Swedish Centre for Worklife Research (Arbetslivscentrum) in Stockholm. After travelling in Finland and Norway with my wife Gwen and daughter Nina, I settled in at the Wenner-Gren Centre for visiting researchers. This was the first time I had lived for an extended period in Sweden since I was a graduate student at the University of Lund in 1967–1968, although I had visited numerous times and maintained contact with Swedish colleagues. The Centre for Worklife Research was established by the Social Democratic government in 1971 during a high point of interest in workplace reforms. The role of the Centre was to conduct applied research into all aspects of working life. It had a tripartite board of management with representatives from unions and employers and government which oversaw its activities. During the next decade, important legislative reforms were introduced on co-determination at work as well as occupational health and safety. The Centre played an important role in evaluating the effects of these reforms on the workplace. Although the Centre was initiated by a Social Democratic government, its role continued under a Conservative Coalition government from 1976 to 1982.

During the period I spent at the Centre in 1990, it had a thriving research programme and had acquired a strong international reputation for the quality of its work. The Centre had its own journal, *Economic and Industrial Democracy*, which published research not only from the Nordic countries but also from around the world. I met Swedish researchers at the Centre with whom I would collaborate in years to come, including Ake Sandberg, Christian Berggren and Lena Gonas. I also met other visiting researchers, including Juhani Pekkola from the Finnish Ministry of Labour, with whom I later undertook projects in Finland.

The main project I pursued while at the Centre was a comparison of productivity and industrial relations in the automotive components industry in Australia and Sweden, using a case study approach. The project was funded by a grant from the Federal Department of Industrial Relations in Australia. The objective of the research was to determine which factors were significant in determining differences in productivity outcomes between similar plants in Australia and Sweden. A case study was initially conducted at BTR Engineering in Sydney and then replicated at a Volvo Components plant in Sweden. Measuring a range of variables, in relation to the production of certain components, it was clear that the Swedish plant achieved much higher productivity and quality than its Australian equivalent.

A number of factors contributed to the superior performance of the Swedish plant, involving both the 'hardware' and the 'humanware'. Of great significance was the fact that the average age of equipment used in the Volvo plant was 10 years compared with 25 years in the BTR plant. There were also striking contrasts in terms of the people and organisational aspects of the two plants. The Volvo plant had a high degree of multi-skilling among its workforce, advanced work group organisation, a relatively flat managerial hierarchy and active consultation between the management and the workforce concerning how the work was organised. There was willingness and capacity among the workers at Volvo to utilise new technology to achieve higher levels of productivity. Although the level of unionisation was similar between the two plants, there was less disputation and interruptions to the work programme at the Volvo plant compared with BTR. The results of the project were published in *Economic and Industrial Democracy* (Lansbury et al., 1992).

While in Sweden, I took the opportunity to refresh my Swedish language skills and enrolled in a course with my former Swedish teacher, Marianne Harry, now retired but teaching Swedish to refugees at an Adult Education Centre in Stockholm. Many of my fellow students were from Kurdish minorities in countries such as Turkey, Iraq and Iran, where they had faced discrimination and persecution. Yet some also complained about their treatment in Sweden. Many were working in jobs which Swedes were reluctant to do, such as home care workers providing services to the sick and elderly. Despite the fact that Sweden offered them safety from regimes they had escaped in their home country, as well as the opportunity to earn a living and to study, many were dissatisfied. They complained of discrimination against them in Sweden and talked of emigrating to countries such as Germany, the United States, Canada or Australia where they imagined that they would have a better life.

As my fellow students pointed out, I did not encounter discrimination as they did as I could pass for a Swede. Our teacher, Marianne, was well aware of the problems that some of her students faced and worked as a volunteer in organisations which sought to assist refugees, particularly women from Islamic and African backgrounds. I should not have been surprised by the complaints of my fellow students as discrimination is a common experience for refugees in many countries. However, Sweden and other Nordic countries took more refugees, in proportion to their population, than most other parts of the world. In years to come, when the flow of refugees increased, there would be a political backlash against allowing entry and the rise of right-wing political parties which would gain strong electoral support.

The Social Democratic government in Sweden lost the general election in 1991. Carl Bildt emerged as Prime Minister leading a conservative coalition which only held office until 1994. The Bildt government merged the Centre for Worklife Research (Arbetlivscentrum) with the much larger Centre for Work Environment to form the National Worklife Institute (Arbetslivsinstitut). The new institute comprised over 400 researchers, most of whom were involved in Occupational Health and Safety. In 2006, a new conservative coalition government announced that the Institute would be closed and that the researchers would be absorbed into the university sector. The 'Conservative Alliance' government, under Prime Minister Fredrik Reinfeldt, held office from 2007 to 2014 and instituted radical reforms including privatisation of some educational and health institutions. Since coming to office in 2014, the minority Social Democratic government, led by Stefan Lofven, has not 'rolled back' many of the previous government's reforms and has declined to reopen the National Worklife Research Institute, although it has agreed to establish an 'Information Bureau' to disseminate the findings of worklife research.

The transformation of global employment relations

In 1990, Tom Kochan and Michael Piore at MIT proposed a large comparative study of changes in industrial relations and human resource policies and practices. Their key research question was whether other countries were experiencing a similar transformation of their industrial relations and human resource systems to the United States. The project utilised the strategic choice framework of analysis from Kochan et al. (1986) and had multiple strands. The focus of the first strand was on industrialised economies. The research team was drawn from 11 countries, mainly from Europe but also included Australia. A planning meeting was held at the Organisation for Economic Cooperation and Development (OECD), Paris in 1992.

The research brief was to investigate the following work and employment practices in a selected number of industries in each country:

- *Changes in work organisation:* including teamwork, working time and work rules, with particular emphasis on the impact of new technology and changes in competitive strategy;
- *Staffing arrangements*: including practices of recruitment, selection and separation, job mobility and career structures, employment security and labour market adjustment;
- *Patterns of skill formation and training*: including the content and delivery of training, the relationship between training and competitive strategy, and the effect of public policy on the training needs of organisations and employers;
- *Compensation arrangements*: affecting the level, structure and forms of compensation of employees; and
- *Governance issues:* including the changing role of industrial relations/ human resource management functions within enterprises and relationships with trade unions, industrial tribunals and other agencies.

These issues were examined in order to show how both institutional arrangements as well as firm strategies made an impact on industrial relations and human resource practices, thereby influencing both economic and social performance.

Industry networks were established by researchers in various countries in the following sectors: automobile manufacturing, airlines, banking, telecommunications, steel and clothing.

The research project was conducted over several years and the results were published in a series of papers and books. The first book dealt with OECD economies (Locke et al., 1995) while the second volume focused on emerging industrialising economies in Asia (Verma et al., 1995). Subsequent books covered industry-level studies in automobile manufacturing (Kochan et al., 1997), banks (Regini et al., 1999) and telecommunications (Katz, 1997). An Australian study tested the transformation thesis in relation to seven industries (Kitay and Lansbury, 1997). Several later books were also influenced by the MIT project (see Bamber et al., 2009; Katz and Darbishire, 2000; Katz et al., 2015).

Although transformation of IR and HR systems appeared to be underway in most advanced economies, there was considerable variation in the pace of change and the degree to which national systems were able to adapt through minor incremental changes versus fundamental transformation. Those countries with institutional arrangements that promoted functional flexibility, such as in northern Europe, appeared to adapt to changes more easily than those with rigid forms of job regulation, as in some Anglo-Saxon countries. Differences were also found between countries that emphasised formal apprenticeship systems as well as continuous skills development and those that did not. Finally, those countries in which the unions were closely tied to job control systems, such as the United States, suffered a greater decline than those countries in which unions played a broader role in society, such as those in the Nordic region.

The MIT project was extended to a number of emerging countries in Asia which were undergoing industrialisation (Verma et al., 1995). The Asian regional project sought to understand the role of the industrial relations and human resource policies, at both the sectoral and national levels, in facilitating economic and social development. It became apparent that no single 'Asian model' existed but that governments played an important role in determining their industrial relations and human resource systems. Some governments responded to growing demands from workers for higher wages and greater voice with suppressive measures that sought to maintain low wages and conditions and to prevent unions from having a stronger role. Other governments responded in more measured ways to accommodate the concerns expressed by the workforce and their representatives.

The Asian project concluded that the successful adaptation to change required alignment of both public and business policies at the firm and the state levels. Adaptation to change at the firm level required greater employee involvement, investment in training and a more flexible work organisation. At the state level, greater investment was required in education and research and development as well as incentives for business to upgrade their operations. A combination of actions by both the state and business, working together, was required to achieve more committed workers, higher skills and greater productivity.

While many changes have occurred in recent years in the industrial relations and human resource management policies and practices in both the OECD and emerging economies of Asia, the findings of these studies from the 1990s were a strong portent of the transformations which would occur during the decades that followed. The ongoing processes of globalisation have meant that economies around the world have experienced similar shocks, from the global financial crisis of 2008–2009 and the more recent COVID-19 in 2020, and their industrial relations and human resource systems have had to adjust to rapidly changing circumstances. Transformation has continued to occur but in a variety of ways and outcomes.

The international automotive industrial relations project

One of the industry networks which emerged from the Global Employment Relations Transformation Project was focused on the international auto industry. The project was initiated by Tom Kochan through his association with the International Motor Vehicle Program (IMVP) which was established at MIT in 1979 to analyse the challenges facing the global auto industry. During the first phase of the IMVP (1979–1990), representatives from auto companies and researchers from universities around the world established benchmarks for comparing manufacturing performance between companies in various countries. In a book, *The Machine that Changed the World* by Womack et al. (1990), based on IMVP research, the authors coined the term 'lean production' to characterise the new paradigm, developed mainly by the Toyota Motor Company, that challenged the long-established mass production system invented by Ford and other companies in the United States and which had become the norm in many countries.

The authors of *The Machine that Changed the World* made the bold prediction that lean production was 'a better way of making things which the world should adopt as soon as possible' (Womack et al., 1990: 225). In their view, lean production was the 'one best way' to organise the production of motor vehicles. Hence, they argued that auto companies would need to adopt lean production in order to compete successfully in any part of the world or fall by the wayside. However, critics of this approach argued that there was not necessarily a single best way to assemble motor vehicles because employment practices vary in different countries according to how workers and managers interact, the way workers and their unions respond to production practices and the nature of the adaptation and innovation process itself.

In 1991, Tom Kochan gathered a team of researchers from a dozen countries to undertake case studies of auto manufacturers in their respective countries to study the effects of employment relations policies and practices on production systems. The project also sought to understand the diffusion and adaptation of lean production and to identify new paradigms which might be emerging. These case studies were combined with analysis of data from the IMVP in a book: *After Lean Production: Evolving Employment Practices in the World Auto Industry* (Kochan et al., 1997).

In *After Lean Production*, IMVP data analysed by John Paul MacDuffie and Frits Pil (1997) from surveys of assembly plants, provided evidence of considerable variation between countries on a number of variables in terms of productivity and work systems. While their data revealed a general trend towards the adoption of lean production principles in auto plants around the world, few companies had adopted the complete set of lean practices, and most had adopted hybrid arrangements which blended elements of both lean and mass production. These findings were supported by evidence from case studies conducted at auto plants in a range of countries. They showed a trend towards greater convergence across countries combined with divergence across and within companies. Hence, Japanese transplants in the United States, United Kingdom and Australia demonstrated that it was possible to achieve high performance outcomes while making few modifications to the lean practices that they had developed in their home country, although their productivity results still fell below that which was achieved in Japan.

The case studies in *After Lean Production* also revealed the important roles played by governments and national institutions in the auto industry. Government economic policies affect the strategies of individual companies and unions by influencing how exposed or protected the domestic market is from international competition and the role the auto industry plays in the development of the domestic economy. Labour policies and the role of industrial relations institutions may also play a significant role in ensuring that workers in the industry receive fair payment and working conditions. Yet domestic auto plants must compete with other plants, often owned by the same parent company, on both cost and quality criteria. In our contribution to the study, we showed how the Australian plants had significantly improved their performance by adopting aspects of lean production. However, these reforms were not sufficient to prevent both the US and Japanese-based companies closing their operations in Australia, ostensibly because the Australian government declined to continue to provide tariff protection and other subsidies to convince the auto companies to remain (see Clibborn et al., 2015).

Industrial relations in South Korea and Australia compared

In April 1990 I received an invitation from the Federal Department of Labour in Canberra to host a half-day seminar at the University of Sydney on Australian industrial relations for a visiting delegation from South Korea comprising representatives of the national employers' association, national trade union officials and government representatives from South Korea. They were particularly interested the Accord between the government and the trade unions, at that time, in Australia. The delegation was led by Dr Young-bum Park of the Korea Labour Institute (KLI), a government 'think tank'. Dr Park had recently returned from Cornell University in the United States where he had gained a PhD in the School of Industrial and Labour Relations. The seminar at the University of Sydney led to a long association with Young-bum Park, the KLI and my continuing involvement with Korean industrial relations during the next 30 years.

The delegation had been invited to Australia by Prime Minister Hawke, who had visited South Korea with Simon Crean, President of the ACTU, and Bert Evans, head of the Manufacturing Employers Association, the MTIA. The reason for the high-level Australian delegation visiting South Korea was recognition of the significant trade relationship between the two countries. South Korea had recently ended a period of military dictatorship, which had lasted for over 40 years. The new democratically elected government was dealing with high levels of industrial disputation now that independent unions had gained legal status for the first time. Prime Minister Hawke suggested to the South Korean President, Roh Tae-woo, that the Accord might have relevance to the problems facing him at that time and invited him to send a delegation to Australia to learn more about its operation.

After the seminar, Dr Park from the KLI asked if we could write a report on industrial relations reforms which South Korea should consider in order to resolve their current problems, drawing on the experience of Australia and other countries. Gianni Zappala, then a research fellow at ACIRRT, and I quickly undertook research on the Korean situation and wrote a report for the KLI setting out options for industrial relations reform which South Korea might consider. Dr Park then invited me to travel to Korea where I discovered that 700 copies of our report had been distributed to members of the government, trade unions, employers and other interested parties (Lansbury and Zappala, 1990). I was closely questioned about our proposals to grant workers and their unions greater rights in their workplaces and to introduce various dispute settling procedures. While our recommendations were not universally endorsed, the visit resulted in ongoing research projects between the KLI and industrial relations academics at the University of Sydney during the next few decades.

With Jim Kitay and Nick Wailes, I subsequently gained ARC grants to undertake comparative research on industrial relations in South Korea and other Asian countries. With South Korean colleagues at UNSW, I later conducted research on industrial relations in Hyundai Motor Company in South Korea and India.

Global HR strategies implode at IBM

In the early 1990s, I was invited by IBM Australia to attend a conference to discuss their global HR strategies. The meeting was held at IBM's headquarters in Armonk, New York, about 60 km from midtown Manhattan. The Global Head of IBM Human Resources, Walter Burdick, hosted the meeting which lasted for several days. Invitees included the IBM Regional HR directors from around the world and about 15 academics from leading Business Schools in the United States, Europe and Asia. We were housed in the IBM Learning Centre which comprised a resort hotel, various amenities and meeting rooms. It was located in a semi-rural area with pleasant trails through 400 acres of woodlands where participants could stroll and converse between meetings.

New horizons at the University of Sydney   121

The invitation from IBM came after I spoke at an annual awards event hosted by the Federal government's Affirmative Action Agency, headed by Valerie Pratt. The HR Director for IBM Australia, who was present at the event, approached me a few days later with an invitation to attend the conference in New York at their expense. Fred Hilmer, Dean of the Australian Graduate School of Management at the University of New South Wales (UNSW), was also invited. Hilmer later became the Vice-Chancellor of UNSW and held a number of senior executive and director roles in major corporations.

The conference at Armonk comprised presentations by Global HR personnel from IBM headquarters as well as by each of IBM's regional HR directors. IBM's European Regional HR director addressed the meeting on industrial relations issues in Germany, where he was located. He explained that while IBM was a non-union employer in the United States, in Germany and some other European countries, they were obliged to recognise and negotiate employment issues with unions. IBM's Asian Regional HR director, based in Japan, discussed the need for IBM to adopt more of an Asian identity and be less 'American' in some of its managerial practices.

Some of us were invited to dinner at the home of Walter Burdick which was located on a hilltop in the wooded area surrounding the IBM complex. He was a genial host and entertained us with some anecdotes from almost 40 years with IBM. Burdick had recently been given the annual Award for Professional Excellence by the US Society for Human Resource Management. He had served on a number of high-level advisory bodies, appointed by President Ronald Reagan, including the National Commission for Employment Policy. He had also been a member an inquiry into CEO salaries in major US corporations, appointed by President Reagan. Burdick assured us that these salaries were not too high as CEOs were like elite sportspeople or movie stars with unique skills. I had noticed that several of the top IBM managers came and went by helicopter to the headquarters, and someone joked that you could tell a person's position in the IBM hierarchy by the size of their helicopters!

However, on the final day of the conference, Fred Hilmer shocked our hosts by commenting that he would not invest in IBM shares because there were ominous signs that the company was heading for major difficulties. This was like 'telling the emperor that he had no clothes'! Hilmer, a former head of McKinsey and Company in Australia, pointed out that IBM had failed to adjust to the end of the dominance of the mainframe computer systems and had not commercialised its invention of the PC, whose market other companies now dominated. Hilmer had read the signals correctly. Within a year, IBM was in deep trouble and speculation was rife that it might not survive.

In 1993, CEO John Akers, a life-time IBM employee, was replaced by Louis Gerstner who had held senior positions at Nabisco, American Express and McKinsey and Company. Gerstner was the first 'outsider' to be appointed to head IBM. He immediately appointed new Heads of Finance and HR as well as replacing three other key executives. Eventually, more than 100,000 IBM employees were laid off, and Gerstner reshaped the organisation by making e-business the focus of the company and withdrawing from areas such as the retail desktop PC market. By the time he retired in 2002, Gerstner had vastly increased IBM's market capitalisation but IBM had lost its once-dominant position in the IT industry.

Another surprise outcome of the conference occurred a year later when I was contacted by an IBM HR manager, whom I had met in Armonk, and was visiting Sydney. Over dinner, he told me that he was now looking for another job, having been a casualty of the near collapse of IBM. Fred Hilmer's intervention at the conference was not a revelation to those working for IBM as they knew that the situation was deteriorating but they were not prepared for the disaster that followed. He also revealed that rumours about the problems at IBM had been circulating on the internal email network. IBM had attempted to suppress any criticisms, and investigations were undertaken to find who was 'leaking' this information. The HR division was closed down and outsourced to a new 'spin off' IBM company called 'People Solutions'.

I maintained my contact with IBM Australia. One of my PhD students was supported by the company for her research on problems facing expatriate managers when they returned to Australia. One of IBM Australia's senior HR managers completed our Master's degree, served on our advisory board for several years and supported the Senior HR Roundtable we established to foster interaction and research with HR practitioners. One of the interesting developments which occurred later in Australia was that IBM was forced to recognise and negotiate with unions after they acquired some unionised businesses. I do not know if any other global HR conferences were ever held at IBM headquarters!

The International Institute for Labour Studies, ILO, Geneva

Prior to arriving in London to commence a PhD, I attended the World Congress of the International Industrial Relations Research Association (IIRA) in Geneva in 1970, on my way to undertaking my doctoral studies at the LSE in the early 1970s. At the congress, I met the late Ken Walker, a former Australian academic, who was Director of the International Institute for Labour Studies at the ILO. He had obtained a PhD at Harvard under the supervision of John Dunlop. Walker visited the LSE on several occasions where I discussed with him the possibility of later joining the Institute. However, Walker had resigned from the ILO by the time I completed my PhD and I accepted an offer to join Monash University as a lecturer. During the next 20 years I visited the ILO on a number of occasions, mainly in relation to activities of the IIRA. I undertook various minor research projects and contributed to ILO publications, but it was not until many years later that I had the opportunity to spend a good part of a year as a visiting scholar at the Institute.

In 1995, Gwen and I travelled to Geneva from Australia via South America and then lived in a small village in France about 40 km from Geneva. I commuted several times a week to the ILO while Gwen worked as a volunteer at the

International Women's Development Agency in Geneva. Our son, Owen, and daughter, Nina, were both enrolled as students at UNSW in Sydney. However, Nina and her boyfriend took a year's leave from university and rode their bicycles from Darwin to Geneva, and then cycled back again, a total of over 7,000 km. Their journey took them through many countries including Indonesia, India, Iran and Turkey. Gwen and I returned to Australia at the end of the year via East Africa where Gwen undertook fieldwork in Tanzanian villages for her doctoral thesis.

It was an interesting but difficult time at the Institute as its continued existence was under threat from the Director-General of the ILO, Michel Hansenne. The reasons given by the Director-General for wanting to close the Institute were economic but his fundamental concern appeared to be that the Institute was too independent of ILO management. The Institute occupied a unique role as a semi-autonomous research unit, which was funded mainly by the ILO but had its own external advisory board. It was established in 1960 with financing provided largely by contributions from several other member countries of the ILO. It had its own research journal, the *Bulletin of the International Institute of Labour Studies* (later renamed *Labour and Society*), an extensive reference library and provided short, quasi-academic courses on industrial relations subjects for students, mainly from developing countries. During its early years, the Director of the Institute held the position of Deputy Director General of the ILO, although this was later changed as the status of the Institute was downgraded.

The Institute played a key role in the establishment of the IIRA, providing it with a secretariat and the Director of the Institute being the Honorary Secretary of the Association. By 1995, the secretariat of the IIRA had been transferred to the industrial relations and labour law department at the ILO, the Institute's library was closed and its collections incorporated into the ILO's main library and the number of researchers at the Institute had been reduced. An informal campaign was conducted by prominent academics, many of whom were former Presidents of the IIRA, who wrote to ILO Director General Hansenne urging him to maintain the Institute's independent existence. This campaign was successful in preserving the Institute. The Institute continued for almost another 20 years and had something of a revival in the early 2000s when a new director was appointed from the OECD. He oriented the research of the Institute towards a stronger emphasis on labour economics and raised the academic quality and standing of *The International Labour Review*. However, the Institute was finally closed by Director-General Guy Ryder in 2014, and some of its functions were taken over by the ILO's Research Department.

Nevertheless, my period as a Visiting Fellow at the Institute gave me an opportunity to gain greater insight of the activities of the ILO as well as work on my own research. I participated in some of the research and teaching activities within the Institute as well as collaborating with researchers in other parts of the ILO, such as Peter Auer in the Employment Division and Muneto Ozaki in the Industrial Relations section. I also gave some lectures at the Institute as well as at the ILO Training Centre in Turin. Towards the end of my period at the Institute, I was invited by the incoming Director of the Institute, Jean Michel-Servais, to join the advisory committee for the World Labour Report. This was a major project and involved assembling a team of researchers from within and outside the ILO to investigate the world of work and employment. The project extended for three years and involved annual meetings of the advisory committee and researchers. However, many of the more radical proposals for industrial relations reform were 'watered down' by higher management in the ILO. The main focus of the final report was on increasing social protection and income security in an era of globalisation but with little detail on how this was to be achieved (ILO, 1998).

I remain a strong supporter of the ILO and believe that their advocacy of core labour standards continues to be important, particularly when governments are put under pressure to adhere to ILO conventions which they have ratified. I have continued to be involved in ILO activities, most recently in Vietnam at the invitation of the ILO Country Director, Dr Chang-Hee Lee. I first met Dr Lee when he joined the ILO in 1996 as a researcher working on the World Labour Report. Dr Lee has worked tirelessly persuading and assisting the government in Vietnam to adhere to the ILO convention on Freedom of Association and permit independent unions to represent workers if they are chosen to do so by the workforce.

ABB: globalisation versus local autonomy in the power transformer industry

In 1990, during my period as a Visiting Fellow at the Swedish Centre for Worklife Research, I met Christian Berggren who had recently written a fascinating doctoral thesis on the Volvo automotive manufacturing system. Berggren worked on the assembly line in the Swedish auto manufacturing industry during the mid-1970s before studying Engineering and Social Sciences at University. Berggren later undertook a detailed study of the Volvo and Saab auto production systems as a doctoral student. In his book *Alternatives to Lean Production: Swedish Work Organisation in the Swedish Auto Industry*, Berggren compared the Swedish approach with that of Toyota Motor Company. He argued that the Swedish auto industry had developed a distinctly different production design and work organisation which offered an alternative to the traditional assembly line and shop-floor hierarchy. Moreover, the Swedish model of teamwork increased independent decision-making and elicited strong union commitment.

In the mid-1990s, I was invited to join a research team which Torsten Bjorkman and Christian Berggren had formed to undertake an international study of the Swedish-Swiss conglomerate Asea Brown Boveri (ABB). The objective was to compare seven plants in six countries, all of which produced the same large power transformers, in order to assess how the company sought to combine a global strategy with local autonomy at the plant level. ABB had adopted 'lean management' principles and had a small head office in Baden, Switzerland. The company was divided into 35 business areas, one of which had responsibility for power transformers. ABB also adopted various 'programs' across each of the business areas to achieve a common approach. These included lean supply, common product, customer focus and total quality management (known as Six Sigma). ABB also practised 'matrix management'.

The ABB conglomerate was formed in 1987 by a merger between two century-old electrical engineering firms: Sweden's ASEA and the Switzerland's Brown Boveri, in order to form one of the largest electro-technical conglomerates in the world. Its main competitors were Siemens in Germany, Alsthom in France and General Electric in the United States. Under the leadership of its first Swedish managing director, Percy Barnevik, the merged company claimed that it would be 'global but local', providing maximum diversity at the local level for its operations in different countries worldwide. The research project involved a series of case studies conducted at the plant level in a wide range of countries to test what the concept of 'being local worldwide' meant in reality.

As part of the global research project, Mark Bray from the University of Newcastle (and formerly at the University of Sydney) in Australia and I spent several years studying three power transformer plants belonging to ABB in Sydney, Australia, Geneva in Switzerland and Vaasa in Finland. The three plants were similar in size, number of employees and products. However, they differed significantly in their levels of performance as measured by productivity, quality and performance. During the period of our study from about 1995–1999, each of the plants had to deal with a worldwide decline in demand for their products due to global changes in the power industry. By the mid-2000s, after our study had been completed, the Australian plant had closed while the Swiss and Finnish plants had successfully restructured and survived.

While there were numerous factors that contributed to the demise of the Australian plant, compared with the success of the other two plants, several significant issues were highlighted by our research. Some factors related to local circumstances while others were global in character. ABB adopted certain aspects of lean production which suited some circumstances but not others. The ABB total quality management programme emphasised the reduction in errors, while the time-based management system focused on the time taken from initial order of a power transformer to its delivery to the customer. However, while ABB encouraged all plants to adopt these programmes to improve their performance, they also allowed local variation in their implementation.

At ABB's power transformer plant in Geneva, new products were developed by its research department, and it became known as the centre of excellence within the Business Area for product innovation. The Finnish power transformer plant in Vaasa adopted new approaches to the organisation of production by eliminating layers of management and introducing extensive multi-functional team working, thereby becoming a centre of excellence for process innovation. Both plants had extensive systems of employee involvement in these decisions, including a works council in the Swiss plant. In contrast to the two European plants, workers at the Australian plant resisted the introduction of new systems to improve their performance and there was a steady decline in orders as well as complaints about poor quality products and failure to deliver on time.

During three years visiting the three plants and getting to know key managers and employees, it became apparent that the Australian plant had suffered from high turnover of managers and failure to invest in new technology, compared with the Swiss and Finnish plants. Eventually, the Business Area management in Europe sent the manager of the Finnish plant to determine if the Australian plant could be 'rescued'. The previous Australian plant manager had moved on to another company but had revealed that ABB was mainly focussed on cutting losses and was considering replacing locally made transformers with cheaper imports from Asia. The new plant manager from Finland explained that without major capital investment in new equipment and upgrading the skills of the workforce, the plant had no future. After a relatively short time, the manager returned to Finland, and the Australian power transformer plant was closed.

Meanwhile, at ABB's headquarters in Switzerland, Percy Barnevik's tenure was coming to a turbulent end. During his eight years as CEO and six years as chairman of ABB, Barnevik had been hailed as a corporate hero by the business press. He was awarded numerous honorary degrees and leadership awards in the United States and Europe. He embarked on a massive acquisition programme during his tenure and achieved record increases in ABB's share price. But one year after he stepped down as chairman, ABB was embroiled in a number of problems, and ABB's stock market value plummeted from 55 to 15 francs. The major contributor to ABB's problems was caused by 'not sticking to their knitting'. Spiralling asbestos claims related to a US firm, Combustion Engineering which ABB purchased in 1990 when Barnevik was CEO. ABB found itself $US10 billion in debt just as demand for its power systems, and industrial robots was hit by an economic downturn. ABB finally managed a turnaround in its fortunes by focusing on power technology and automation and returned to profitability in 2005.

The ABB research project demonstrated the need to investigate beyond the corporate rhetoric and slogans to understand the inner workings of a multinational corporation at both the headquarters and subsidiary levels. Although ABB was hailed as 'the most successful cross-border merger since Royal Dutch linked up with Britain's Shell in 1907', the research project raised doubts about the reality of ABB's global success under the 'messianic' leadership of Percy Barnevik. Nevertheless, the case studies of the power transformer plants in three countries revealed that at the local level, there were noteworthy successes. The Swiss plant was able to thrive by leveraging its expertise as a product innovator while the Finnish plant showed how process innovation underpinned its success. Sadly, the closure of the Australian plant underlined the failure of local management to produce power transformers at both sufficient quality and price to survive in a competitive global market.

Life beyond Sydney in the Hunter Valley

Since leaving Melbourne, we missed having a weekend house in the country to which we could retreat. Gwen was a regular squash player with a woman in

Avalon who would tell her of hard-working but stimulating weekends which she and her family spent on a farm at Paynes Crossing near Wollombi in the Hunter Valley of NSW. The family had joined a group of friends, mainly from Avalon, and purchased an old farm with a nearly derelict sandstone house built by a former convict, Thomas Paine, in the 1840s. The group had restored the house over a period of time but maintained many of its simple original features. However, she said to Gwen that she was now selling her share in the farm and would we be interested in buying it. We did!

From 1988 to 2000, we became part-owners, along with four other families, of the Paynes Crossing Pastoral Company – which was a grand title for a run-down farm with about 20 cattle and several horses. Most of the other families had children, and it became an opportunity for all of us to experience being weekend farmers. It turned out to be a very unprofitable venture as we usually bought cattle at the local Wollombi saleyards at high prices and sold when the market was in decline. It was also hard work looking after the cattle and keeping the fences repaired. However, we had great fun and our children became lovers of the bush as they roamed the hills and valleys adjacent to the farm.

The house had been restored to something like its original state by the time we joined the group. There were few concessions to the twentieth-century comforts. The 'drop' toilet was in a tin shed in the paddock, and the bathroom was in a separate building with a bucket shower. However, one day Gillian Armstrong, a well-known film producer, came by and asked if she could use our house in a film based on Peter Carey's novel, *Oscar and Lucinda*, which is set in the 1840s. The film starred Cate Blanchett, in her first major role, and the well-known British actor Ralph Fiennes. Unfortunately, despite several weeks' filming at our place, the film only included a couple of brief sequences from our house and farm. However, we did receive sufficient payment for the use of our property to enable us to purchase an ecologically designed toilet which we, of course, named 'Oscar and Lucinda'.

By 2000, we decided to sell our share and buy our own cottage on smaller block of land nearby. This proved to be a wise decision as it gave us greater access to a weekend 'retreat' which we could use at any time. It also freed us from having to care about the cattle while still maintaining horses. We have now owned 'Nurumbinya' for over 20 years and visit most weekends, which sometimes extend into the following week. We have become part of the small community and have observed the decline of farming and extension of vineyards along the valley. Much of this book was written there!

8 A broader role in academic research and leadership (2000–2009)

During the latter part of the 1990s, I became more involved in wider university activities. I was elected as President of the University of Sydney Association of Professors (USAP) which represented professorial level academics across the university. It was traditional for the executive of USAP to meet quarterly with the Vice-Chancellor and other senior members of the university's administration to discuss matters of mutual interest. For the most part, this comprised congenial discussions about issues facing the university but occasionally USAP would make suggestions or seek improvements in the conditions of employment for the professoriate. USAP did not undertake any collective bargaining functions, which were the province of the National Tertiary Education Union (NTEU). However, at the request of the University of Sydney Branch of the NTEU, I facilitated a meeting to encourage members of USAP to join the union and to foster greater cooperation between the NTEU and USAP.

Gavin Brown was appointed as Vice-Chancellor of the University of Sydney in 1996. Early in his term of office, the first round of enterprise bargaining commenced between the University of Sydney and the NTEU. Negotiations reached a stalemate, and members of the NTEU threatened to withhold exam results unless their demands were met. Gavin Brown sought my advice on how to end the deadlock. I contacted Jim Macken, a retired Judge of the Industrial Relations Commission of NSW, who met with the parties informally and resolved the dispute through mediation. Soon after this, I was asked if I would be interested in applying for the newly created position of Pro-Vice-Chancellor for Industrial Relations. However, in order to gain a better understanding of the role, I was invited to undertake a review of the Human Resource and Industrial Relations functions at the University. This proved to be an interesting experience as it revealed the complexity and unwieldy nature of the office in charge of these matters, which was in need of reorganisation. After consideration, I decided not to proceed with an application for the position as my long-term interest was in continuing my academic career rather than moving into University administration.

Peter Wolnizer was appointed Dean of the Faculty of Economics at the end of the 1990s marking a significant change from the previous era under Stephen Salsbury. Wolnizer had gained a PhD in Accounting at the University of Sydney and departed for the University of Tasmania in 1987 to become Professor of

Accounting. Later, he became Dean of a combined School of Business and Law at Deakin University in Victoria and raised the profile and reputation of Deakin in both fields. Peter Wolnizer proceeded carefully in his first year as Dean at Sydney, with extensive discussions about future directions involving the Heads of existing Departments. As a result of these deliberations, two Schools were created: the School of Business with a strong emphasis on Accounting and Finance, and the School of Economics and Politics, within a renamed Faculty of Economics and Business. Departments were recast as Disciplines.

Peter Wolnizer offered me two roles in the new Faculty: initially as Head of the new Business School and later as Associate Dean of Research across the two schools. I chose the latter and greatly enjoyed the next six years serving as Associate Dean with occasional stints as Acting Dean. Both Peter Wolnizer and I retired after a tumultuous decade of growth within the Faculty. During this period, there was major expansion in the number of fee-paying international students, mainly from China. The number of students undertaking both undergraduate and Masters' degrees increased substantially as did the number of academic staff, including those in Work and Organisational Studies. I accompanied the Dean on visits to China and South Korea to establish formal links with leading universities both to facilitate research as well as attracting students to our postgraduate programmes.

The increase in fee-paying students enabled more resources to be made available for academic staff to undertake research and to attend international conferences. Our success rate in attaining competitive research grants increased substantially, and the number of PhD students grew steadily. For several years, our Faculty was ranked second among Australian universities in attaining the top category of competitive grants from the Australian Research Council (ARC). With colleagues in Work and Organisational Studies, as well as from several other universities, I obtained a number of Discovery Grants from the ARC to undertake international and comparative research in the airline, automotive manufacturing and banking industries.

The Hyundai Motor Company's global strategy

My interest in South Korea grew during the 1990s when I visited several times at the invitation of the Korean Labour Institute (KLI) and as part of the MIT project on industrial relations in Asia. I was fortunate to have an excellent graduate student from Korea, Seoghun Woo, who began as a Master's student and later undertook research on industrial relations in the Korean auto industry for a PhD. With the assistance of Youngbum Park at the KLI, Woo gained access to Kia Motor Company and undertook a detailed case study of how it adapted lean production systems to Korean conditions and negotiated the required changes with the trade unions (Lansbury and Woo, 2001; Lansbury et al., 2006). Seung-Ho Kwon, a friend and former classmate of Woo, was undertaking a similar doctoral research project at Hyundai. These projects were well-timed as the Korean auto companies were just emerging as important international competitors, albeit at

130 Broader role in academic research

the lower-priced end of the market. After gaining a PhD, Woo returned to South Korea and became a successful consultant in the human resources field, while Kwon joined the Korea-Australia Research Centre (KAREC) and began to undertake further studies of the internationalisation of Korean companies

In the late 1990s, I successfully applied for an ARC Discovery Research grant with Seung-Ho Kwon and Chung-Sok Suh, from UNSW to undertake a three-year study of Hyundai Motor Company (HMC)'s emerging global strategy. This was an opportunity to observe and analyse how Hyundai expanded from being a domestic manufacturer in South Korea to becoming a global company with plants around the world, with particular reference to how they managed human resources and industrial relations policies and practices (Lansbury et al., 2006).

The HMC is one of Korea's most globally successful family owned conglomerates known as chaebols (Kwon and O'Donnell, 2001). It began as a complete knock down (CKD) assembler in 1968, under an agreement with the Ford Motor Company. In 1976, it produced its first originally designed model, the *Pony*, using a low-cost strategy. Less than ten years later, in 1985, HMC opened its first overseas plant in Canada in order to assemble the mid-sized, front wheel drive *Sonata* model. However, HMC closed the plant in 1993 after prolonged operational and industrial relations problems.

In 1996, HMC established a 100 per cent owned subsidiary in Chennai, India, and constructed a plant designed to build 120,000 passenger cars per year. Our ARC funded project followed the progress of this plant from 1996 to 2001 in order to examine the inter-relationship between the production systems, human resources and employment relationships. Hyundai Motors India (HMI) aimed to expand production beyond the Indian domestic and export to the region. Our project involved visits to the plant in Chennai as well as to HMC's head office in Seoul, South Korea, where we conducted extensive interviews with a wide range of managers and workers as well as union officials.

During its first five years of operation, HMI was very successful at both producing and selling its cars in India. It appeared to have learned from its negative experience in Canada by working closely with Indian authorities and appointing Indians to some senior roles, such as the head of Human Resources and Employment Relations. However, HMI also employed a large number of Korean managers and technicians to work alongside their Indian counterparts. HMI collaborated with Indian parts suppliers in order to raise the quality of their products to the level required, although it continued to source vital components from Korea due to problems finding parts of sufficiently high quality in India. However, our research identified human resources and employment relations as potential weaknesses for HMI going forward (Lansbury et al., 2007).

HMI's entry strategy was to use a semi-mechanised, labour-intensive production system with a low-cost, non-unionised workforce. This partly replicated the approach used by HMC during its early stage of development in Korea. However, during its initial days of operation in Korea, there was a military dictatorship, the official unions were under the control of the government and high import tariffs on foreign vehicles meant that the Korean car industry was protected from international competition. This is not the case in India where there is a strong and independent trade union movement and HMI had to compete with other international auto companies which had already established operations in India using more highly automated and mechanised assembly systems. Senior management at HMI claimed that the company would not have to deal with unions as the industrial relations authority in Chennai would not permit unions to organise workers in the plant. However, this changed in the years immediately following our study when unions succeeded in enrolling members at HMI and the company was forced to recognise collective bargaining rights for the workers, albeit with an enterprise-based union which only covered workers in the Chennai plant.

We concluded from our study that Hyundai had succeeded thus far in India where, unlike its strategy in Canada, it was pursuing a mixture of company-specific practices and adaptations to local conditions and local institutional pressures and constraints. HMI did not simply replicate the 'lean production' techniques of Toyota, which relied on tightly coupled supply chains, but developed a 'hybrid' approach using both local parts suppliers supplemented by components from Korea. HMI's shopfloor practices were more hierarchical and less team-oriented than Toyota and relied more on close supervision by Korean managers of the Indian workforce. Furthermore, while HMI appointed an Indian to head Human Resources and Industrial Relations in Chennai, the Korean line managers exercised tight control over the workforce in line with their production strategies. It may have been due the fact that Hyundai head office in Korea was determined to succeed in India, after their failure in Canada, but it was apparent that the Chennai plant was closely monitored and controlled from Korea. It was clear from our interviews with the Korean managers in the Chennai operations that they were committed to spending a number of years in India in a 'hardship post' in order to secure promotion within Hyundai once they returned to Korea.

Reviewing our book in 2009, several years after our research was completed, Dong-One Kim from Korea University noted that we were correct in our prediction that the HMI plant in Chennai would become unionised in the longer term. In 2007, after a series of strikes, HMI were forced to recognise and negotiate a collective agreement with a union representing the workforce in the Chennai plant. The non-union Works Committee, established as an alternative to a union by HMI, was ultimately transformed into a local union. Kim also noted that the HMI case illustrated that not all auto manufacturing companies were converging towards the Toyota lean production system and that many hybrid forms existed which blended different forms of auto production (Kim, 2009: 191).

The book attracted attention several years after its original publication and was reprinted as a paperback edition by Routledge in 2007. Then in 2016, the book was translated into Portugese and published in Brazil as Hyundai's expansion of production in Brazil attracted attention in that country (Lansbury et al. 2016)

Another of my students, Mimi Zou, undertook a study of the HMC in Beijing while she was an exchange student undertaking Masters' level courses at

Tsinghua University in Beijing. While undertaking her research, the workers in the Beijing plant went on strike for better wages and conditions. This was much to the consternation of Hyundai management who believed that the Chinese government would prevent any industrial disruption by workers at the plant. The dispute was resolved after negotiations involving the Beijing municipal authorities, and the company resulted in most of the workers' demands being met. This case demonstrated that, under certain circumstances, workers in foreign-owned companies were willing to take industrial action against the opposition of the official Chinese unions and the government (Zou and Lansbury, 2009). Mimi Zou completed a PhD in Law at Oxford University and currently holds an academic position there teaching in the field of Chinese labour law.

Globalisation and employment relations in the auto and banking (GERAB) industries

During the early to mid-2000s, Jim Kitay, Nick Wailes and I gained two ARC Discovery Grants to study the impact of globalisation on the automotive manufacturing and retail banking industries, for which we used the acronym GERAB. In collaboration with researchers in nine countries, we compared changes in employment relations practices in these two industries. Australia and the United States were used as examples of liberal market economies (LMEs), Germany and Sweden exemplified coordinated market economies (CMEs), while Japan, South Korea, Singapore, Hong Kong and China represented Asian market economies. Our objective was to ascertain whether there was systematic variation in the impact of globalisation on employment relations across different types of market economies in these two industries. Jim Kitay coordinated the retail banking segment of the research (Kitay et al., 2007) while I focused on the auto manufacturing studies (Lansbury et al., 2008).

An important development in comparative analysis of the impact of international economic changes on industrial relations, at the time our research was conducted, was the emergence of theories of capitalist diversity (for an overview, see Deeg and Jackson, 2007). The most influential of these studies was the *Varieties of Capitalism* (VoC) approach of Hall and Soskice (2001). The VoC and similar approaches developed from the field of political economy but included references to industrial relations and have been widely adopted by comparative industrial relations scholars. Hall and Soskice (2001: 6–9) argued that in market economies, firms are faced with a series of coordination problems, both internally and externally. They distinguished between two ideal types that resolve these coordination problems by different means. LMEs rely on market-based forms of industrial relations with limited commitments by employers to workers. By contrast, CMEs base their industrial relations on collective agreements which reflect longer-term commitments by employers to their employees. The United States is seen as an exemplar of an LME while Germany is regarded as a CME.

While the VoC framework is seen as helpful for comparative analysis of industrial relations, critics have argued for a wider range of varieties to accommodate economies that do not neatly fit the duality of LME and CME

(Rhodes et al., 2007). VoC has also been criticised as too deterministic and leaving little room for agency and conflict to shape social outcomes. Nor does it account for change when an economy defined as a CME (such as Japan) gradually adopts more characteristics of an LME. The framework gives little attention to international factors and seems to infer that all economies are relatively closed.

Further criticism of the VoC framework relates to its limited applicability to developing countries that have a large informal economy and a labour market that relies more on traditional uncoded norms, conventions and behaviours. This argument is particularly relevant to the gap that exists between the formal composition of institutions and the actual practice of industrial relations in much of Asia (Ford and Gillan, 2016: 172). In his study of *Divergent Capitalisms*, Whitley (1999) argued that Asian and Western business systems differ on a broad range of variables ranging from forms of property law and capital market structures, cultural patterns and beliefs. Yeung (2000: 408), who extended Whitley's work, coined the term *Asian business systems* and showed how these can be differentiated from LMEs and CMEs because of their strong business networks, the heightened role of personal relationships and the close involvement of the state in economic activity. In our study, we used the category of *Asian business systems* as separate from CMEs and LMEs. However, it is difficult to place all Asian countries, such as China and South Korea, in the same category, so this needs further investigation.

The auto industry studies

The focus of our global automotive research was on major firms which assemble automobiles. We selected two auto manufacturers in each country for in-depth study. The global auto assembly industry is dominated by a small number of very large companies with many parts suppliers of varying sizes. We used a common research protocol based on the framework which was adopted by the MIT–IMVP auto project (Kochan et al., 2007). Where possible, the researchers visited the headquarters as well as assembly plants to interview managers as well as union officials and assembly line workers.

The findings of our project suggested that there were systematic differences in the impact of globalisation on industrial relations in liberal, coordinated and, to a lesser extent, Asian market economies. In both LMEs and CMEs, pressures associated with globalisation reinforced rather than eroded some of the distinct features of industrial relations under these regimes. In the United States, for example, increased global competition appeared to have reinforced the tendency for union avoidance, particularly by foreign-owned transplants in the southern 'sunbelt' states. By contrast, in Germany and Sweden, industry-wide collective bargaining had been maintained although these were signs of change towards some forms of decentralised bargaining. In Germany, increasing emphasis was on securing 'opening clauses' in collective agreements to give individual companies and plants more local flexibility. In Asian market economies, the response to globalisation was less clear. Industrial relations in the Japanese auto industry, for example, has changed considerably during recent decades. As Japanese economy stagnated, long-held work practices, such as life-time employment and seniority-based wages, were increasingly difficult to maintain. Similarly, as the Korean auto company, Hyundai expanded production to other countries, such as the United States and India, pressure increased on the Korean autoworkers' union to agree to employment concessions in order to retain jobs in Korea-based plants.

There also appeared to be considerable within-variety diversity in industrial relations processes and outcomes in European and North American-based auto companies. Within Germany, for example, although the major manufacturers all continued to maintain high levels of skill training, and works councils retained an important role in decision-making at the plant level, there were significant differences in how these policies were applied in different firms. Similarly, within the United States, while GM and Ford continued to bargain with the UAW in their long-established plants in the north, the newer plants in the south tended to be non-union like their foreign-owned counterparts. Even greater diversity was apparent between companies in the Asian market economies, from high levels of unionisation in Korean companies in their domestic plants compared with their operations elsewhere, such as the United States and India.

The retail banking industry studies

The retail banking industry studies adopted a similar research protocol to the auto manufacturing industry studies which, in turn, was derived from the MIT–IMVP project (Kochan et al., 2007). Where possible, the researchers visited head offices as well as branches of each bank in each country. Similar countries representing liberal and CMEs in the auto project were used in the banking studies. However, Sweden was omitted while two additional countries were included from Asian market economies: Hong Kong and Singapore.

In LMEs, such as Australia and United States, competitive pressures produced significant erosion of labour conditions and employment security. Unions had a declining role in enterprise governance. In a CME like Germany, however, the retail banking system remained relatively coordinated, and institutions of co-determination and skill formation continued to play an important role. In the Asian market economies, there were considerable changes in employment relations. However, in all the Asian countries in our study, the state continued to play an important role when banking systems were firmly under the control of national governments. Hence, the impact of globalisation on retail banking was largely indirect. These findings indicated that, in retail banking, the nation state continued to play an important role in determining the relationship between globalisation and employment relations.

Implications of GERAB research findings

The results of our research suggested the need to adopt a more 'variegated' view of industrial relations, in both the automotive manufacturing and retail banking industries, which are under pressure from globalisation. While it is evident that institutions at the national level continue to provide important regulatory structures, within which employers and unions interact, there are differences in relation to the auto and retail banking industries.

In retail banking, international sources of competition and foreign capital (either in the form of foreign direct investment or equity) play a significant role in some countries but national governments still exercise strong controls over banks operating in their domestic market. In the auto industry, the influence of multinational auto companies has increased as companies have expanded their operations around the world. As new markets develop in emerging economies like China, where the government exercises significant control over how companies operate, and where unions currently act as agencies of the state, foreign auto companies will continue to be constrained in how they can operate and manage their workforce.

As Asia becomes increasingly significant as an auto producing region, it will be important to analyse what kinds of systems of labour regulation emerge and whether workers gain a stronger collective voice in the terms and conditions of their employment. Our research suggested that the future of the global auto industry in Asia and elsewhere will depend not only on the production systems they develop through technological change but also on whether employers, unions and governments can forge a social contract with the people whose interests they serve.

Flying high and low? Strategic choice in the airline industry

In the early 2000s, Tom Kochan initiated a study of industrial relations and firm performance in the international airline industry and invited scholars from various countries to join in the project, including Greg Bamber and myself from Australia. The book which resulted from the multi-country study contrasted the 'high' and 'low'-road approaches taken by various airlines, with Southwest Airlines exemplifying the 'high road' and Ryanair taking the 'low road' (Bamber et al., 2009). The 'high road' strategy was characterised by high levels of cooperation and commitment between employers, workers and their unions. By investing in their workforce, organisations were more likely to achieve increased productivity and the creation of higher quality products and services, while increased profits would enable firms to pay their employees higher wages. Conversely, a 'low road' strategy focused on minimising wage costs, avoiding or opposing unions, investing less in skills development and creating a relationship with the workforce. This was based on control rather than mutual commitment (Kochan, 2006: 16).

The global airline research project adopted the strategic negotiations framework of Walton et al. (1994) which argued that employers make deliberate choices about how they will interact with their employees and the unions that represent them. Employers can either promote employment relationships that simply encourage *compliance* with the terms of the employment contract or collective

136 *Broader role in academic research*

agreement or seek to enhance the level of *mutual commitment* and generate interdependence between management and labour. Employers have a range of choices in relation to how they deal with unions. They can seek to *avoid* dealing with unions, they can *accommodate* unions by engaging in collective bargaining to achieve an equitable outcome or they can *cooperate* with unions by pursuing mutual goals and seeking an integrative outcome. As shown in Figure 8.1, the employment relations strategies of various airlines can be viewed dichotomously: relationships with unions and with employees. As noted below, our research on two Australian airlines, Qantas and Jetstar, revealed that the employment relations strategies adopted by management of these airlines changed during the course of our study (see Sarina and Lansbury, 2013).

As part of the global research project, Troy Sarina and I examined the strategic choices made by Qantas, a full-cost legacy airline, and its low-cost carrier (LCC), Jetstar, in regard to industrial relations during the period 2000–2011. Although our initial study was part of the global project, we continued to monitor the two airlines during the following decade in order to gain a more dynamic view of how industrial relations strategies can change in response to circumstances. In October 2011, the Australian aviation industry gained international attention when Qantas suspended all flights and 'grounded' its fleet in response to a breakdown in negotiations with some of its key unions over the terms of their enterprise agreements. Although the industrial dispute was resolved by arbitration and Qantas resumed its services, it marked a shift in relations between Qantas management and its unions from cooperation to conflict. It also had implications for the way in which Qantas had differentiated its approach to industrial relations from Jetstar.

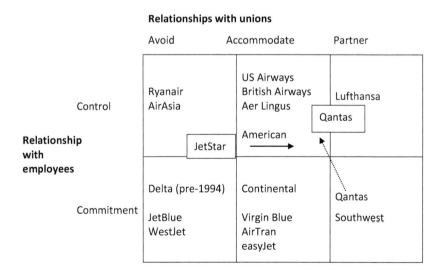

Figure 8.1 Employment-relations strategies of selected airlines.

Qantas is Australia's main domestic and international carrier. It operated as a government-owned enterprise from 1947 to 1995 when it became a publicly listed company following a decision by the federal government to deregulate Australia's airline industry. Qantas had long positioned itself as an airline providing a high-quality service and displayed characteristics of a 'high-road' industrial relations strategy by offering market-leading wages and conditions to its employees. However, in 2000, Qantas faced the prospect of significant competition from a newly established carrier, Virgin Blue. Its business model was delivering 30 per cent lower operating and labour costs than Qantas. To respond to this challenge, Qantas created Jetstar in 2004, a wholly owned 'low fares' or 'low-cost carrier' (LCC) based on a similar business model to Virgin Blue.

By offering a 'no frills' service, Jetstar displayed traits of a 'low-road' strategy by offering relatively low wages coupled with high levels of managerial control. Jetstar also sought to take advantage of changes to Australian industrial relations laws which encouraged the use a combination of collective, non-union and individual-based agreements to regulate its workforce. Alan Joyce, the founding CEO of Jetstar, argued that the 'mixed' approach provided the airline with the flexible operation base required to operate an LCC which could compete on a 'level playing ground' with Virgin Blue. A 'flying committee' overseeing the operation of Qantas and Jetstar developed an aggressive market segmentation strategy or 'pincer' movement to contain the competitive threat from Virgin Blue.

By the mid-2000s, Qantas faced further competition from low-cost carriers. Tiger Airways, a subsidiary of Singapore Airlines, commenced flying to a number of Australian airports with even lower fares than Virgin Blue. Air Asia X, another regional low-cost carrier, began to compete with Qantas on a number of Asian routes, including to Malaysia and Japan. Under the brand name V Australia, Virgin Blue challenged Qantas's predominance of the lucrative trans-Pacific route with daily flights. Qantas also faced fluctuating fuel costs and the global recession of 2008–2009. It made 2000 employees redundant while offering voluntary redundancy to over 7000 cabin crew. In November 2008, the CEO of Jetstar, Alan Joyce, was appointed as head of Qantas after the retirement of Geoff Dixon. It was widely expected that Joyce would introduce 'Jetstar reforms' into Qantas. Initially, however, Joyce indicated that the 'two-branded strategy and segmentation' business model would be maintained for the 'sake of the company's future'.

Under Joyce as CEO, the industrial relations strategies of Qantas and Jetstar moved closer together in a 'hybrid' model that drew on both the high and low roads. On the one hand, Qantas adopted human resource practices such as the provision of training and 'social' benefits to foster greater commitment by employees to organisational goals. However, Qantas also created conflict with its unions by outsourcing certain functions to reduce costs by employing cheaper labour and took a 'hard line' in negotiations to 'bring wage and conditions back to market'. Similarly, Jetstar adopted a 'mixed' approach by relaxing its opposition to unions and agreeing to negotiate a collective agreement with the airline pilots' union. Hence, after five years of operation, the policies and practices of the two airlines were converging, particularly in regard to their industrial relations strategies. This has continued to be the case, with Jetstar expanding its operations, often at the expense of Qantas.

The International Labour and Employment Relations Association (ILERA)

My involvement in industrial relations began when I attended my first World Congress of the then International Industrial Relations Association (IIRA) held at the ILO in Geneva in 1970. I was just commencing as a doctoral student at the London School of Economics and had little knowledge of industrial relations. My experience of attending the IIRA congress in 1970 not only exposed me to the field of industrial relations but also to academics, employers and union officials who were in attendance. This was only the second World Congress of the IIRA, which had been founded four years previously by academics representing industrial relations associations in the United States, United Kingdom and Japan. Key people involved in the establishment of the IIRA were Robert Cox from the ILO, John Dunlop from Harvard and Ben Roberts from the LSE, who was the foundation President.

One of the aims of the founders of the IIRA was to assist in establishing the legitimacy of industrial relations as an interdisciplinary field of knowledge and practice. As Roberts noted in his Presidential address to the congress in 1970, while industrial relations had been long established in some major universities, particularly in the United States, 'in many others, it has only recently been accepted as a branch of learning in its own right' (Kaufman, 2004: 323). The ILO provided a modest secretariat for the IIRA, and the honorary secretary of the IIRA was usually a senior official from the ILO. During the past 50 years, the IIRA has grown from a membership comprising 10 national industrial relations associations and 160 individual members to more than 50 national associations and over 1,000 individual members. In 2007, the Association changed its name to the International Labour and Employment Relations Association (ILERA) on the grounds that the new name signalled a broader range of interests among its members to include areas such as human resource management and organisational behaviour. However, industrial relations remains the core area of interest and activity for ILERA.

In 2003, I became the President-elect of ILERA. This meant that Australia would be responsible for hosting the World Congress of ILERA in Sydney in 2009. I was fortunate that John Niland, former Vice-Chancellor of UNSW, had held the position of ILERA President in 1992 and organised the first World Congress of ILERA which was held in Australia. My nomination as President was made by the Industrial Relations Society of Australia (which later changed its name to ALERA) at the initiative of the Honorary Secretary, Joe Catanzariti, who committed the Society to host the World Congress. At that time, Joe was a senior partner in a prominent law firm and put considerable time and effort into ensuring that the congress was a success. Joe convened an organising committee with representatives from employers, unions and academics which met regularly for several years planning for the congress. Joe also raised funds from the state Industrial Relations Societies as well as other sources. My colleague at the University of Sydney, Nick Wailes, undertook the formidable task of organising the programme for the congress.

The ILERA World Congress in 2009 coincided with the global recession, and it was uncertain whether there would be sufficient attendees to enable the congress to proceed. However, offers of over 500 papers were received and more than 1,000 people attended, of whom half were from outside Australia. The congress opened with a major forum on the implications of the global recession for industrial relations, with leading experts from the Americas, Europe, Asia and Africa. This attracted considerable media attention and was well attended. The congress was opened by Julia Gillard, the Minister for Industrial Relations who would later become the Prime Minister of Australia. The congress offered the opportunity for participants to review extensive industrial relations reforms which had just been introduced in Australia by the Labor government under the Fair Work Act. This Act sought to restore the role of unions in collective bargaining and to strengthen the powers of the Federal industrial relations tribunal. Many other countries represented at the congress were also going through major changes in their industrial relations system and demonstrated the importance of ILERA providing a forum where ideas could be shared.

Since the Sydney World Congress, ILERA has expanded its activities around the world. China was admitted as a national member in 2012 and hosted the Asian regional congress in Beijing in 2018. The World Congress in 2015 was held in Capetown, South Africa and in Seoul, South Korea in 2018. Latin America held its first World Congress in Lima, Peru, in 2006. However, there remain many challenges to expanding membership in regions such as Asia where major growth in population and economic development is occurring. Although unions exist in most Asian countries, the right to join unions and engage in collective bargaining is limited, and industrial relations, as an academic field, has only a minor presence in universities. The situation is even worse in many African and Latin American countries. ILERA is seeking to play a greater role in developing regions of the world by providing support for research and conference attendance by scholars in these countries, but the majority of ILERA members and activities remain in Europe, North America and Australia. A symposium on ILERA, with reflections by former presidents of the association, was held at the World Congress in South Korea in 2018 and subsequently published as a book (Kim, 2020).

9 Research and travels in retirement (2010–2020)

After my retirement from the University of Sydney in 2009, I did not expect to maintain an active role in research and teaching. However, during the past ten years I have continued to do both, albeit at a slower pace. When David McAllister undertook a gradual departure from his role as artistic director of the Australian Ballet, he described the process as 'a lovely descent through the hills to the sea-levels of retirement'. I think this is an apt description of my experience of retiring from academia.

I have remained involved in research projects in two of the most interesting areas of the world, Asia and the Nordic region, and have continued to be engaged in various aspects of Australian industrial relations. My recent research in Asia was undertaken in collaboration with two long-term colleagues Byoung-Hoon Lee in South Korea and Ng Sek-hong in Hong Kong. In the Nordic countries, I was invited by Jan Johansson and Lena Abrahamsson at Lulea Technical University (LTU) to participate in an EU-funded project on sustainable mining, which involved research in the northern areas of Sweden and Finland as well as Poland. I was also a member of an international team reviewing research on work organisation in Swedish universities for Forte, the Swedish Research Council on Health, Working Life and Welfare. These projects enabled me to engage in stimulating research activities during the period 2010–2020.

Perspectives on industrial relations in Asia

As an undergraduate student at the University of Melbourne, I met students from a variety of Asian countries, became active in the International Club and the World University Service and was appointed director of international student welfare for the National Union of Australian University Students. My first overseas travel, as a 20-year old, was to India and Southeast Asia, and I thought that my future career might involve living and working in Asia. As it transpired, I became more engaged in Europe and the Nordic countries during my postgraduate studies. However, in later years I was drawn back to Asia, particularly through research on the Korean auto industry, and brief periods as a visiting academic at Nanyang Technological University in Singapore and the University of Science Malaysia, as an Adjunct Professor at the Open University of Hong Kong as well as visits to China and Vietnam. Through the auspices of the ILO, I also became engaged in projects involving industrial relations in the Asian region. As President of ILERA, I helped negotiate the entry of China as a member of the association. I also suspect that the latent influence of my doctoral supervisor at LSE, Keith Thurley, a specialist in Japanese workplace issues, stimulated my ongoing interest in the region.

In the early 1990s, I collaborated with Anil Verma and Tom Kochan on a research project which presaged the book *Employment Relations in the Growing Asian Economies* (Verma et al., 1995). This was part of the MIT Global Transformation project and focused on emerging economies in Asia which were undergoing industrialisation. The countries in the project included India, China, Taiwan, Hong Kong, Singapore, Malaysia, South Korea and the Philippines. The objective of the project was to improve understanding of the role of the industrial relations and human resource policies at both the sectoral and national levels in facilitating economic and social development in Asia.

The project revealed that governments in Asia played a varied but significant role in determining their industrial relations and human resource systems. Some governments responded to growing demands from workers for higher wages and greater voice by suppressing the rights of workers and organised labour. This resulted in wages being kept low and prevented unions from having a stronger role. Other governments, however, responded in more measured ways to accommodate the concerns expressed by the workforce and their representatives.

The Asian project with Verma and Kochan concluded that the successful adaptation to change required alignment of both public policies and business strategies at the firm and national levels. Adaptation to change at the firm level required employers to foster greater employee involvement, invest in training and introduce more flexible systems of work. At the national level, greater investment was needed by governments in education and research and development as well as incentives for business to upgrade their operations. A combination of actions by both governments and business, working together, was necessary for workers to become more committed, acquire greater skills and achieve higher productivity.

In 2015, 20 years after the MIT project, I was approached by Ng Sek-hong in Hong Kong with a proposal that we undertake research on trade unions and labour movements in Asia and publish the results in a book in honour of the late Keith Thurley, who had supervised both our doctoral studies. Keith Thurley's life-long interest in Asia began in the early 1950s when he was assigned to Japan as a national serviceman. Based on research which he undertook in the Asian region, Thurley argued that there were distinctive features of unions and labour movements in Asia which were different from the West and could be characterised as 'Asian unionism'. Thurley claimed that unions in many Asian countries utilised 'patriotic sentiments' to collaborate with the state and capital for advancing the national economy rather than being oriented towards class consciousness (Thurley, 1988).

Ng Sek-hong proposed that we invite scholars with expertise in various Asian countries to explore the changing nature of unions and labour movements in Asia-Pacific. I had previously co-edited a symposium with Byoung-Hoon Lee, from Chung-Ahn University in South Korea, on 'refining varieties of labour movements' in the Asia-Pacific, published by the *Journal of Industrial Relations* (Lee and Lansbury, 2012). I suggested to Sek-hong that we invite Byoung-Hoon to join us in this venture. Twelve Asian countries were selected: China, Taiwan, Japan and South Korea from East Asia; Indonesia, Singapore, Malaysia, Thailand, Vietnam and the Philippines from Southeast Asia; and India from South Asia. Two of the researchers who participated in the MIT Asia project 20 years previously from Singapore and the Philippines were included. Australia was incorporated into the project on the grounds that it represented a Western model in the Pacific.

We decided to adopt the 'varieties of unions' framework developed by Frege and Kelly (2004) in their study of unions in advanced industrial economies, with particular reference to the challenges faced by unions in each country and the strategies which they had adopted to secure their future. We extended the study beyond the traditional trade unions to inquire into other organisations which were part of the labour movement or labour-oriented NGOs. Byoung-Hoon Lee kindly hosted a workshop, attended by most of the research team, at Chung-Ahn University. We also presented our preliminary findings at the World Congress of ILERA held in Seoul.

Our research concluded that Thurley's conception of 'Asian unionism' was an intriguing attempt to capture the distinct orientations of Asian unions, which can be contrasted with their Western counterparts. However, there was a great variety of unions and labour movements in the Asia-Pacific. These included state-dominated, political, business, social partnership, militant and NGO-style advocacy unionism. Three factors which constrained unionism and labour movements in the Asia-Pacific were the state, market forces and religious traditions. The state continued to be the key actor in the Asia-Pacific as it shaped the regulatory setting of employment relations and labour associations. The growing dominance of market forces was observed in many countries in the region. This was prompted not only by globalisation but also by government policies on deregulation. Religion was observed to have a persistent effect of encouraging dependence on paternalistic company management and the state, inhibiting the growth of independent union movements and undermining workers' demands for labour rights. Other important factors that contributed to the weakness of unions in the Asia-Pacific were the large share of the workforce who work in the informal sector, the fragmented nature of work in the formal sector and the spread of non-regular employment.

Yet, even in the face of historical union weakness, there were some successful attempts at union revitalisation and union growth in some countries such as India and Vietnam. Unions in a number of countries also drew strength from NGOs and other civil society organisations. Strengthening bonds between formal unions and informal worker associations may be the result of resistance by governments and employers to traditional unions and the strong desire of workers to forge a collective voice through non-traditional means. Our study concluded that there is a need to further develop theoretical frameworks in order to identify and explain the commonalities of non-Western worker movements as well as classifying varieties of Asian labour movements in a taxonomic form. As noted by Cooper and Ellem in relation to unions in Australia, crises can create the need for a new strategy leading to survival and renewal (Cooper and Ellem, 2020).

Mining in the Swedish Arctic and the Australian desert

In 2005, my long-standing interest in the Nordic region was rekindled by an invitation from Jan Johansson and Lena Abrahamsson, from LTU in the far north of Sweden, to participate in a conference in the mining town of Kiruna with the intriguing title of 'From Grounded Skills to Sky Qualifications'. The participants in the conference presented papers on new approaches to skills development in a variety of industries around the world. Our Swedish colleagues from Lulea were interested in how mining in the Arctic region of Sweden was becoming increasingly automated and required workers with different skills than was previously the case. The 'sky qualifications' referred partly to the European Space Program's installation near Kiruna which stimulated new jobs in the aerospace industry and brought new skills to the region (Abrahamsson and Johansson, 2006).

The LKAB iron ore mine in Kiruna is one of the largest, deepest and most automated in Europe. As noted earlier, I first visited the mine as a student in 1968 while it was still an open cut or open cast operation and before it became a very deep mine. In the early 1990s, when I was undertaking a project for the Australian government on how to stimulate new economic development in the declining mining town of Broken Hill, I used the example of Kiruna to demonstrate how the Swedish government stimulated new economic activity in the Norrbotten region. This was to ensure that there would be other jobs available when there was a recession in mining. By contrast, Broken Hill had failed to diversify and was facing economic difficulties as mining declined (Lansbury and Breakspear, 1995).

When I revisited the LKAB mine in Kiruna, it was in the process of adopting 'autonomous' systems to undertake mining tasks. It was estimated that fewer workers would be needed in the future but those who remained would need to acquire new technical skills to operate and maintain the automated equipment. The nature of mining work was being transformed. Arduous physical labour underground was being replaced by remote-controlled machines. Hence, the 'grounded skills' of the traditional underground miners were being replaced by IT workers with 'sky qualifications'.

In 2014, Jan Johansson nominated me to be a member of an advisory board for a major research project, entitled *The Intelligent Mine of the Future*, which was funded by the European Union (EU). The project sought to assist member states, involved in deep mining, to develop new technologies and make the transition to autonomous mining. The long-term objective was to enable the mining industry to minimise environmental damage and reduce accidents by eliminating the need for people to undertake extremely dangerous work in the mines. The project brought together representatives of mining companies, firms which supply equipment and technology to the mines, and academic researchers. My role on the board was to provide advice in relation to the effects of technological change on work organisation, skills, health and safety and other human resource aspects of the project. During the next four years, from 2014 to 2018, we met at a different mine each year where inspections were conducted and discussions held on progress towards new automated technologies. This enabled me to observe mines in Sweden, Finland and Poland where research projects were being conducted.

The EU project gave me an appreciation of how the metalliferous mining in Europe was entering a new technological age involving remotely operated and autonomous mining equipment. This was profoundly changing how minerals are mined and processed. I was surprised that automation had come much later to mining than other industries such as auto manufacturing. Commentators noted that until recently progress towards automation in mining had been piecemeal and focused mainly on using technology to improve traditional 'manned-systems'. However, robotics enabled mining to be undertaken in a completely new way which involved not only the use of new technologies but also different approaches to managing the workforce (Dunnant-Whyte, 2010). According to a report by McKinsey Global, 'the mining industry is at an inflection point, in which digital technologies have the potential to unlock new ways of managing, but only if they change the way people work' (McKinsey and Company, 2015). Autonomous mines will require fewer workers but those who remain will need to be multi-skilled. According to Bassan et al. (2011), 'technology-assisted workers will perform the jobs of two or three traditional roles, with only a skeleton workforce remaining on site'.

In Australia, the mining industry has taken an optimistic view regarding the effects of automation on employment in mining. The Australian Institute of Mining and Metallurgy has promoted the adoption of automation and other forms of technology as 'unlocking' productivity and efficiency as well as enhancing health and safety by eliminating high risk roles. The Institute claims that automation will not lead to a loss of jobs but concedes that mining will need to 'employ different types of people with different skills' and that 'an entirely new cohort of professionals across a range of disciplines (will be needed) in the resources sector over the next decade'. However, the mining union believes that automation will cost jobs and impact negatively on mining communities (see Darren Gray in the *Sydney Morning Herald*, 27 April 2019).

A report in the *New York Times* claimed that 'Sweden presents the possibility that, in the age of automation, innovation may be best advanced by maintaining ample cushions against failure'. The article quotes the case of a former miner sitting at a computer screen driving a loader, which is deep in the mine, from a computer in the control centre on the surface. It also claims that in Sweden, unions generally embrace automation as it gives a competitive edge that makes jobs more secure. Furthermore, should someone lose their job, there are generous unemployment benefits and extensive job retraining programmes (Peter Goldman in the *New York Times*, 27 December 2017).

While European mines are on the threshold of autonomous mining, major companies in Australia such as Rio Tinto and BHP claim to be well advanced in this field. Rio Tinto, for example, currently has one of the world's most automated mining systems in the world. Operators in Perth control driverless trucks in the Pilbara many thousands of kilometres away. It is forecast that Rio Tinto will ultimately be able to operate mines remotely from Perth in other parts of the world (Gollschewski, 2015). However, most automated mining operations in Australia occur in open-cut iron ore mines, unlike the deep underground mines in Sweden and other parts of the world.

Comparing Australian and Swedish approaches to industrial relations in mining

The Australian and Swedish mines in our comparative study were all located in remote areas: the Swedish Arctic region and the Australian desert. However, they took different transition paths to autonomous mining (see Cooney and Lansbury, 2018). In some mines in Queensland, control activities were being removed from mine sites and located in a control centre in Brisbane, almost 1,000 kilometres away. The strategy of the mining companies in the Australian example, which we studied, was to gradually reduce the workforce at the mine and to hire mostly new staff with IT skills to operate the control centre in the capital city. Most of the regular mine workers were employed on a 'fly-in-fly out' or 'drive-in-drive out' basis and lived in regional or capital cities remote from the site. Approximately 50 per cent were contractors and supplied to the mining company by a labour hire firm. Although some employees at the mine site were offered positions in the control centre in the capital city, most decided to look for mining jobs with other companies. Although many of the workers at the mines belonged to a union, there was little consultation between the company and the unions in regard to the transition arrangements.

In the Swedish mines, the transition strategy was completely different. Most of the mine workers lived nearby, and almost all were employed directly by the mine. The Swedish mining company experimented with various configurations of autonomous technology and decided to place the control activities on-site and to retrain existing mine workers in IT skills as much as possible. The mines included both surface and underground operations, and mine workers were provided with training to learn to operate multiple types of equipment. Most of the workforce was unionised, and the unions were involved in planning and executing the transition to more autonomous mining operations. However, the Swedish mining companies expressed concerns about deficits in the education and technical skills of the workforce and were providing training to enable the current mine workers to adapt to the new technologies.

About one year after we completed our study, one of the Australian mining companies we had studied announced that it was slowing down the transition to autonomous mining and that only three of its five active open-cut mines would be fully automated in the next three years. The company also announced that rather than centralising all of its control activities in the capital city, it was experimenting with a 'digital hub-and-spoke operating model that would see control centres set up around (the region of the mines)'. This potential change of strategy on the part of the mining company in Australia acknowledged that a successful transition pathway to autonomous mining requires attention to the social context in which technological change occurs.

Our comparative study of transitions to autonomous mining in Australia and Sweden highlighted the continued relevance of a socio-technical systems approach to such phenomena. Socio-technical systems theory, developed by researchers at the Tavistock Institute in the United Kingdom, was initially applied to the transition from manual work to mechanisation in the British coal mines in the immediate post-war era (Trist and Bamforth, 1951). The Tavistock researchers were interested in the psycho-social aspects of industrial work and showed how changes in technology interacted with social systems. Their approach was influential in the Nordic countries during the 1970s when democratic approaches to work design and the management of workers were being introduced in a range of industries (Emery and Thorsrud, 1976). More recent research has nested socio-technical systems theory within national institutions and global markets. This has connected individual workplaces within the context of broader system pressures (Geels, 2005). Hence, in our comparison of Australian and Swedish mines, we emphasised the importance of co-evolution of both technological and social systems as companies sought to make the transition to autonomous mining (Cooney and Lansbury, 2018).

In parallel with our fieldwork studies of the transition to autonomous mining in Australia and Sweden, my colleague Bradon Ellem collaborated with two academics in Lulea comparing industrial relations in the iron ore industry in the Malmfalten area northern Sweden and the Pilbara in Western Australia from the 1960s to the present day (Ellem et al., 2020). Ellem et al. concluded that industrial relations in the iron ore sectors of both countries had been transformed over the past 60 years by technological changes and the decentralisation of industrial relations. However, change in Sweden had been gradual and incremental with the Malmfalten region remaining fully unionised and unions retaining a significant role in mining company activities. By contrast, in the Pilbara, multinational mining companies had succeeded in de-unionising their workforce and unions had lost their influence in the region. Although commuting to the mines from other towns had increased in Malmfalten, this was of minor significance compared with the 100 per cent 'fly-in-fly-out' workforce in the Pilbara.

While some of the mining towns in Malmfalten were losing population, efforts were made to make them more attractive and create new sources of employment in order to maintain the towns. By contrast, no new towns were created in the Pilbara during the past 40 years, and there was little support to maintain existing towns by either the mining companies or the government. The mining companies in the Pilbara adopted 'lean production' methods to reduce the workforce. By contrast, in Malmfalten, the mining companies used 'process optimisation' to improve their operations without major job losses. Finally, 'the Swedish model' of industrial relations, involving high levels of unionisation and cooperative relations between employers and unions, remained relevant to the mining industry of the Malmfalten region.

Restoring Swedish leadership in work and industrial relations research

To many scholars and policy makers in the field of work and employment relations, Sweden has long been regarded as a leader in innovative policy-related research. This was particularly the case during almost four decades, from 1970 to the early 2000s, when the National Institute for Worklife Research (Arbetlivsinstitut) was an international 'beacon' of research in this field. Among the qualities which characterised research on work and employment relations in Sweden and other Nordic countries, during this period, were cooperation between the social partners: employers, unions and government, significant financial support from the state and an emphasis on applied research in the socio-technical systems tradition (Graversen and Lansbury, 1988; Sandberg, 2013; Scott, 2014). At the Arbetslivsinstitut there was a high level of interaction and collaboration between Swedish and visiting international researchers and valuable comparative research undertaken in worklife research (e.g. Lansbury et al., 1992).

Although Sweden continues to perform strongly in work and employment relations research, various factors have led to a decline in the importance of this field in comparison with other emerging areas of social science (Abrahamsson and Johansson, 2013; Hakansta, 2014). The closure of the National Institute for Worklife Research in 2007 by the Conservative Swedish government was controversial as it was a world-renowned research organisation with more than 450 employees and an annual budget of 300 million SEK. Although the Institute included only 20 per cent of the total number of researchers in the field of working life, and some of its research funding was subsequently reallocated to university departments and other centres working in this field, its closure was a major shock to researchers in this field and to those who had benefited from its work. There was a strong international reaction to the closure of the institute not only because the government undertook this action with little consultation with interested parties but also because it effectively reduced the total funding for working life research (Westerholm, 2007).

In 2013, I was invited to join a panel of international scholars to undertake an evaluation of Swedish research on work organisation, covering the period 2007–2013, for the Swedish Research Council for Health, Working Life and Welfare (Forte, 2015). The brief given to the panel was first to evaluate the quality and coverage of research on work organisation in Sweden in relation to both scientific worth and application. Second, to evaluate the development of the research considering past and current trends and to make recommendations on future directions, funding structures and resources, and research infrastructure, indicating their relevance for policy makers, funding agencies and researchers.

The evaluation team was provided with discussion papers, background information on research publications, results of a questionnaire survey of Swedish researchers (in which they nominated their ten best publications), a list of PhD dissertations dealing with issues related to work organisation which had been completed at Swedish universities since the 1960s, and a bibliometric analysis of research in this field as recorded in the Web of Science and interviews with researchers, employers and unions. Site visits were undertaken of a sample of organisations in the private and public sectors to investigate how they utilised the results of research on work organisation and interacted with academic researchers in this field.

The results of the evaluation revealed a high level of activity by Swedish researchers in work organisation. There were 74 active research groups across Sweden, predominantly in universities, conducting work in this field. Approximately 450 researchers were engaged in work organisation studies, including more than 100 current PhD students. Two thirds of researchers worked in groups of more than 10 members, and 22 per cent of the groups included researchers from three or more disciplines.

Productivity of Swedish researchers in this field was shown to be relatively high in terms of both numbers of publications and impact. However, although there was overall growth of research in this field during the period 2007–2013, the focus shifted from research based on traditional socio-technical systems design to more management-oriented topics such as lean production and quality management. This mirrored the experience of organisations which were visited during the review and asked what kinds of research they were utilising. The topics assigned the most importance by academic researchers surveyed by Forte were organisational change, management and leadership. Of medium priority were equality issues, work and health, and new forms of employment. The area of employment relations, which was a core concern to the traditional Swedish model, was assigned a lower priority by researchers.

In order to gain some insights into how Swedish organisations were utilising research on work organisation and interacting with academic researchers, site visits were undertaken by Olle Hammarstrom and myself to a variety of organisations including the LKAB mine in Kiruna, Scania Bus and Truck Manufacturing in Sodertalje, BT Toyota in Mjölby and Gustavsberg Vårdcentral (a Primary Health Clinic). In each case, collaboration had been established between the organisation and research institutions. However, in most cases, the connections with researchers were generally of a short-term duration. While the organisations all reported satisfaction with the research collaboration, the relationships tended to be one between client and consultant and focused on specific problems rather than longer-term research projects which would result in scientific publications. The research projects also tended to focus on 'technical' issues rather than having a broader social science approach.

Nevertheless, there were some examples of deeper and longer-term engagement such as Gustavsberg Vårdcentral, which had embarked on a major reorientation of the way in which mental disorders were detected and treated, in collaboration with researchers from the Karolinska Institute in Stockholm. Similarly, LKAB had extensive research collaboration with researchers at LTU who were undertaking joint projects on a wide variety of issues related to work organisation such as socio-technical aspects of work and organisation design, work safety, gender equality and employment relations. The LKAB-LTU research collaboration not only resulted in organisational change but also in a large number of research publications. It is difficult to ascertain the impact that research had on work organisation in Gustavsberg Vardcentral and LKAB but there appeared to be significant commitment to research collaboration with academic institutions (Lansbury, 2016).

While it was difficult to gain a complete and accurate picture of research funding for the area of work organisation, concern was expressed by academic researchers about funding issues. Public funding of work organisation research, by government and research agencies, has declined during the past decade, even though there are signs of a partial recovery of funding by Forte and universities in recent times. There is general agreement that current funding is not sufficient to support the development of new researchers as the older generation retires. This is illustrated by the continuing decline in the number of PhD theses in this field since the early 2000s.

Findings of the review of work organisation research in Sweden

The Forte Report (2015) concluded that while there was considerable research activity concerned with work organisation, Sweden had lost its former pre-eminence, and urgent action was needed to rebuild research capacity. The report recommended a strategic reorientation of research to focus on developing a 'new Swedish model' which could demonstrate how work organisation issues could play an effective and socially responsible role in a social market economy. It also called for strengthening research infrastructure and a new funding system to support basic and innovative cross-disciplinary research over a longer time span and a structured PhD programme on work organisation to build a new generation of researchers in this field.

While Swedish researchers have been concerned with labour market problems, such as rising unemployment and underemployment and the growth of non-standard and contingent work, there, less attention has been given to traditional industrial relations issues, such as collective bargaining and union-management relations, as well as fewer studies of work organisation in a broad perspective. The initial enthusiasm for the concept of 'good work', which was initiated by the Swedish union movement, has been eclipsed in recent years by the focus on management-oriented concerns to introduce 'lean management' and associated approaches to reorganising work (Johansson and Abrahamsson, 2009; Sandberg, 2013).

There are many reasons for the decline in industrial relations research in Sweden as well as across a range of countries. In most mature industrialised economies, the percentage of the workforce who are unionised has declined, particularly in the private sector, and this has resulted in a smaller proportion of the workforce covered by collective bargaining. Laws have become more restrictive in relation to collective action, such as strikes, and the number of formal industrial disputes has declined. Labour markets have been progressively deregulated and collective agreements have been replaced by more individualised forms of employment contracts. Many of the institutions which supported the role of unions in bargaining and dispute resolutions have declined or been dismantled. This has given employers and governments greater power to unilaterally set wages and conditions of the workforce while unions are declining in influence.

The Forte Report argued for a 'higher level of funding over greater time spans to support and improve the research, strengthen the infrastructure and reinforce PhD and post-doctoral research'. It warned that failure to provide a greater level of support for work organisation research risked a 'loss of intellectual and social capital and erosion of Sweden's international position and reputation'. The Report also recommended the development of a 'new funding framework by Forte, preferably in collaboration with Vinnova and AFA Insurance to produce synergistic effects and enhance greater coherence, continuity and impact' (Forte, 2015: 51).

There are lessons which can be derived from earlier examples of Swedish worklife research in which there was strong interaction between the researchers and the social partners. This was exemplified by researchers at the National Institute for Worklife Research who were major contributors to conceptualising the Nordic 'model' of work organisation (see Sandberg, 2013). There needs to be incentives and support for longer-term academic research which is more exploratory and innovative, like these earlier examples, rather than short-term projects which aim principally at quick publication of results in academic journals.

However, to obtain a significant improvement in work and employment relations research, the establishment of a new, dedicated funding body in Sweden is required. The current organisational arrangements are inadequate to deliver a strong and coherent approach to research in this area. Leading Swedish and international scholars have made submissions to the Swedish government requesting that a new institution be formed, with representatives of the unions, employers and research community to provide the vision for future research and provide long-term funding needed to renew Sweden's leadership in this field. While it may not be appropriate to return to the organisational structure of the former National Institute for Working Life, a national centre is required to support vital research in this field. Such a national centre would provide a link between researchers in Sweden and other countries which have interests and expertise in similar fields. This would help to revitalise and restore Swedish leadership in the world of work and employment relations research which has been absent in recent years.

The future of national work and employment relations systems in Australia and Denmark

In recent years, a research partnership has been forged between Work and Organisational Studies (WOS) at the University of Sydney and the Centre for Research on Work and Employment Relations (FAOS) at the University of Copenhagen, initiated by Marian Baird and Chris Wright. The Director of FAOS, Soren Kaj Andersen, was a distinguished visiting scholar at WOS. Along with my colleagues in WOS, I gained the opportunity to visit the University of Copenhagen and collaborate with researchers in FAOS, which is located in the Institute of Sociology. This had special significance for me as I was a visiting graduate student at the Institute for six months in 1970, before I began my doctoral studies at the London School of Economics.

An initial study compared the different paths taken in each country towards decentralised collective bargaining and consequent outcomes (Andersen et al., 2017). The Australian system places greater emphasis than the Danish on a legalistic approach to labour-management regulation and enforceability of employment contracts. While the bargaining level has shifted from the national or sectoral level to the enterprise level, the Fair Work Commission still plays an important role in setting minimum wages through the award system. However, there has been a distinct trend towards individual rather than collective regulation of wages and working conditions.

The Danish system retains much of its voluntaristic social partnership approach, subject to a complicated interplay between collective agreements and legislation as well as EU regulations. Although there has been a shift from centralised bargaining to a mixture of industrial and company-level collective agreements, the unions and employer associations retain a relatively high degree of wage coordination. However, the autonomy of the Danish social partners in relation to bargaining has been challenged by EU regulation, including directives and rulings by the European Court of Justice.

Our study also examined the degree to which the industrial relations changes in each country were examples of 'path dependency' insofar as they were products of historical legacies. While we concluded that there was strong influence from the past, there was a complex interaction between factors which fostered a more decentralised approach to bargaining and remnants of the former centralised system. There has also been divergence between each country in terms of the way in which decentralised bargaining occurs. We concluded that the voluntaristic, agreement-based approach in Denmark produced a stronger partnership approach between employers, employees and unions than the more regulated and legalistic Australian case.

A formal Partnership Collaboration Award was secured between the Universities of Sydney and Copenhagen in 2019 to undertake a multi-level study of *The Future of National Systems of Work and Employment Relations in Australia and Denmark*. The overall hypothesis is that both Australia and Denmark are moving towards more diversified labour markets characterised by rapid changes in skills and labour needs, reflecting the disappearance of existing jobs and the creation of new ones. This, in turn, affects incomes because emerging jobs are in both high-paid fields, such as ICT and finance, and low-paid work, such as private services. Tensions have also emerged between employers seeking increased flexibility in the organisation of working time while workers need greater predictability of working time due to family commitments. The research project is investigating how the two contrasting 'most different' employment relations systems of Australia and Denmark are responding to these trends towards diversification.

The project comprises comparative case studies of three core work processes. The first case study examines trends in pay, particularly during a period of low pay growth, as determined though collective bargaining and government regulation. Investigating the attitudes of the parties to the low pay growth is an important part of this case study. The second case analyses labour supply, particularly in terms of skill formation, labour migration and collective strategies. The third case focuses on the organisation of working hours, particularly as it relates to gender, work and family dynamics. The findings of the project will assist organisations and policy makers in both Australia and Denmark adapt to future work-related challenges. The case studies will also help to advance the field of comparative employment relations.

Is industrial relations still relevant to the world of work?

The future of work has been a popular topic of discussion and debate in recent times with numerous articles in both the popular press and academic journals as well as special reports by the ILO and various governmental and private bodies. This interest has been driven by economic and social trends such as 'gig work', 'platform businesses' and the 'sharing economy', all of which have challenged established ways of performing work. This is a global phenomenon, with consumer platforms such as Uber and Airbnb expanding quickly around the world. Workers engaged on these platforms may or may not be covered by employment laws and regulations which apply to people performing work in more traditional organisations. There are widely varied estimates of the percentage of the workforce who are engaged in platform-related work. The Global McKinsey Institute estimates that up to 20 per cent of the adult workforce in the United States and Europe are involved in some form of independent work such as the gig economy (Manyika et al., 2016). However, this is based on a very broad definition of independent work, and the US Treasury estimated that less than 1 per cent of the US workforce can be legitimately classified as being engaged in alternative work arrangements (Jackson et al., 2017). The coexistence and interaction of different forms of employment has important implications for the future of work and its regulation.

The future of industrial relations as a field of knowledge and practice has also been widely discussed, with frequent predictions of its imminent demise. This debate tends to be most prevalent in Anglo-Saxon countries such as North America, the United Kingdom and Australia, where industrial relations has been a subject studied in undergraduate and graduate degree programmes. In the United States, many programmes were initiated by state governments after the Second World War when there was a major increase in strikes and conflict, particularly in manufacturing, transportation and maritime industries. Institutes for Labour and Industrial Relations education and research were established in prestigious private universities such as Cornell, Harvard, MIT, Michigan and Chicago as well as in many state 'land grant' universities such as Wisconsin, Illinois and California (at UCLA and Berkeley). Many of these institutes have now been scaled back or closed down as union membership has declined, industrial disputes have withered away and fewer students undertake degrees in the subject. Similar experiences have occurred in the United Kingdom where the older universities, such as Oxford and Cambridge, as well as the LSE, Warwick, Leeds and Cardiff, all had thriving programmes until the past 20 years. In Australian universities, the 1980s and 1990s were a 'golden age' for industrial relations programmes but many of these have now declined. Yet there continue to be courses in industrial relations taught in universities, and research is still being carried out, albeit within other disciplines such as political science, economics, sociology and human geography.

Various reasons have been advanced for the decline of industrial relations as a popular field of study. In the United States, according to Strauss, 'mainstream industrial relations positioned itself rather narrowly, focusing primarily on the union-management relationship and its impacts. Only secondary attention was given to individual workers, individual relationships between workers and managers, and relationships between groups, except as occurred through collective bargaining'. With the decline of strikes and union coverage, 'the field's reason for existence became less clear' (Strauss, 1987). By the 1990s, according to Cappelli, 'having narrowed its focus over the years to union-management relations, and having excluded consideration of other models, industrial relations researchers suddenly had little to say that other constituent groups cared to hear' (Cappelli, 1991: 6). However, concerns about the long-term future of the field were voiced even at the inaugural meeting of the Industrial Relations Research Association in the United States, where C. Wright Mills (1948) warned of pitfalls if industrial relations became captive to the 'sophisticated conservatism' of American managers and their enthusiasm for 'human relations'. This warning was prescient as courses on human resource management (HRM) became increasingly prevalent and, to some extent, replaced industrial relations. HRM takes a more 'unitarist' view of relations between employees and employers in contrast to the more 'pluralist' and critical perspectives of industrial relations as a field of study (see Bray et al., 2018).

There are many reasons why industrial relations as a field of study remains highly relevant to the contemporary world of work. In the United Kingdom, Sisson has argued that industrial relations is not only a vibrant field of intellectual inquiry but it 'delivers' something of practical value:

> the subject is able to impart ideas and provide insights that inform policy and practice, present evidence that tests their explanatory power and maps

developments in the field that add richness to the discourse of the employment relationship as a multi-faceted phenomenon.

(Sisson, 2008)

The British Universities Industrial Relations Association (BUIRA) issued a statement to refute the argument that the subject was outmoded arguing that 'the future of industrial relations remains challenging but promising' and that it can effectively address issues of increasing complexity such as 'a diverse workforce, radical change in technology and organisation of work, the shift towards a service economy, new contractual arrangements and patterns of working and the pressures of the global economy' (BUIRA, 2008).

Drawing on the experience of the United States, McKersie argues that academic programmes which have broadened their approach to work and employment relations can 'take centre stage in the social sciences and everyday practice and policy where industrial relations was once situated'. McKersie draws attention to the fact that the field of negotiations and conflict management, on which much of his research has focused, has shown robust development and that this is an area in which industrial relations scholars have considerable experience. He also notes that as 'organisations have become more complex, achieving consensus across interests and boundaries has become elusive…(and) we need savvy individuals who can help opposing parties find integrative outcomes in a mixed-motive world that has become intensively distributive' (McKersie, 2019: 205). This argument is relevant to other countries, such as Australia and the United Kingdom, where the expertise which industrial relations scholars and practitioners have acquired in dispute resolution can be applied to other areas of conflict in the workplace. Alternative methods of providing a voice and influence for employees at their placed of work should be a natural province of industrial relations specialists (Lansbury, 2009).

Not all industrial relations programmes have adapted to these new challenges which McKersie has outlined. However, the WOS Discipline at the University of Sydney has been moving in this direction. In her introduction to *Contemporary Issues in Work and Organisations: Actors and Institutions*, Marian Baird notes that:

> a strength of the Sydney group has been its ability to respond to changes in the nature of work, its organisation and the demographics of the workforce, engage in policy debates about employment, and chart shifts in the theoretical and conceptual domains framing these inquiries.
>
> (Baird, 2020: xi)

Taking this book as an example of research and scholarship in this field in Australia, it is interesting to observe that while only 4 of the 15 chapters focus directly on the role of collective actors in industrial relations, most of the chapters deal with the concerns of people about work and working life. In the concluding chapter of the book, Howell notes that the former 'accepted wisdom' of industrial relations scholars that conflicts of interest between labour and capital could be resolved by collective bargaining and the institutions which supported the system, no longer applies. However, the contributions by scholars in this book, argues Howell, provide a valuable analysis of how 'contemporary capitalism has produced new forms of precarity, inequality and risk, for individual workers and for the planet and humanity as a whole' (Howell, 2020: 240). These are all relevant issues for industrial relations scholarship.

The future of work and industrial relations

In order to analyse the current and future changes in Work and Industrial Relations in a period of rapid and global technological change, Wright and Lansbury (2020) have proposed a 'dynamic work systems' framework that focuses on institutions which govern the employment relationship as well as the forces of continuity and change which influence outcomes. Their framework also emphasises the interaction between national, sectoral and transnational institutions (see Figure 9.1). At the national level, various policy arrangements determine the conditions under which workers are employed. The roles that unions and employer associations play representing their members and how conflicts between labour and capital are resolved through institutions, such as industrial tribunals, are also determined at a national level.

At the sectoral level, institutions representing the interests of an industry play a stronger or weaker role depending on the preferences of the parties, the nature of the product and labour markets, and the technological and regulatory features of specific sectors. Manufacturing employers, for example, are likely to be more

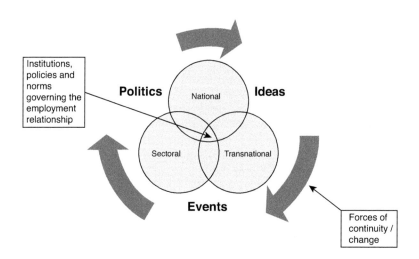

Figure 9.1 A multi-scalar institutional framework for analysing work and employment relations.

tolerant of unions and prefer coordinated employment relations arrangements. By contrast, employers in the service sector are likely to favour more 'flexible' employment relationships, including non-union workplaces. Sectoral institutions cut across national systems, thereby enabling greater diversity in employment relations within countries (Bechter et al., 2012). Finally, transnational institutions are involved where there are multilateral forms of governance or other actors who transcend national boundaries. Multinational enterprises, for example, sometimes attempt to implement common industrial relations policies around the world, while global institutions such as the ILO promote labour standards across different countries. These three levels or types of institutions may respond differently to changes in the nature of work, and industrial relations and their importance may vary over time.

While an institutional approach is helpful in explaining continuity, it is less so in relation to changes arising from politics, ideas and events. Policies and policy making are central to understanding how laws and institutions respond to changing circumstances. Ideas and ideology are often responsible for initiating change. Events which result in crises and/or critical junctures can produce major historical changes at the national, sectoral and/or transnational levels. Many reforms to industrial relations policies and practices have followed dramatic and cataclysmic events, such as those experienced in many countries after the Second World War. The industrial relations systems of Japan and Germany, which are now taken for granted, were the result of the Allied powers imposing changes in the immediate post-war period. In the United States, the 'New Deal' introduced by President Roosevelt in 1932 was a response to the Great Depression which engulfed the world at that time. The subsequent industrial relations reforms, which were part of the New Deal, had ramifications for at least the next 50 years.

The effects of the COVID-19 pandemic on the health and economy of nations around the world is being compared to the consequences of the Second World War. The full long-term effects, which the unforeseen disaster of the virus will have on Work and Industrial Relations, are yet to be realised but the immediate effects have been devastating. It remains to be seen whether the labour market institutions governing employment relations in various countries will be adequate to resolve the problems arising from the virus.

The dynamic work systems framework provides a means of analysing how the forces of continuity and change play out when a major disruptive event such as the COVID-19 pandemic occurs. There are transnational institutions such as the World Health Organization (WHO) and the ILO which attempt to assist nation states to deal with both the health and workforce outcomes. However, the WHO has been under attack by the Trump administration in the United States for not being more effective in warning against the virus and compelling China to act earlier and more decisively. While this criticism seems to be motivated to find a scapegoat for the inability of the United States to contain the virus, it also reflects the difficulties faced by UN institutions which are limited in what they can achieve without the support of member nations.

National governments respond with actions to ameliorate the outcomes of COVID-19, but these are experienced in different ways across industrial sectors. Hence, while global supply chains are disrupted and international aviation thrown into chaos, some industries which are more domestically based are likely to proceed with less interruption. However, the complexities of a global pandemic, like COVID-19, make it difficult to choose a single theory or framework to explain the past or predict the future. Nevertheless, the dynamic work systems approach can assist in understanding the changes to work and employment relations because it examines the interaction between the national, sectoral and transnational dimensions.

10 Concluding observations on Work and Industrial Relations

In *A Field in Flux: Sixty Years of Industrial Relations* (2019), eminent US academic Robert McKersie describes his career as an 'industrial relations journey'. Using a life-cycle approach, he describes his journey from apprentice, to journeyman, to managing the shop and, finally, returning to the bench. He includes a quote from Pope Francis: 'Journeying is an art...If we stop, we don't go forward and we also miss the goal'. My goal in this book has been to use my own 'journey' and experience to reflect on changes in the field of Work and Industrial Relations through the lens of my research and experiences over the past 50 years. My hope is that the description of my journey may be of interest not only to those who have experienced these changes but also to current and future generations who will have to deal with the legacy of Work and Industrial Relations which my generation of scholars and policy makers leave behind.

I was drawn to industrial relations as a field of research and teaching because I found it intrinsically interesting. It offered me opportunities to undertake research on issues which profoundly affect the lives and work of people around the world. As the previous chapters have illustrated, industrial relations also brought me into contact with scholars, practitioners and policy makers whose words and actions have influenced the way that industrial relations are practised. With the appropriate regulatory framework, industrial relations can play a key role in making working life fairer, more fulfilling and productive for all concerned. However, industrial relations laws can also be framed and applied in a way that results in negative outcomes. Some countries, such as those in the Nordic region, have chosen to have minimal labour laws and encourage employers and unions to rely on negotiated agreements rather than regulations imposed by governments. The challenge for academics is to undertake research and advocate reforms which can achieve positive results for people at work and the broader community.

In recent decades, industrial relations have been radically transformed in countries around the world. In many Western market economies, where unions expanded their activities during the first few decades following the Second World War, membership density has now declined along with collective bargaining coverage. Collective agreements previously negotiated by unions have been replaced by individual employment contracts. Labour markets have been progressively deregulated, and the proportion of the workforce engaged contingent forms of work has increased. Labour laws have become more restrictive in relation to collective forms of action, such as strikes, and the number of formal industrial disputes has declined. Yet issues related to Work and Industrial Relations have become increasingly important to economic and social progress.

The traditional approach to teaching industrial relations, which often focused rather narrowly on collective bargaining and industrial conflict, has changed in recent years. As noted previously, the Discipline of Work and Organisational Studies at the University of Sydney has taken a broader approach to issues related to work and the employment relationship, and courses connect micro-level concerns at the workplace level with macro-level issues in society and the economy. Newer social actors, such as NGOs and community organisations, actively concerned with issues at work and the workplace, are being included alongside unions and employers, when discussing contemporary industrial relations. Alternative or complementary means of providing workers with a voice and influence in the workplace are also being explored. The research agenda of academics and doctoral candidates in Work and Organisational Studies includes topics such as work and family, the gig economy, wage theft and compliance, migrant labour and insecure work. But collective bargaining issues are also still examined. This wide range of subjects covered by Work and Organisational Studies research is represented in the recent publication *Contemporary Issues in Work and Employment Relations* (Lansbury et al., 2020). The expertise which industrial relations scholars and practitioners have developed in dispute resolution between unions and employers can also be applied to other areas of conflict in society.

The international dimension of industrial relations, which has been the focus of much of my research, has become more important in an era of globalisation. There are some, such as the United States, which are turning away from international organisations and becoming more protectionist in their economic policies. However, the United Nations and related organisations such as the World Trade Organization (WTO) and the International Labour Organization (ILO) will continue to be supported by the majority of member nations. Multinational corporations are likely to be the locus of employment for increasing numbers of people and will exert considerable influence on the future of Work and Industrial Relations. Although Western systems of industrial relations will continue to be important, the newly industrialising economies in Asia and elsewhere are developing their own approaches and institutions to regulate industrial relations which reflect their particular traditions and political systems. In Asia, labour-oriented NGOs are playing an increasingly important role, particularly where unions have been restricted in their roles and/or been ineffective for various reasons.

Influences on my approach to Work and Industrial Relations

The opening chapters of this book were devoted to my early life because I believe that our later careers are strongly influenced by the values we gain from our family, mentors and peers as well as our education.

From my family, I gained the view that people should be treated with respect and equality irrespective of their class, status or wealth. My teachers inculcated a thirst for knowledge and encouraged me to undertake higher education. From my classmates at high school, I learned the importance of being both collaborative as well as competitive. My university days were important not only from what I learned from the studies in which I undertook but also other student activities in which I participated. Contact with international students enhanced my interest in world affairs. My mentors, Alan Davies and Leon Peres, opened my eyes to new fields of learning and instilled confidence in me to achieve academic success. They also gave me my first job opportunities in higher education and influenced my choice of topics for Masters' and Doctoral research. I learned a great deal from students whom I supervised for honours and postgraduate research theses. One of the highlights of my academic career was receiving the Vice Chancellor's award at the University of Sydney for supervision of higher research degrees.

Although my academic career may appear to be marked by continuous success, it has been a combination of hard work and good fortune. I had my share of disappointments. I found it difficult to obtain my first tenured lecturing position and gain promotion early in my career. I had doubts about my ability to manage both an academic department and a research centre. I learned the importance of building networks of support among my colleagues, not just in my home institution but also in other universities in Australia and overseas. I found it valuable and fulfilling to build connections with officials in unions, employers and their associations and with public servants at both the state and federal levels of government. This added greatly to my enjoyment of teaching and research in industrial relations because it provided me with insights into practice and policy making. I began to receive invitations to undertake research and consulting activities for unions, employers and governments. I was also appointed to advisory boards and inquiries by a variety of governments at both state and federal levels. In time, this also led to undertaking projects and participating on advisory bodies for international bodies, such as the ILO, OECD and European Union. Some of my most satisfying research experiences were collaborating with colleagues around the world who invited me to be part of their teams on major projects, such as the International Motor Vehicle Program at MIT and the EU Sustainable Mine of the Future project with colleagues in Sweden.

My choice of research topics has been driven by my curiosity and interest in a variety of issues. This has been problematic at times, particularly during my early career, because I was perceived to have a 'scattergun' approach to research. As a postgraduate student, I was strongly influenced by my supervisors. Hence, my research on leisure in the new suburbs on Australia and Sweden built on a project initiated by my supervisor Alan Davies. However, this research was also driven by my interest in writers during the mid-1960s who predicted that many market economies were on the verge of an 'age of leisure' brought about by advances in technology which would free us from the burdens of work. According to commentators at the time, the new suburban developments would provide the locus for spending increased leisure in community and family activities. These utopian visions were not achieved and look much less likely now. This project focused my attention on the meaning of work and changes in advanced economies which made it possible to replace working time with greater leisure. During the following decades, trade unions in many countries, including Australia, mounted campaigns for reductions in the standard 40 hours working week which were partially successful.

My doctoral research was strongly influenced by Leon Peres for whom I worked as a tutor. Leon's interest in the sociology of science, based on his previous career at the CSIRO, led me to focus on the emerging role of information technologists in management services at British European Airways. My research highlighted how new occupational groups, introducing technological change, were transforming the airline. This led to subsequent studies in other industries including auto manufacturing, banking and mining and retailing, often comparing how changes were introduced and implemented in different countries. A common theme in these studies was the role of trade unions in responding to the introduction of new technologies which affected the jobs of their members. In some countries, such as Sweden, unions had an influential role in how changes were introduced including retraining of workers for the new technology and redesign of work to assist the workers to undertake new tasks. In other countries, unions were not consulted or involved in decisions regarding changes and took an opposing position.

Industrial democracy or worker participation in decision-making has been my abiding interest over the past four decades, although it has waxed and waned as an issue of public policy. I became interested in the topic during the mid-1970s when the Swedish automotive industry, Volvo and Saab, came to prominence with redesigning their work systems in collaboration with their workers and unions. The Swedish Social Democratic government passed legislation to require companies to consult with their workforce, and consensus was reached between employers and unions on the need for more collaboration in the workplace. During the Hawke Labor government in Australia, there was considerable discussion between unions and employer associations about developing a joint approach to worker and employee participation.

By 1980, when I published an edited volume on *Democracy in the Workplace*, I was able to draw on a number of case studies of enterprises in Australia which were undertaking initiatives on worker participation, many in cooperation with unions. I became involved with government officials who were drafting policies which appeared likely to lead to legislation. However, the political turbulence of the mid-1990s, which included the defeat of the Keating Labor government, ended any interest in legislative change. Unions became focused on internal issues as their membership density declined and the Howard Coalition government passed legislation which sought to further weaken union power and influence. Nevertheless, the issue of employee participation and engagement remains a key concern for many employers. Research on high performance work systems continues to show that where workers have a genuine influence over decisions which affect them, quality and productivity are enhanced.

Unitarist and pluralist approaches to industrial relations revisited

One of the first and most influential publications I read when I began my doctoral research at LSE was *Industrial Sociology and Industrial Relations*. Alan Fox wrote this brief research paper in 1966 for the *Royal Commission on Trade Unions and Employer Association*, chaired by Lord Donovan in the United Kingdom. Fox described the significance of two 'frames of reference' in the resolution of industrial conflict. The 'unitarist' approach assumes that employees and employers have shared interests and can resolve any differences that arise between them without the involvement of third parties, such as unions. Fox argued that this approach was unrealistic because it denied the legitimacy of conflict between the parties. The 'pluralist' approach recognises that differences exist which can lead to conflict, but that this can be resolved by negotiation between unions and employers. However, this assumes that bargaining power between the parties is relatively equal. Later, Fox added a 'radical' frame of reference which held that inequality of power between employers and employees, which lies at the heart of the capitalist system, makes it difficult to resolve conflict between the parties, except on a temporary basis (Fox, 1974). More recently, Craddon (2011) has argued that while the essence of Fox's theory remains valid, there is a need to broaden his work with a greater variety of frames of reference.

As an aside, I visited Alan Fox when I was a doctoral student, to ask him more about his 'frames of reference' which I was trying to apply to my own research. I located him in a small office in an old building housing the Department of Social and Administrative Studies at Oxford. I recall that he was quite self-effacing but generous with his time and seemed to be more interested in discussing my research than his own. I later discovered that he had left school at 14 and worked in a variety of jobs, served in the RAF during the Second World War and was awarded a Distinguished Flying Medal. This was before he gained his degree at Ruskin College, Oxford, in his late 20s. Alan Fox published his autobiography 30 years later, in 1990, appropriately titled *A Very Late Development*.

My conceptual approach to Work and Industrial Relations has generally been pluralist. However, with the rise of inequality in most countries, the bargaining power of workers has declined while that of employers has increased. This inequality of power has been exacerbated by neo-liberal governments which have sought to further weaken the power and influence of organised labour. Hence, unitarist approaches have become dominant, and the case for more radical reforms to restore the balance between the parties in industrial relations is compelling. While the concept of a social contract at work may appear to be more of a pluralist approach, it requires a radical shift towards greater equality of rights between employees and employers. This is in keeping with the views of Alan Fox in *Beyond Contract: Work, Power and Trust Relations* (1974), which are still pertinent to current circumstances.

In recent research, Bray et al. (2018) have coined the phrase 'collaborative pluralism' to describe examples where unions and employers have used interest-based negotiations to achieve enterprise agreements and organisational change, with the Fair Work Commission playing an important facilitative role. They cite examples from the Newcastle and Hunter region of NSW where cooperative arrangements have existed between employers and unions for several years. They contrast this with 'unitarist consultation' in which cooperation is solely between managers and individual workers on employers' terms, without involving unions representing the interests of workers. The successful examples of organisational transformation cited by Bray et al. mostly involve unions playing a key role in achieving positive outcomes. Yet these examples of collaboration have had to 'swim against the tide of adversarialism' which has characterised much of the history of industrial relations in Australia.

My research in Work and Industrial Relations over the past three decades has convinced me that if Australia and other countries are to survive both domestic and global crises, such as the COVID-19 pandemic and its economic consequences, there has to be greater commitment by all parties to a 'social contract'. This is required to underpin future social and economic development and must be accompanied by a willingness to create a more democratic workplace. The concept of a social contract has been used and adapted by many writers since Jean-Jacques Rousseau's book in 1762, entitled *On the Social Contract or Principles of Political Rights*. Rousseau's work was inspired by the revolutionary ferment and the Age of Enlightenment in Europe, and he argued against the established view at that time that monarchs were divinely empowered to legislate. A modern interpretation of the social contract is provided by political scientist Tony Palfreeman (2017: 214) as 'a notional contract between the people and their government' in which the people grant the government rights to collect taxes and act on their behalf. But, in return, the people expect the government to provide them with 'social order, economic wellbeing, security and overall good governance'. This concept can be applied to the workplace in which there are mutual rights and obligations between workers, employers and government, as outlined below (see also Baird and Lansbury, 2007; Kochan, 2016; Lansbury, 2009).

The way forward: a new social contract at work

If long-term improvement in life at work is to be achieved, not only is goodwill between the social partners required but labour market institutions also need to be strengthened. In Australia and a number of other countries, such as the United States, systems of industrial relations and labour laws have been under sustained attack, usually from radical conservative interests. The pillars of the social contract at work need to be more firmly established. Thomas Kochan has defined the social contract, in the context of the workplace, as

> the mutual expectations and obligations that employers, employees and society at large has for work and employment relations.... It is a set of norms

that holds us all accountable for adding value at work and providing work that is a productive, meaningful life experience.

(Kochan, 2016)

The concept of a social contract at work is not new to Australia. In the early 1900s, at the time of Australia's federation, a historic compromise was reached between the interests of labour and capital. A system of conciliation and arbitration system was established which recognised both the prerogatives of employers and the collective bargaining rights of workers through their unions. Paul Kelly (1992) used the term 'social settlement' to describe this period when not only was an industrial relations compact achieved but also tariff protection was provided to domestic manufacturing, so that local industry could develop without undue foreign competition undercutting the costs of production. Australia may be facing the greatest crisis since the Second World War, due to COVID-19. Kelly argues for a new 'social compact' because 'there is a new spirit of concord (and) the crisis has transformed awareness of our interdependence as a community. We realise, as never before, how much society and economy need each other' (Kelly, 2020).

A new social contract at work in Australia should rest on three pillars: a full employment policy coupled with a strong safety net for those unable to work; a comprehensive vocational training and education system which provides retraining for those who need or wish to change their employment; industrial relations reforms to provide a stronger voice for workers in decisions affecting them in the workplace. As outlined below, these pillars should be based not only on the historical experience of Australia but also draw on successful examples from other countries. The Nordic countries, for example, rely less on legal protections for workers and more on collective bargaining between unions and employers, with little intervention by government. The Nordic systems are based on high levels of unionisation that provide a greater equality of bargaining power than is found in most other advanced market economies.

The Nordic countries also provide a wider range of opportunities for workers to influence decisions by management at the enterprise level through works councils and other workplace institutions. Compared with Australia, the Nordic countries have greater gender equality at work. Addressing this and other inequalities is essential if a new social contract at work is to be achieved. During previous eras, Australia has adopted innovative approaches to employment policies, training and education, and industrial relations. It is time for Australia once again to take the lead in crafting a new social contract at work.

Pillar one: commitment to full employment

Comparisons have been made between the COVID-19 crisis and the challenges which Australia experienced during and after the Second World War. Commitment to full employment was one of the key planks of the policy platforms adopted by the Australian Labor Party and enacted by Prime Minister

Ben Chifley after he commissioned *The White Paper on Full Employment* by Dr H.C. Coombes in 1945. The Coalition government, which held power from 1949 to 1972, enjoyed a period of mostly low unemployment, aided by the 'long economic boom' which prevailed at this time. However, in recent decades, governments of both major political parties appear to have largely given up trying to maintain full employment and have accepted levels of 5 or 6 per cent unemployment as acceptable.

The current COVID-19 crisis has revealed not only the persistence of historically high levels of unemployment, particularly among younger people but also at least a third to a quarter of the workforce being in 'non-standard' forms of employment. These include people working on fixed-term, casual and part-time, on-call, freelance arrangements, often for temporary employment agencies. While there are some workers who prefer temporary to more permanent forms of work, surveys consistently demonstrate that there is a high level of 'underemployment' among workers who are seeking more paid hours of work. Many workers report that they are seeking greater security of employment and full-time employment with sufficient hours to provide an adequate income. Wage subsidies to protect jobs, during the COVID-19 crisis, have revealed high labour turnover within the increasingly 'gig'-oriented labour market. More than one million workers were ineligible to receive wage subsidies during the crisis because they had not been in continuous employment during the previous 12 months.

Successive Australian governments have scaled back or abandoned active labour market programmes designed to achieve full or near to full employment. Earlier attempts at job creation programmes have been started and then curtailed after changes of government. Long-term stability of employment programmes is needed, whether they involve wage subsidies to private employers or creation of public works. Such programmes must involve education and training so that participants are provided with the skills required to find work in the regular labour market. The Danish system of 'flexicurity' is an example where long-term unemployment was reduced by providing employers with greater freedom to hire or dismiss employees, for just cause, but adding an obligation that education and training be provided to workers who are displaced because of changes in technology or the nature of the business. This has meant that while labour turnover has increased in Denmark, the proportion of workers who obtain new jobs in a reasonably short period of time has also improved.

Our system of care for children and the elderly also needs to be thoroughly reformed so that quality care becomes the norm. The Nordic countries again provide examples of universal systems of care which create more egalitarian societies by ensuring there are ample opportunities for people to participate in paid work as well as in other aspects of society.

Pillar two: revitalising vocational education and training

Vocational education and training systems in Australia have staggered from one crisis to another during recent decades. State governments have reduced spending on technical and further education, closed state-run colleges and transferred responsibility to private providers, many of which have proved to be inefficient and unreliable. In the past, government departments and instrumentalities, particularly those providing electricity, gas, water and transportation, were major employers and trainers of apprentices and supplied skilled labour to the rest of industry. With privatisation, outsourcing and the rationalisation of services, governments have reduced their commitment to apprenticeships and traineeships. Although federal governments expanded shorter traineeships under the title of 'new apprenticeships', there has been criticism of the quality of both the work and training provided by these schemes. Furthermore, employer contributions to training of skilled workers have stagnated, and the hours of training have declined as shorter-length traineeships have replaced traditional apprenticeships. Non-completion and attrition rates of apprenticeships have remained as high as when we undertook our study of skills training in *Ticket to Nowhere: Education, Training and Work in Australia* during the mid-1970s. Australia is simply not keeping up with the level and quality of training provided in a range of occupations provided by most other advanced economies.

University enrolments in Australia have boomed during the past decade, but much of the increase has been generated by international students, particularly from China. Furthermore, as the federal government has reduced the percentage of spending on higher education, universities have been forced to rely on fee-paying students from overseas as well as from Australia. The fees for undertaking tertiary education have significantly increased in recent decades so that fees charged for degree courses at Australian universities are higher than equivalent state universities in the United States. Furthermore, the pathways from vocational courses offered at Institutes of Training and Further Education are difficult to navigate and only a handful of Australian universities have comprehensive programmes to facilitate mobility of students from vocational to degree level education. Unlike Germany and other European countries, where students can proceed more easily from skilled apprenticeship training to degree programmes, Australian systems remain divided between different streams of post-secondary education with little opportunities for students to transfer from one to the other.

Pillar three: reform of industrial relations through collective voice and representation

A revitalised union movement is essential not only for establishing a social partnership between labour and capital but also for maintaining a democratic society. During the COVID-19 crisis, the federal government sought cooperation of both the union movement and employer associations for its initiatives to keep people employed by introducing wage subsidies and more flexible working arrangements. This was a recognition of the importance of social partnerships and tripartite cooperation between the government, employers and unions in order to address both national health and economic crises. The government also requested the Fair Work Commission to implement changes in awards and agreements necessary to keep most of the workforce employed and protected during the crisis period. Reforms are needed not only to guarantee union rights to engage in various industrial activities, including collective bargaining with employers, but also to strengthen the role of the Fair Work Commission as the independent tribunal and labour market regulator. There is a need for new systems of worker representation at the enterprise level, such as works councils, which are well-established in Germany and other European countries.

Since the 1990s, unions have faced legislative changes by both Labor and Coalition governments which have made it difficult to carry out their traditional functions of representing the interests of workers and negotiating wages and conditions through collective bargaining. The Hawke and Keating Labor governments presided over the shift to enterprise agreements without the safeguards which existed under the previous industry-wide awards. This was followed by the so-called *Work Choices* legislation by the Coalition government, led by John Howard, which enabled individual non-union agreements to replace awards, introduced restrictions on union activities and reduced the role of the Fair Work Commission. Although the subsequent Rudd and Gillard Labor governments repealed the most controversial aspects of Work Choices, including restoring workers' rights to appeal against unfair dismissal, it maintained the pre-eminence of the enterprise-based bargaining system. The award system, in which unions had exclusive rights to represent workers, was not restored even though a system of 'modern awards' was introduced to provide an additional 'safety net' for most workers (Bray, 2011).

Unionisation rates are now perilously low, having fallen from 49 per cent in 1990 to around 15 per cent in 2020 and less than 10 per cent in the private sector. There are many factors which have contributed to the long-term decline of union membership, not just in Australia but also in most other OECD countries. Changes in the structure of the economy are estimated to account for about half of the decline in unionisation. This includes the decline in sectors, such as manufacturing and the public sector, where unionisation was traditionally strongest. Other factors include hostility from employers and government which make it difficult for unions to organise. However, removal of institutional arrangements enshrined in the previous arbitration system, such as the encouragement of union and employer organisations as representative bodies within the industrial relations system.

Unions have tried various strategies to increase their membership such as developing organising skills to revitalise workplace unionism and forging alliances with NGOs and the broader community. However, to increase their membership density, unions need to have a stronger institutional role in the industrial relations system to act as the primary or exclusive representation of workers in award and agreement making. Industry-wide bargaining also should be restored so that unions can establish agreements which extend beyond the enterprise where this is required. Although there has been a trend towards decentralised bargaining in many countries, German and Nordic systems have retained industry and national level bargaining, thereby enabling unions and employers a greater choice in agreement making. Finally, while collective bargaining will remain the bedrock of industrial relations in many countries, other forms of employee representation and voice at the workplace need to be considered.

The European Union has been at the forefront of creating new opportunities for workers to be involved in decision-making irrespective of whether or not they are unionised. Since 1996, European Works Councils (EWC) have provided an additional channel for employee representation for employee participation in decision-making. The EU has also established statutory mechanisms for information and consultation between employees and employers. However, final decision-making powers remain with management. At various times in Australia's history, there have been examples of joint consultation and works councils which have been successful, although they waxed and waned over time (Markey and Patmore, 2009). It appears, from international experience, that legislation is important to ensure that workers have a right to establish works councils or similar bodies and that their roles and functions are clearly prescribed.

COVID-19 has highlighted great inequalities in the societies around the world which are a challenge to achieving a new social contract at work. A statement entitled *Humans are not resources: Coronavirus shows why we must democratise work*, was signed by many academics from universities and research centres around the world and published in *The Guardian Newspaper* (16 May 2020). The authors of the statement noted that Article 23 of the *Universal Declaration of Human Rights* states that everyone has the right to work, to free choice of employment and to just and favourable conditions of work and protection against unemployment. The statement also demanded that firms be democratised by giving employees greater rights, than currently exist, over decisions affecting them at work. One means by which this could be achieved is extending the powers of works councils over decisions by boards of management. The statement also called on the EU to extend job guarantees to workers in European firms so that they can 'play a crucial role in assuring the social, economic and environmental stability of our democratic societies'.

Industrial Relations as a field of knowledge is relevant to current issues facing workers, employers and policy makers in relation to work and employment. While the material conditions of many people across the world have greatly improved during the past 50 years, the gap has widened between those who have gained the most compared with those who have gained the least. There are significant challenges which face the current and future generations entering the workforce. A new social contract at work is necessary in order to make the transition to a fair and equitable outcome for all.

Afterword

Before I read this amazing rendition of Russell Lansbury's life, I thought I knew about most of his legendary achievements as a researcher, teacher, leader, and public citizen. But I should have known better. As I said when urging him to write his memoir, "nobody in our field has a more extensive mental rolodex of the people, places, and projects that shaped our field." As these pages attest, that was an understatement.

Russell Lansbury has touched more people with his warmth, inquisitiveness, and range of interests than anyone I have met in our field of industrial relations—current and past generations included. Reading these pages was like a typical afternoon's conversation with Russell. Stories are told of his jaunts to interesting places around the world, but always with a focus on what *he* learned from *them*. The truth is the balance of trade often tipped in the other direction; Russell was as much if not more the teacher than the student.

And, with Russell, no lesson learned, time or place of its origin, or comrade in arms is ever forgotten. All get recorded in his memory, ready to be put to good use as needed. We read, for example, how his early exposures to information technology and professional employees at British Airways was put to use in his dissertation, later in his work with us on the US and Australian airline industries, and more recently in writing about technological change in the global industry. His early work on Sweden laid the foundation for becoming the international expert on call when that country and its European neighbours needed an adviser for numerous government studies and academic research projects.

Russell and Gwen Lansbury have been gracious hosts to more international visitors at their homes near Sydney and in Wollombi than I'm sure they can count. Visitors like my wife Kathy and I would always be treated to brisk walks, great food, conversations, and often another visitor or two they would invite over to make sure we met more of their friends and professional contacts. And as a bonus, they would make sure we would meet one or more of Russell's students, many of whom, like Marian Baird, have become life-long friends. That is the Lansbury touch we have been privileged to experience first-hand and the one that comes through so vividly in the life story told here.

We live in a time when too many of the values, principles, and lessons of industrial relations are being stressed to their limits. But reading about the many ways Russell has used these attributes to improve the world of work inspires us all to carry on with the optimism and steady hand of this world class scholar, gentleman, and dear friend.

Thomas A. Kochan
George Maverick Bunker Professor of Management
MIT Sloan School of Management
Co-director, MIT Institute of Work and Employment Research
Massachusetts Institute of Technology
Cambridge, USA

Acknowledgements

Writing this book has reinforced my sense of how much I owe to my family, teachers, colleagues, students and others who have provided me with advice and support over many years. I am grateful to my parents for their love and guidance from my childhood through to adulthood. However, the greatest influence on my life is Gwen, my wife of over 50 years, for whom no words can adequately express my gratitude. Not only did Gwen sacrifice many things for my career but she also gave birth to our children and cared for them during my numerous absences. We are both very proud of Owen and Nina who have given us four wonderful grandchildren. This book is dedicated to Gwen and our family.

It is invidious to acknowledge only a few of the many people who have assisted me during the course of my life and I apologise to those whom I have not named. At high school, Graham Worrall was an inspiring history master and debating coach who motivated me to become a teacher. At the University of Melbourne, I met Harvey Williams who has been my friend and confidante for more than 50 years. I was fortunate to have Alan Davies as teacher and mentor who put me on the pathway to becoming an academic. Alan not only gave me the opportunity to pursue postgraduate studies but also appointed me to my first full-time academic job as a tutor and acting lecturer in Political Science at the University of Melbourne. At the London School of Economics, Keith Thurley gently guided me through my doctoral research. The influence of both Alan and Keith has remained with me throughout my career, not only in terms of their ideas but also their kindness and support.

During my first appointment as a lecturer at Monash University, Di Yerbury was my mentor and Ed Davis was my first research student. Both became my life-long friends and colleagues. At the University of Sydney, I have had many wonderful colleagues who became close friends, over more than 30 years, including Marian Baird, Mark Bray, Ron Callus, Stephen Clibborn, Rae Cooper, Bradon Ellem, Dimitria Groutsis, Suzanne Jamieson, Anya Johnson, Jim Kitay, Di van den Broek, Mark Westcott, Chris F. Wright and Keith Whitfield. I am particularly grateful to Rawya Mansour for many years of support and assistance. The late Peter Gilmour was co-author of three books, and we worked together at both Monash and Macquarie universities. Greg Bamber, a fellow doctoral student at LSE, and I jointly edited our book on *International and Comparative Industrial Relations* through six editions over a period of 30 years.

Dexter Dunphy and the late Bill Ford at the University of New South Wales provided advice and friendship from the very beginning of my academic career and smoothed my transition from Melbourne to Sydney. I also wish to acknowledge the inspiration and support I have received from two of the 'fathers' of industrial relations in Australia: Keith Hancock from Adelaide and Flinders universities and the late Joe Isaac from Monash and Melbourne universities. John Niland assisted me in my role at the University of Sydney when he held the Chair of Industrial Relations and later became Vice-Chancellor at UNSW.

I have learned a great deal from my doctoral students over the years. I particularly wish to acknowledge Marian Baird, Stephen Clibborn, Debra Da Silva, Etsuko Hayashi, Anya Kirsch, Robin Kramar, Teresa Shuk-Ching Poon, Chi Do Quynh, Nick Wailes and Seoghun Woo. All subsequently made valuable contributions in academia, business, government and NGOs in Australia and around the world. It was a privilege to work with them on their research projects and become friends during the process.

I have been most fortunate to have collaborators and friends around the world with whom I share interests in work and industrial relations. In the United States, I am particularly grateful to Tom Kochan who welcomed me to MIT in the mid-1980s and has been a close friend and colleague ever since. At MIT, I also began long-term friendships with Bob McKersie, Harry Katz and Joel Cutcher Gershenfeld. I have enjoyed a long association and friendship with Janice Bellace, at the Wharton School, University of Pennsylvania, particularly through our shared interests in the ILERA and ILO. In Sweden, my long-term friend, Olle Hammarstrom, a former trade union leader, and our families have been close since we met in the early 1970s.

I am also grateful to Lena Abrahamsson and Jan Johansson at Lulea Technical University, Christian Berggren at Linkoping University, Mia Ronnmar at Lund University and Ake Sandberg at Stockholm University for their collaboration over many years. In Denmark, it has been my pleasure to work with Soren Kaj Andersen at the University of Copenhagen as well as the late Gert Graversen at the University of Aarhus. At the ILO in Geneva, I have been engaged in a number of projects, dating back to the 1970s, particularly with Muneto Ozaki, Chang-Hee Lee and Peter Auer. Byoung-Hoon Lee at Chung Ahn University, Youngbum Park, formerly at the Korea Labor Institute, and Chang-Hee Lee have deepened my knowledge of Korean culture and industrial relations and have been valued colleagues for many years.

I am indebted to several valued friends and mentors who died during the past year. Jim Stern hosted my first study leave at the University of Wisconsin-Madison in 1970s and introduced me to industrial relations in the United States. Willy Brown of Cambridge University was a friend from my days as a doctoral student at the LSE and was a frequent and welcome visitor to Australia. Bill Ford was a mentor throughout my career. Joe Isaac was a 'legend' in industrial relations in Australia and revered by many of us in the field. I was particularly grateful for Joe's advice and guidance. Each of these scholars was not only important in my life but also made significant contributions to research and practice in industrial relations. They will be greatly missed.

Finally, I wish to thank many people who kindly read and provided advice on the draft of the book. I am particularly grateful to Graeme Dean and Derek McDougall, both of whom read and annotated the whole manuscript. Ron Callus also made substantial contributions to the final work. I am also indebted to others for their insightful comments: Soren Kaj Anderson, Marian Baird, Greg Bamber, Adrian Boddy, Richard Cooney, Ed Davis, Dexter Dunphy, Bradon Ellem, Joel Cutcher Gershenfeld, Graeme Gill, Nina Hall, Olle Hammarstrom, Jim Kitay, Tom Kochan, Gwen Lansbury, John Lewer, Jim Nicol, Greg Patmore, Peter Sheldon, Rod Tiffen, Alex Veen, Harvey Williams and Chris F. Wright. Responsibility for the final words, however, is mine alone.

Last but not least, I wish to thank Yongling Lam at Routledge who encouraged me to write this book and agreed to publish it!

Bibliography

Abrahamsson L and Johansson J (2006) From grounded skills to sky qualifications. *The Journal of Industrial Relations* 48 (5): 657–676.

Abrahamsson L and Johansson J (2013) One hundred years of inertia: An expose of the concept of psychosocial work environment in Swedish policy and research. *The Nordic Journal of Working Life Studies* 3 (1): 5–16.

Andersen SK, Kaine S and Lansbury RD (2017) Decentralised bargaining in Denmark and Australia: Voluntarism versus legal regulation. *Australian Bulletin of Labour* 42 (1): 45–70.

Ausubel D (1965) *The Fern and the Tiki: An American View of New Zealand National Character, Social Attitudes and Race Relations.* New York: Holt Rinehart and Winston.

Australia Council of Trade Unions and Trade Development Council (1987) *Australia Reconstructed.* Canberra: Australian Government Publishing Service.

Baird M (2020) Preface. In Baird M, Hancock K and Isaac JE (eds) *Work and Employment Relations: An Era of Change – Essays in Honour of Russell Lansbury.* Sydney: The Federation Press: xviii–xix.

Baird M, Hancock K and Isaac JE eds (2011) *Work and Employment Relations: An Era of Change – Essays in Honour of Russell Lansbury.* Sydney: The Federation Press.

Baird M and Lansbury RD (2004) Broadening the horizons of HRM: Lessons for Australia. *Asia Pacific Journal of Human Resources* 42 (2): 147–155.

Baird M and Lansbury RD (2007) Reworking or restoring the American dream? *Labour History* 48 (3): 347–354.

Bamber GJ, Gittell JH, Kochan TA and von Nordenflycht A (2009) *Up in the Air: How Airlines Can Improve Performance by Engaging their Employees.* Ithaca, NY: Cornell University Press.

Bamber GJ and Lansbury RD (1986) Codetermination and technological change in the German automobile industry. *New Technology, Work and Employment* 1 (2): 160–171.

Bamber GJ and Lansbury RD (1987) *International and Comparative Industrial Relations: A Study of Developed Market Economies.* First edition. London and Sydney: Allen and Unwin.

Bamber GJ and Lansbury RD (1988) Managerial strategy and new technology in retail distribution: a comparative case study. *Journal of Management Studies* 23 (3): 197–216.

Bamber GJ and Lansbury RD (1989) *New Technology: International Perspectives on Human Resources and Industrial Relations.* London: Allen and Unwin.

Bamber GJ and Lansbury RD (1991) Organisational and technological change in retail distribution. In Legge et al. (eds) *Case Studies in Information Technology. People and Organisations.* Oxford: Blackwell: 124–146.

Bamber GJ and Lansbury RD (1993) *International and Comparative Industrial Relations: A Study of Industrialised Market Economies.* Second edition. London and Sydney: Allen and Unwin.

Bamber GJ and Lansbury RD (1998) *International and Comparative Industrial Relations: A Study of Industrialised Market Economies.* Third edition. London: Sage Books; Sydney: Allen and Unwin.

Bamber GJ, Lansbury RD, Wailes N and Wright CF eds (2016) *International and Comparative Employment Relations: National Regulation, Global Changes*, Sixth edition. Sydney: Allen and Unwin and London: Sage Books.

Bassan J, Srinivasan N and Tang A (2011) The augmented mine worker. *Proceedings of the Second International Future Mining Conference.* Melbourne: Australian Institute of Mining and Metallurgy.

Bechter B, Brandl B and Meardi G. (2012). Sectors or countries? Typologies and levels of analysis in comparative industrial relations. *The European Journal of Industrial Relations* 18 (3): 185–202.

Berg IE (1970) *Education and Jobs: The Great Training Robbery.* New York: Praeger Publishers.

Berggren C (1992) *Alternatives to Lean Production: Work Organisation in the Swedish Auto Industry.* Ithaca, NY: Cornell ILR Press.

Berlanger J, Berggren C, Bjorkman T and Kohler K eds (1999) *Being Local Worldwide: ABB and the Challenge of Global Management.* Ithaca, NY: Cornell University Press: 119–130.

Blain ANJ (1972) *Pilots and Management: Industrial Relations in the United Kingdom Airlines.* London: Allen and Unwin.

Blainey G (2019) *Before I Forget.* Melbourne: Penguin Hamish Hamilton.

Bray M (2011) The distinctiveness of modern awards. In Baird M, Isaac JE and Hancock K (eds) *Work and Employment Relations: An Era of Change.* Sydney: Federation Press: 17–33.

Bray M and Lansbury RD (1999) ABB in Australia: Local autonomy versus globalisation? In Berlanger J, Berggren C, Bjorkman T and Kahler C (eds) *Being Local Worldwide: ABB and the Challenge of Global Management.* Ithaca, NY: Cornell University Press: 119–130.

Bray M, Macneil, J and Stewart A (2018) *Cooperation at Work: How Tribunals Can Help Transform Workplaces.* Sydney: Federation Press.

Brown WA (2016) 'Foreword' to Bamber GJ, Lansbury RD., Wailes N, and Wright CF eds *International and Comparative Employment Relations: National Regulation, Global Challenges.* London: Sage and Sydney: Allen and Unwin.

BUIRA (British Universities Industrial Relations Association) (2008) *What's the Point of Industrial Relations?* London: BUIRA.

Callus R and Lansbury RD (2019) Obituary: Farewell Bob Hawke. *The Journal of Industrial Relations* 35 (3): 475–476.

Callus R, Morehead A, Cully M and Buchanan J (1991) *Industrial Relations at Work: The Australian Workplace Industrial Relations Survey.* Canberra: Australian Government Publishing Service.

Cappelli P (1991) Is there a future for the field of industrial relations in the United States? In Lansbury RD (ed) *Industrial Relations Teaching and Research: International Trends.* Sydney: Australian Centre for Industrial Relations Research and Teaching, University of Sydney.

Chelius J and Dworkin J eds (1990) *Reflections on the Transformation of Industrial Relations.* Metuchen, NJ: Rutgers University and Scarecrow Press.

176 Bibliography

Clibborn S, Lansbury RD and Wright CF (2015) Who killed the Australian automotive industry: The employers, government or the trade unions? *Economic Papers* 35 (1): 12–15. Also in Covarrubias A, Yates C and Ramirez S (eds) *The New Frontiers of the World Auto Industry*. London: Palgrave: 255–276.

Colvin AJS and Darbishire O (2013) Convergence in industrial relations institutions: The emerging Anglo-American model? *The Industrial and Labor Relations Review* 66 (5): 1047–1077.

Cooney R and Lansbury RD (2018) Socio-technical transitions in mining: Sweden and Australia compared. *Proceedings of the SASE 30th Annual Conference*. Tokyo: Doshisha University.

Cooper R and Ellem B (2020) Australian unions: Crisis, strategy, survival. In Lee BH, Ng SH and Lansbury RD (eds) *Trade Unions and Labour Movements in the Asia-Pacific Region*. London and New York: Routledge

Craddon C (2011) Unitarism, pluralism, radicalism and the rest? *Working Paper* no. 7. Department of Sociology, Geneva: University of Geneva.

Davies AF (1958) *Australian Democracy: An Introduction to the Political System*. London: Longmans.

Davies AF (1966) *Private Politics: A Study of Five Political Outlooks*. Carlton: Melbourne University Press.

Davies AF (1967) *Images of Class: An Australian Study*. Sydney: Sydney University Press.

Davies AF (1973) *Politics as Work*. Parkville: Melbourne Politics Monograph, University of Melbourne.

Davis EM and Lansbury RD eds (1996) *Managing Together: Consultation and Participation in the Workplace*. Melbourne: Addison Wesley Longman.

Deeg R and Jackson G (2007) Towards a more dynamic theory of capitalist variety. *The Socio-Economic Review* 5 (1): 149–179.

Delbecq AL and Elfner ES (1970) Local-cosmopolitan orientations and career strategies for specialists. *Administrative Science Quarterly* 13 (4): 373–387.

Dunnant-Whyte H (2010) *Transforming the Mining Industry Globally*. Sydney: Australian Centre for Field Robotics, University of Sydney.

Ellem B (2017) *The Pilbara: From the Deserts Profits Come*. Crawley: UWA Publishing

Ellem B, Sandstrom J and Persson C (2020) Neoliberal trajectories in mining: Comparing Malmfalten and the Pilbara. *The European Journal of Industrial Relations* 26 (3): 297–312.

Emery FE and Thorsrud E (1976) *Democracy at Work: The Report of the Norwegian Industrial Democracy Project*. Leiden: Martinus Nijhoff.

Emery FE and Trist E (1969) Socio-technical systems. In Emery FE (ed) *Systems Thinking*. London: Penguin Books.

Encel S (1984) Social implications of technological change. In Lansbury RD and Davis EM (eds) *Technology, Work and Industrial Relations*. Melbourne: Longman Cheshire: 224–233.

Evans G (2017) *Incorrigible Optimist: A Political Memoir*. Melbourne: Melbourne University Press.

Ford GW (1984) Human resources and the balance of skills. In Lansbury RD and Davis EM (eds) *Technology, Work and Industrial Relations*. Melbourne: Longman Cheshire: 213–223.

Ford M and Gillan M. (2016) Employee relations and the state in southeast Asia. *The Journal of Industrial Relations* 58 (2) 167–182.

Forte (Swedish Research Council for Health, Working Life and Welfare) (2015) *Swedish Research on Work Organisation: An Evaluation Covering the Period 2007–2013*. Stockholm: Forte.

Fox A (1966) *Industrial Sociology and Industrial Relations*: Research Paper No. 3, Royal Commission on Trade Unions and Employers' Associations. London: Her Majesty's Stationery Office.
Fox A (1974) *Beyond Contract: Work, Power and Trust Relations*. London: Faber and Faber.
Freeman R and Medoff J (1984) *What Do Unions Do?* New York: Basic Books.
Frege C and Kelly J (2004) *Varieties of Unionism: Strategies for Union Revitalisation in a Globalising Economy*. Oxford: Oxford University Press.
Galbraith JK (1967) *The New Industrial Estate*. Boston: Houghton Mifflin.
Ganesh J (2019) Make memories not savings in your 20s. *The Financial Times*, 10 November.
Geels FW (2005) *Technological Transitions and System Innovations: A Co-evolutionary and Socio-technical Analysis*. Cheltenham: Edward Elgar Publishing.
Gilmour P and Lansbury RD (1978) *Ticket to Nowhere: Education, Training and Work in Australia*. Ringwood: Penguin Books.
Gilmour P and Lansbury RD (1984) *Marginal Manager: The Changing Role of Supervisors in Australia*. St Lucia: University of Queensland Press.
Gilmour P and Lansbury RD (1977) *Organisations: An Australian Perspective*. Melbourne: Longman Cheshire.
Gollschewski M (2015) Mining case study. In *Automation and Australia's Future Workforce*. Melbourne: Committee for the Economic Development of Australia.
Graversen G and Lansbury RD eds. (1988) *Technological Change and Industrial Relations in Scandinavia*. London: Gower.
Gregory A (2011) *Woodfull: A Gentleman and a Scholar. A Life of William Maldon Woodfull*. South Yarra: The Langley Courtis Thompson Library Trust.
Gustavsen B (2012) The Nordic model of work organisation. *The Journal of the Knowledge Economy* 2 (4): 463–480.
Hakansta C (2014) Former glory and challenges ahead: The definition of working life research in Sweden. *The Nordic Journal of Working Life Studies* 4 (4): 3–20.
Hall PA and Soskice D eds (2001) *Varieties of Capitalism: The Institutional Foundations of Comparative Advantage*. New York: Oxford University Press.
Hancke B, Rhodes M and Thatcher M (2007) Introduction. In Hancke B, Rhodes M and Thatcher M (eds) *Beyond Varieties of Capitalism: Conflict, Contradictions and Complementarities in the European Economy*. Oxford: Oxford University Press: 3–38.
Hancock K (1984) *Report of the Committee of Review into Australia Industrial Relations Laws and System*. Canberra: Australian Government Publishing Service.
Hawke RJL (1994) *The Hawke Memoirs*. Sydney: Heinemann Australia.
Heery EJ (2008) Introduction: The field of industrial relations. In Blyton P, Bacon N, Fiorito J and Heery EJ (eds) *The SAGE Handbook of Industrial Relations*. London: Sage: 1–32.
Horwood R (1981) Review of Professionals and Management: A Study of Behaviour in Organisations. *British Journal of Industrial Relations* 19 (2): 262–263.
Howell C (2003) Varieties of capitalism: And then there was one? *Comparative Politics* 36 (1): 103–124.
Howell C (2020) Labouring under the new capitalism. In Lansbury RD, Johnson A and van den Broek D (eds) *Contemporary Issues in Work and Organisations: Actors and Institutions*. London: Routledge: 239–254.
Hyden G (1968) *TANU Builds the Country*. Lund: Political Science Department Monograph.
International Labour Organisation (1998) *World Labour Report*. Geneva: ILO.

Bibliography

Jackson E, Looney A and. Ramnath S (2017) The rise of alternative work arrangements: evidence and implications for tax filing and benefit coverage. *Office of Tax Analysis Working Paper* 114. Washington CD: US Department of Treasury.

Johansson J and Abrahamsson L (2009) The good work: A Swedish trade union vision in the shadow of lean production. *Applied Ergonomics* 40 (4): 775–780.

Jones BO (1982) *Sleepers, Wake! Technology and the Future of Work*. Sydney: Oxford University Press.

Katz HC (1997) *Telecommunications: Restructuring Work and Employment Relations Worldwide*. Ithaca, NY: Cornell University Press.

Katz HC and Darbishire O (2000) *Converging Divergences: Worldwide Changes in Employment Systems*. Ithaca, NY: Cornell University Press.

Katz HC, Kochan TA and Colvin AJS (2015) *Labor Relations in a Globalising World: An Introduction Focused on Emerging Countries*. Ithaca, NY: Cornell University ILR Press.

Kaufman B (2004) *The Global Evolution of Industrial Relations*. Geneva: International Labour Organisation.

Kelly P (1992) *The End of Certainty. The Story of the 1980s*. Sydney: Allen and Unwin.

Kelly P (2020) Team Australia our new normal. *The Australian Newspaper*, 4 April: 15.

Kim, D-O (2009) Review of Lansbury RD, Suh CS and Kwon SH (eds) The global Korean motor industry: The Hyundai Motor Company's global strategy. *The British Journal of Industrial Relations* 47 (1): 189–191.

Kitay J, Cutcher L and Wailes N eds (2007) Globalization and employment relations in banking. *Bulletin of Comparative Labour Relations*. No. 63. Alphen aan den Rijn: Kluwer Law International.

Kitay J and Lansbury RD eds (1997) *Changing Employment Relations in Australia*. Melbourne: Oxford University Press.

Kleingartner A (1967) *Professionalism and Salaried Worker Organisation*. Madison: University of Wisconsin, Industrial Relations Research Institute.

Kochan TA (2006) Taking the high road. *MIT Sloan Management Review* 47 (4): 16–19

Kochan TA (2016) *Shaping the Future of Work*. New York: Business Experts Press.

Kochan TA, Katz HC and McKersie RB (1986) *The Transformation of American Industrial Relations*. Ithaca, NY: Cornell ILR Press.

Kochan TA, Lansbury RD and Macduffie JP eds (1997) *After Lean Production: Evolving Employment Practices in the World Auto Industry*. Ithaca, NY: Cornell University Press.

Kochan TA and Piore M (1990) A proposal for comparative research on industrial relations and human resource policy and practice. Unpublished manuscript. Cambridge MA: MIT.

Kwon SH and O'Donnell M (2001). *The Chaebol and Labour in Korea: The Development of Management Strategy in Hyundai*. London: Routledge.

Lansbury RD (1970a) The suburban community. *The Australian and New Zealand Journal of Sociology* 6 (2): 131–138.

Lansbury RD (1970b) Leisure in the new suburbs. *Sociologiske Meddeleleser* 14 (1–2): 79–92.

Lansbury RD (1972) *Swedish Social Democracy*. Young Fabian Society Pamphlet 29. London: Fabian Society.

Lansbury RD (1974) Performance against promise: The Labor government and industrial relations. *Journal of Industrial Relations* 17 (3): 288–295.

Lansbury RD (1978a) The return to arbitration: Recent trends in dispute settlement and wages policy in Australia. *International Labour Review* 117 (5): 611–634.

Lansbury RD (1978b) *Professionals and* Management: *A Study of Behaviour in Organisations*. St Lucia: University of Queensland Press and Hemel Hempstead, UK: Prentice Hall International.
Lansbury RD ed (1980) *Democracy in the Workplace*. Melbourne: Longman Cheshire.
Lansbury RD (1994) Changing Nordic approaches to bargaining and participation: Some implications for Australia. *Economic and Labour Relations Review* 5 (2): 3–13.
Lansbury RD (2004) Work, people and globalisation: Towards a new social contract for Australia. *The Journal of Industrial Relations* 46 (1): 102–115.
Lansbury RD (2009) Work and industrial relations: Towards a new agenda. *Relations Industrielles/Industrial Relations*, 64 (2): 326–339.
Lansbury RD (2016a) Varieties of transformation in industrial relations: An international perspective. *Industrial and Labor Relations Review* 69 (5): 1288–1294.
Lansbury RD (2016b) Renewing Swedish leadership in work and employment research. In Sandberg A (ed) *Pa Jakt Efter Framtidens Arbetet* (Searching for the Work of the Future). Stockholm: Tanksmedjan Tiden: 30–42.
Lansbury RD and Breakspear C (1995) Closing down the mine: a tale of two communities and their responses to mining closures in Australia and Sweden. *Economic and Industrial Democracy* 16 (2): 275–290.
Lansbury RD and Davis EM eds (1986). *Democracy and Control in the Workplace*. Melbourne: Longman Cheshire.
Lansbury RD, Hammarstrom O and Sandkull B (1992) Industrial Relations and Productivity: Evidence from Sweden and Australia. *Economic and Industrial Democracy* 13 (3): 295–329.
Lansbury RD, Johnson A and van den Broek D eds (2020) *Contemporary Issues in Work and Organisations: Actors and Institutions*. London: Routledge.
Lansbury RD, Kwon SH and Suh CS (2006) Globalisation and employment relations in the Korean auto industry: The case of Hyundai Motor Company in Korea, Canada and India. *Asia Pacific Business Review* 12 (2): 131–147.
Lansbury RD, Kwon SH and Suh CS (2007) *The Global Korean Motor Industry: The Hyundai Motor Company's Global Strategy*. London and New York: Routledge.
Lansbury RD, Kwon SH and Suh CS (2016). *E Estrategia Global Da Hyundai: A Evolucao da Industria Coreana de Automoveis*. Porto Alegra and Sao Paulo: Bookman Editora Ltda.
Lansbury RD, Lee BH and Ng SH (2020) Refining varieties of unions and labour movements: Perspectives from the Asia-Pacific Region. In Lee BH, Ng SH and Lansbury RD (eds) *Trade Unions and Labour Movements in the Asia-Pacific Region*. London: Routledge: 3–13.
Lansbury RD and Macdonald D (1992) *Workplace Industrial Relations: Australian Case Studies*. Melbourne: Oxford University Press.
Lansbury RD and Ng SH (1987) The workers' congress in Chinese enterprises. In Warner M (ed) *Managerial Reforms in China*. London: Francis Pinter: 149–162.
Lansbury RD and Prideaux GJ (1978) *Improving the Quality of Working Life*. Melbourne: Longman Cheshire.
Lansbury RD and Wailes N (2008) Employee involvement and direct participation In Blyton P, Bacon N, Fiorito J and Heery E (eds) *The Sage Handbook of Industrial Relations*. London: Sage Books: 434–446.
Lansbury RD, Wailes N and Kirsch A (2009) Globalisation and varieties of employment relations: An international study of the automobile assembly industry. *Labour and Industry* 20 (1): 89–106.
Lansbury RD, Wailes N, Kitay J and Kirsch A eds (2008) Globalisation and employment relations in the auto assembly industry: A study of seven countries.

Bulletin of Comparative Labour Relations. No. 62. Alphen aan den Rijiin: Kluwer Law International.

Lansbury RD and Woo S (2001) Production systems, human resources and employment relations in Korea: The case of Kia Motors. *Asia Pacific Journal of Human Resources* 39 (2): 54–66.

Lansbury RD and Zappala J (1990) *Recent Developments in Industrial Relations: General Perspectives for Korea with Special Reference to Australia.* Seoul: Korea Labor Institute.

Lee BH (2016) Employment relations in South Korea. In Bamber GJ, Lansbury RD, Wailes N and Wright CF (eds) *International and Comparative Employment Relations: National Regulation, Global Changes* (6th ed). London: Sage Books

Lee BH and Lansbury RD eds (2012) Refining varieties of labour movements: Perspectives from the Asia-Pacific region. A symposium. *The Journal of Industrial Relations* 54 (4): 433–442.

Lee BH, Ng SH and Lansbury RD eds (2020) *Trade Unions and Labour Movements in the Asia-Pacific Region.* London: Routledge.

Lewer J and Larkin R (2020) Death of industrial relations greatly exaggerated. *Presentation to the Annual Conference of the Association of Industrial Relations Academics (AIRAANZ)*, Queenstown, New Zealand.

Locke RM, Kochan TA and Piore M eds (1995) *Employment Relations in a Changing World Economy.* Cambridge MA: MIT Press.

Macduffie JP and Pil F (1997) Changes in auto industry employment relations: An international overview. In Kochan TA, Lansbury RD and Macduffie JP (eds) *After Lean Production: Evolving Employment Practices in the World Auto Industry.* Ithaca, NY: Cornell ILR Press.

McCallum R (2019) *Born at the Right Time.* Sydney: Allen and Unwin.

McKersie RB (2019) *A Field in Flux: Sixty Years of Industrial Relations.* Ithaca, NY: Cornell University Press.

McKinsey and Company (2015) *Mining's Next Performance Horizon: Capturing Productivity Gains from Innovation.* Sydney: McKinsey and Company.

Manyika J, Lund S, Bughin J, Robinson K, Mischke J and Mahajan D (2016). *Independent Work: Choice, Necessity and the Gig Economy.* McKinsey Global Institute.

Markey R and Patmore G (2009) Employee participation and labour representation: ICI works councils in Australia, 1942–1975. *Labour History* 97: 53–74.

Marginson P (2015) Coordinated bargaining in Europe: From incremental corrosion to frontal assault? *European Journal of Industrial Relations* 21 (2): 97–114.

Meidner R (1978) *Employee Investment Funds: An Approach to Collective Capital Formation.* London: George Allen and Unwin.

Merton RK (1968) *Social Theory and Social Structure.* New York: Free Press.

Mills C Wright (1948) The contribution of sociology to studies of industrial relations. In Derber M (ed) *Proceedings of the First Annual Conference of the Industrial Relations Research Association.* Urbana: University of Illinois: 199–222.

Mills C Wright (1953) Two styles of research in current social studies. *Philosophy of Science* 20 (4): 11–32.

Murad A and Hook L (2015). Uber's international expansion chief steers for the exit after regulatory blows. *Financial Times*, 1 June.

Nankervis A, Compton R, Baird M and Coffey J (2011) *Human Resource Management: Strategies and Practice.* Melbourne: Cengage.

Palfreeman T (2017) *From the Whangpoo to the Wollombi.* Melbourne: BookPOD.

Regini M, Kitay J and Baethge M eds (1999) *From Tellers to Sellers: Changing Employment Relations in Banks.* Cambridge, MA: MIT Press.

Reisman D, Glazer N and Denney R (1950). *The Lonely Crowd: A Study of the Changing American Character*. New Haven, CT: Yale University Press.

Rhodes M, Hancke B and Thatcher M (2007) *Beyond Varieties of Capitalism: Conflict, Contradictions and Complementarities in the European Economy*. Oxford: Oxford University Press.

Russell B (1935) *In Praise of Idleness and Other Essays*. London: George Allen and Unwin.

Ryder G (2015) The International Labour Organization: The next 100 years. *The Journal of Industrial Relations* 57 (5): 748–757.

Sandberg A (1985) Socio-technical design, trade union strategies and action research. In Mumford E, Hirschheim R, Fitzgerald G and Wood-Harper T (eds) *Research Methods in Information Systems*. Amsterdam: Elsevier: 73–86.

Sandberg A ed. (2013) *Nordic Lights: Work, Management and Welfare in Scandinavia*. Stockholm: SNS Forlag.

Sandberg A ed. (2016) *Pa Jakt Efter Framtidens Arbetet* (Searching for the Work of the Future). Stockholm: Tanksmedjan Tiden.

Sarina T and Lansbury RD (2013) Flying high and low? Strategic choice and employment relations in Qantas and Jetstar. *Asia Pacific Journal of Human Resources* 51 (1): 437–453.

Scott A. (2014) *Northern Lights: The Positive Policy Example of Sweden, Finland, Denmark and Norway*. Clayton: Monash University Publishing.

Sheldrake PF (1971) Orientations to work among computer programmers. *Sociology* 5 (2): 209–224.

Sisson K (2008) Putting the record straight: Industrial relations and the employment relationship. *Warwick Papers in Industrial Relations* No. 87.

Strauss G (1984) Foreword to Gilmour P and Lansbury RD (1984) *Marginal Manager: The Changing Role of Supervisors in Australia*. St Lucia: University of Queensland Press.

Strauss G (1987) Industrial relations: what should our basic course cover? *Organisational Behaviour Teaching Review* 9 (4): 115–119.

Takamiya S and Thurley K (1985) *Japan's Emerging Multinationals*. Tokyo: Tokyo University Press.

Thelen K (2014). *Varieties of Liberalization and the New Politics of Social Solidarity*. New York: Cambridge University Press.

Thurley K (1988) Trade unionism in Asian countries. In Yao YC, Levin D, Ng SH and Sinn E (eds) *The Labour Movement in a Changing Society: The Experience of Hong Kong*. Hong Kong: Centre for Asian Studies, University of Hong Kong.

Thurley K and Hamblin A (1963) *The Supervisor and his Job*. London: DSIR and HMSO.

Thurley K and Takamiya S (1985) *Japan's Emerging Multinationals*. Tokyo: Tokyo University Press.

Thurley K and Widernius H (1973) *Supervision: A Reappraisal*. London: Heinemann.

Thurley K and Widernius H (1989) *Towards European Management*. London: Pitman.

Thurley K and Wood S eds (1983) *Industrial Relations and Management Strategy*. Cambridge: Cambridge University Press.

Triggs G (2018) *Speaking Out*. Melbourne: Melbourne University Press.

Trist E and Bamforth K (1951) Some social and psychological consequences of the long-wall method of coal-getting. *Human Relations* 4 (3): 3–38.

Verma A, Kochan TA and Lansbury RD eds (1995) *Employment Relations in the Growing Asian Economies*. London: Routledge.

Wailes N (2011) Still the exception? Australian employment relations in comparative perspective. In Baird M, Hancock K and Isaac JE (eds) *Work and Employment*

Bibliography

Relations: An Era of Change – Essays in Honour of Russell Lansbury. Sydney: The Federation Press: 141–152.

Wailes N, Lansbury RD, Kitay J and Kirsch A (2008). Globalization, varieties of capitalism and employment relations in the automotive assembly industry. In Lansbury RD, Wailes N, Kitay J and Kirsch A (eds) *Globalization and Employment Relations in the Auto Assembly Industry: A Study of Seven Countries*, Kluwer: Alphen aan den Rijin: 1–11

Walter J (2007) Alan Fraser Davies 1924–1987. *Australian Dictionary of Biography.* Volume 17. Melbourne: Melbourne University Press.

Walton RE, Cutcher Gershenfeld J and McKersie RB (1994) *Strategic Negotiations: A Theory of Change in Labor-Management Relations.* Boston, MA: Harvard Business School Press.

Webb S and Webb B (1897) *Industrial Democracy.* London: Longman.

Westerholm P (2007) Closing the Swedish National Institute for working life. *Occupational and Environmental Medicine* 6: 787–788.

Wheeler H (1987) Management-labour relations in the United States. In Bamber GJ and Lansbury RD (eds) *International and Comparative Employment Relations.* London and Sydney: Allen and Unwin: 57–80.

Whitley R (1999) *Divergent Capitalism: Structuring and Change of Business Systems.* New York: Oxford University Press.

Whyte WF (1948) The social structure of the restaurant. *American Journal of Sociology* 54 (1): 302–310.

Womack JP, Jones DT and Roos D (1990) *The Machine that Changed the World.* New York: Rawson Associates.

Wright CF and Lansbury RD (2010) A dynamic work systems approach for analysing employment relations. In Lansbury RD, Johnson A and van den Broek D (eds) *Contemporary Work and Employment Relations: Actors and Institutions.* London: Routledge: 12–26.

Wright CF and Lansbury RD (2014) Trade unions and economic reform in Australia, 1983–2013. *Singapore Economic Review* 59 (4): 1–22.

Wright CF, Wailes N, Lansbury RD and Bamber GJ (2016) Conclusions. Beyond varieties of capitalism: Towards convergence and internationalisation? In Bamber GJ, Lansbury RD, Wailes N and Wright CF (eds) *International and Comparative Employment Relations: National Regulation. Global Changes.* London: 341–361.

Yeung H (2000) The dynamics of Asian business systems in a globalising era. *Review of International Political Economy* 23 (10): 15–30.

Zhu XY and Chan A (2005) Staff and workers' representative congress: An institutionalized channel for expression of employees' interests? *Chinese Sociology and Anthropology* 37 (4): 6–33.

Zou M and Lansbury RD (2009) Multinational corporations and employment relations in the People's Republic of China: The case of Beijing Hyundai Motor Company. *International Journal of Human Resource Management* 20 (11): 2349–2369.

Index

Note: *Italic* page numbers refer to figures.

Abrahamson, Lena 36, 140, 143
academic research and leadership: airline industry 135–138, *136*; ARC 129; GERAB industries (*see* globalisation and employment relations in the auto and banking (GERAB) industries); Hyundai Motor Company's global strategy 129–132; ILERA 138–139; NTEU 128; USAP 128
'active labour market' policies 66
ACTU 85, 87, 108–109
Adams, Philip 41
Adelaide team 21
Agreements Database and Monitor (ADAM) 106
All-China Federation of Trade Unions (ACFTU) 84–85
Allen, Geoff 86
Amalgamated Metal Workers' Union (AMWU) 60
Anderson, Don 88
Asea Brown Boveri (ABB) 124–126
Association of Industrial Relations Academics of Australia and New Zealand (AIRAANZ) 3
Australia 154, 160; *Australian Democracy* 18; aviation industry 136; Communist Party members 58; conscription policy 7; COVID-19 164; economy 86; *The Fern and the Tiki* (Ausubel) 29; fund-raising activities 20; ILERA 138; industrial democracy 73–75; industrial relations 59–60, 82, 95–96, 104–105, 113, 114, 140, 163; IBM 122; Labor government 54, 139; labour market programmes 87–88; Liberal-Country Party coalition government 18; *Marginal Manager: The Changing Role of Supervisors in Australia* 63–65; military 28; mining 143–147; national work and employment relations systems 151–152; *Organisations: An Australian Perspective* 63; plant 125–126; Productivity Promotion Council 62; Qantas in 44, 137; Rotary International 38; social and economic issues 81; *vs.* South Korea industrial relations 119–120; standards 40; *vs.* Sweden, leisure 33–35; *Ticket to Nowhere: Education, Training and Work in Australia* 65–67, 166; transformation thesis 117; 'uncouth' 44; in Vietnam War 22; vocational training 87–88, 165–166; workplace reform 107–108
Australian Boys Choir 14
Australian Broadcasting Commission (ABC) 20
The Australian Centre for Industrial Relations Research and Teaching (ACIRRT) 104–107, 111, 112, 120
Australian Chamber of Commerce and Industry (ACCI) 111
Australian Competition and Consumer Commission (ACCC) 56
Australian Democracy (Davies) 18
Australian Department of Foreign Affairs 19
Australian Dictionary of Biography (Davies) 18
Australian Graduate School of Management (AGSM) 79
Australian History and Social Studies 16
Australian Human Rights Commission 4, 20
Australian-Indonesian relations 21

184 Index

Australian Labor Party (ALP) 58
Australian Manufacturing Workers Union (AMWU) 58
Australian National Mental Health Commission 56
Australian Research Council (ARC) 129
Australian Security and Intelligence Office (ASIO) 19–20
Australian Workplace Industrial Relations Survey (AWIRS) 105
Australia *vs.* Sweden leisure 33–35
auto industry studies 133–134

Ball, W. Macmahon 19
Bamber, Greg 92, 93, 96–98, 135
Barnevik, Percy 126
Batavia Insurance Company 7
BEA Personnel Planning and Research Department 2
Benjamin, Colin 23
Berggren, Christian 114
Bjork, Gillis 35–36, 42
Booth, Anna 112
Booth, John 27
Born at the Right Time (McCallum) 3–4
Box Hill Rotary Club 27
Bray, M 162–163
British European Airways (BEA) 41–42, 46–48
British experience: BEA 46–47; Callaghan Labour government 46; Fabian Society 50–52; Heath Conservative government 46; job evaluation, airline 44; LBS 45; London School of Economics 49–50; London Stock Exchange 45; Management Services Division 44; *The Nation* 52–53; research outcomes 47–49; Swedish Social Democracy 50–52; Thatcher Conservative government 46; WGH 45; Wilson Labour government 45
The British Journal of Industrial Relations (Horwood) 48, 50
British Overseas Airways Corporation (BOAC) 47, 48
British Universities Industrial Relations Association (BUIRA) 154
Brown, Gavin 128
Bryant, Gordon 23
Buchanan, John 107
Bureau of Labour Market Research 88
Burton, Montague 101
Business Council of Australia (BCA) 86–87
Bussell, Sue 112–113

Cairns, Jim 22–23
Callus, Ron 102, 104, 112
Cameron, Clyde 55, 60
Campbell, George 89
Carmichael, Laurie 59–61, 81
career: academic 1, 4, 5, 19, 22, 23, 31, 49, 56, 61, 62, 128, 160; African politics 37; employees development 68; industrial relations 112, 113, 158; orientations 47, 48
Catholic schools 10
Centre of Industrial Relations Research at the University of Sydney (CIRRUS) 104–105
Charles University 32
Charlesworth, Max 17
Chifley, Ben 164–165
Chinese Academy of Social Sciences (CASS) 83
Cochrane, Donald 57, 63
Cole, GDH 73
Collins, Keith 61–62
Committee of Inquiry into Technological Change in Australia (CITCA) 95
Commons, John R 3, 73
Conrad, Joseph 3
Conservative Student Association 37
coordinated market economies (CMEs) 132, 133
Corina, John 101–102
Cornell University 57, 59
COVID-19 2, 34, 118, 156, 157, 163, 165, 166, 168
Craddon, C 162
Crean, Simon 60, 76, 120
Crosland, Tony 51
Cultural Revolution 83, 84

Danish National Health Service 42
D'Arcy, Eric 17
Davies, AF 17, 31, 33, 38, 39, 160; *Australian Democracy* 18; *Australian Dictionary of Biography* 18; *Images of Class* 18, 41; *Politics as Work* 18; *Private Politics* 4, 18; *Skills, Outlooks and Passions* 18
Deakin University 79
Debating Society 21–22
Democracy in the Workplace 74
Dolan, Cliff 85, 89–90
Duke, Graham 13–14
Duke University 18, 56
Dunlop, John 91, 138
Dunphy, Dexter 79
dynamic work systems framework 155

Elliott, John 61
employers: arbitration system 57; collective bargaining 167; and employees 2, 112, 153, 162, 168; employment relationship 135, 156; 'fighting fund' 111; organisations and 116; private, wage subsidies 165; superannuation 87; unions and 56, 74, 75, 83, 85–87, 89, 94, 98, 100, 106–108, 136, 147, 148, 159; to workers 132
employment relations/industrial relations 3, 99; airlines 136, 136; Asian market economies 134; Australia and Denmark national work 151–152; globalisation 99, 116–118, 132; human resources 130; labour associations 142; policies and practices 118; trade unions 85; work and 2, 147, 150, 154, 155, 159, 163
Ennis, Philip 29, 35
Erlander, Tage 36
Europe 30–31
European Economic Community 52
European Works Councils (EWC) 168
Evans, Bert 110–111, 120
Evans, Gareth 13, 20–23; *Incorrigible Optimist: A Political Memoir* 4

feeder school 11
A Field in Flux: Sixty Years of Industrial Relations (McKersie) 3
Fingleton, Jack 12
Ford, Bill 79
Fraser Coalition government 95
Fraser, Malcolm 58, 59, 61, 62, 67, 77, 89–90, 95
From the Whangpoo to the Wollombi (Palfreeman) 4
fund-raising events 20

Galbraith, JK 29, 46
Ganesh, J 1
German auto industry 93–94
German economy 94
Gershenfeld, Joel Cutcher 92
Gillard, Julia 108, 139
Gilmour, P 50, 59, 63–66, 79; *Organisations: An Australian Perspective* 63; *Ticket to Nowhere? Education, Training and Work in Australia* 65–67, 166
globalisation and employment relations in the auto and banking (GERAB) industries: auto industry studies 133–134; capitalist diversity 132; CMEs 132, 133; implications 134–135; LMEs 132, 133; retail banking industry studies 134; VoC approach 132, 133
'golden age,' industrial relations 102–104
Gonas, Lena 114
Gorton, John 23, 41
government 141, 163; academics and 83; Australian 7, 21, 27, 119, 143, 165; Callaghan Labour government 46; Chinese unions 132; Coalition 55, 58, 59, 61, 67, 77, 107, 110, 165, 167; 'Conservative Alliance' 115–116; economic policies 63, 119; federal 22, 87, 89, 104, 105, 137, 166; Fraser government 62, 95; Hawke Labor government 41, 60, 67, 74, 75, 82–83, 87, 95, 161; Heath Conservative government 46, 52; Howard government 111; Indonesian 38; Keating 60, 77, 108, 161, 167; Labour government 30, 56; LiberalCountry Party coalition 18; neo-liberal 162; social contract 4; Social Democratic government 72, 114, 115; Swedish 40, 53, 72, 143, 147, 150; Thatcher Conservative government 46; Whitlam government 23, 51, 55, 57, 58, 60, 63, 66–68, 77; Wilson Labour government 30, 45, 50
Gregorian University 17
Gregory, A: *Woodfull: Gentleman and Scholar* 12

Hall, PA 132
Hammarskjold, Dag 35, 36
Hancock Report, industrial relations reform 86–87
Hansenne, Michel 123
Harry, Marianne 27, 115
Hartnett, Bruce 23
Harvard Trade Union Program 90–91
Harvard University 1, 28–30, 80, 90–93
Hawke, Bob 55
Hawke/Keating era: Advanced Management Program 80, 81; Australian industrial relations 82; 'balance of skills' 95–96; CITCA 95; employment relations 99–100; 'entertainment venues' 80–81; FIET 98; Fraser Coalition government 95; German economy 94; globalisation 99; Great Depression 81; Harvard Trade Union Program 90–91; Hawke Labor government 82; HRM 92, 99; humanisation of worklife 94; IIRA 97; international economy 100;

labour-management studies 85–90; Macquarie management mission, China 83–85; Macquarie University 80–83; Management's Crisis of Legitimacy 82; MIT 90–92; post-industrial revolution 95; quasi-domestic services 95; retail distribution 96–97; Senior Fulbright Scholarship 90–93; 'social partnership' approach 98–99; social wage 83; team teaching approach 82; technological change 93–94, 96–97; third industrial revolution 96; UNSW 79, 80; 'varieties of capitalism' approach 99
Hawke Labor government 41, 60, 67, 74, 75, 82–83, 87, 95, 102, 161
Heath, Edward 45, 50–51
Hegarty, David 17–18
home-related activities 34
Howard, Bill 56–57
Howard, John 58, 62, 82, 109–110
Howie, John 75
Howson, Peter 22–23
Human Resource Management (HRM) 49–50, 55, 92, 99, 121, 153
Hunter Valley 126–127
Hyden, Goran 37
Hyundai Motors India (HMI) 130–131

IBM, global HR strategies 120–122
Images of Class (Davies) 18
Improving the Quality of Working Life (Lansbury and Prideaux) 70
Incorrigible Optimist: A Political Memoir (Evans) 4
India 25–26
Indian universities 26
Indonesian YMCA 38
The Industrial and Labor Relations Review 92
industrial democracy 43, 71, 76, 88–89, 161; Australia 73–75
industrial relations 1–4, 101–102, 132, 138–139, 152, 155–156, 158–161; ACIRRT 106–107; in Asia 140–143; Australian 59–60, 82, 95–96, 104–105, 113, 114, 140, 163; career 112, 113, 158; COVID-19 166; decision-making 92; globalisation 133; 'golden age' 102–104, 153; Hawke Labor government 82, 90; Heath government 52; human resource systems 117, 118, 130; IIRA 97, 123; international automotive project 118–119; international dimension 97–100; Jetstar 136; labour economics 56; management and 50; market-leading wages 137; mining 145–147; 'New Deal' era 91; 'players' 59–62; policy 76, 77, 154; practitioners and policy makers 108–114; reform, Hancock Report 86–87; South Korea 119–120; Swedish leadership 147–149; technological change 95–96; unitarist and pluralist approach 162–163; workplace 104–105; *see also* employment relations/industrial relations
Industrial Relations Bill 51
Industrial Relations Commission 103
Industrial Relations Research Association (IRRA) 72
Industrial Relations Research Institute (IRRI) 71
Industrial Sociology 41
Intergovernmental Panel on Climate Change (IPCC) 10
International Club 18–19, 22, 25, 26
International Crisis Group 13
International Federation of Commercial, Clerical, Professional and Technical Employees (FIET) 98
International House in Lund 36
International Industrial Relations Association (IIRA) 97, 122–124, 138
International Labour and Employment Relations Association (ILERA) 93, 111, 138–139
International Labour Organization (ILO) 1, 122–124, 159
International Motor Vehicle Program (IMVP) 118–119
International Relations 19
Isaac, Joe 1, 68, 71, 105

Jackson, Keith 42, 44
Japan Airlines (JAL) 40
Japan's Emerging Multinationals (Takamiya and Thurley) 49
Jarring, Gunnar 35
Jetstar 137
Johansson, Jan 36, 140, 143
Jones, Barry 41, 95
The Journal of Industrial Relations 55, 101, 142

Katz, Harry 91, 92
Kelly, Paul 164
Kelty, Bill 59–61, 76, 111, 113
Kemp, David 21, 62
Kennan, Jim 51, 75
Kennedy, Edward 28
Kirby, Michael 27, 108

Kirby Report 88
Kirby, Richard 56
Kleingartner, Archie 45
Kochan, Tom 91, 92, 116, 118, 135
Korea-Australia Research Centre (KAREC) 130
Korean Labour Institute (KLI) 129–132

Labor Premier of South Australia 21
labour-management studies, Macquarie University: employee participation 88–89; Hancock Report, industrial relations reform 86–87; industrial democracy 88–89; labour market programmes 87–88; McGill University 85; superannuation reform 87; vocational training 87–88; wages and prices 86
labour market 3
Laffer, Kingsley 101, 106
Lansbury, Frank 9
Lansbury, Freda 5–6
Lansbury, George 52
Lansbury, Gwen 6, 9–10, 39–42, 44, 45, 50, 52, 54, 75, 76, 79, 80, 83, 90, 114, 122–123, 126–127
Lansbury, Len 5–8, 15
Lansbury, Russell D 66, 155
Larkin, R 3
LaTrobe team 21
La Trobe University 67
Law and Medicine 18
Law and Social Sciences 85
Lee Kwan Yew 25
Lewer, J 3
Lewin, Kurt 77
Liberal-Country Party coalition government 18
liberal market economies (LMEs) 132, 133
Liberal National Party Coalition 55, 58, 67
life-cycle approach 158
London Business School (LBS) 45
London School of Economics (LSE) 2, 45
The Lonely Crowd: A Study of the Changing American Character (Reisman) 29
Loveridge, Ray 45
Ludowke, Jeremy 12
Lulea Technical University (LTU) 140

McAllister, David 140
McCallum, R 3–4
McDougall, Derek 18
MacDuffie, John Paul 119

McKern, Bruce 79, 80, 83, 85
McKersie, RB (Bob) 3, 90–92, 154, 158; *A Field in Flux: Sixty Years of Industrial Relations* 3
McMichael, Tony 27
Macphee, Ian 59, 61–62
Macquarie Advanced Management Program 83
Macquarie management mission, China 83–85
Macquarie University 6, 9, 79, 80–83
McQueen, Johnny 8
Margaret, Dame 8–9, 52
Marginal Manager: The Changing Role of Supervisors in Australia 63–65
'mass observation' movement 17
McGill University 85
Meidner, Rudolf 72, 73
Melbourne University Debating Society 21
Menzies, Robert 18, 25
Merton, Robert: *Social Theory and Social Structure* 32
Metal Trades Industry Association (MTIA) 110
Metcalf, David 93
Michel-Servais, Jean 124
Mills, C. Wright 153
MIT 1, 3, 49, 90–92, 116, 117
Mollison, James 14, 41
Monash University, Whitlam and Fraser eras: academia 62; ACCC 56; ad hoc 'Melbash' intervarsity 54–55; ALP politics 77; AMWU 58; arbitration system 57; *Australia Reconstructed* 75; *Democracy in the Workplace* 74; France and United States 70–73; Hawke Labor government 74, 75; HRM 55; *Improving the Quality of Working Life* 70; industrial democracy 71, 73–75; Industrial Relations 54; *The Journal of Industrial Relations* 55; Labor government 54; labour market training 57; Liberal National Party Coalition 55; *Marginal Manager: The Changing Role of Supervisors in Australia* 63–65; National Wage Cases 56; Organisational Behaviour 55, 59; organisational consulting 77–78; *Organisations: An Australian Perspective* 63; *Performance Appraisal: Managing Human Resources* 67–70; 'players,' industrial relations 59–62; 'radical campus' 54; self management 73–74; Sudreau Report 71; Swedish Social Democrats 71; *Ticket to Nowhere? Education, Training and*

188 *Index*

Work in Australia 65–67; trade union movement 74; union theory 57; wage freeze 55; worker control 75
Moore, Sir John 104, 108
Morawetz, David 13
Morris, Richard 102
Moynihan, Daniel Patrick 29, 46
Myers, Rupert 95
Myrdal, Alva 36, 72

National Council of Churches (NCC) 29
National Employment and Training Scheme 57
National Tertiary Education Union (NTEU) 58, 128
National Union of Australian University Students (NUAUS) 25–27
National Wage Cases 56
Nazi-occupied territories 35
The New Statesman 51, 52
Nordic countries 39, 43, 61, 65, 114, 115, 117, 140, 143, 146, 147, 158, 164, 165; *see also* Nordic exposure
Nordic exposure: Australia *vs.* Sweden leisure 33–35; Danish health system 41; global economic power 41; industrial democracy 43; International House in Lund 36; internationalism 35; public intellectuals 41; Rotary Club of Lund 35–36; Rotary International 38; social reforms 33; Swedish Communist Party 37; Swedish politics 39–40; Swedish suburban community 32; University of Copenhagen, Denmark 40–43; University of Melbourne 38–39; University of Uppsala 32

Organisational Behaviour: The Australian Context (Spillane and Lansbury) 81–82
Organisation for Economic Cooperation and Development (OECD) 116–118
organisations 154, 159; Australian 63, 95; Christian 15; civil society 142; community 34; consulting 77–78; goals 137; Japanese and British management 50; individual 69; industrial relations 81; political 111; private-sector 68–69; and society 48; student 18–19, 21, 64; theory 83; youth 38; work 46, 65, 97, 107, 117, 124, 144, 147–150
Organisations: An Australian Perspective (Gilmour and Lansbury) 63

Palfreeman, Tony 163; *From the Whangpoo to the Wollombi* 4
Palme, Olof 33, 51–53
Papandreo, George 36
Parliament of Youth 13
Paterson, John 22
Patmore, Greg 102–104, 109
Paton, George 20
Peacock, Andrew 21–22
Pekkola, Juhani 114
Performance Appraisal: Managing Human Resources 67–70
Perlman, Selig 73
Pil, Frits 119
Piore, Michael 116
politics 7, 17, 18, 37, 39–40, 68, 75–77, 156
Politics as Work (Davies) 18
power transformer industry 124–126
Presbyterian Church, social activity 15
Prideaux, Geoffrey: *Improving the Quality of Working Life* 70
Private Politics (Davies) 4, 18

Qantas Airways 47, 49, 112–113, 136, 137
quality of work life (QWL) 62–63, 70, 73

Rawson, Don 86
Rehn-Meidner model 72
Reinfeldt, Fredrik 116
Reisman, David: *The Lonely Crowd: A Study of the Changing American Character* 29
research: at Macquarie University 81–83; at Monash 55–57; outcomes 47–49; publish/perish 62–70; workplace industrial relations, Australia 104–105; *see also* academic research and leadership; retirement
retail banking industry studies 134
retail distribution 96–97
retirement: Australian and Swedish mines 145–147; BUIRA 154; dynamic work systems framework 155; Global McKinsey Institute 152; 'golden age' 153; industrial relations, Asia 140–143; 'land grant' universities 153; LTU 140; multi-scalar institutional framework 155, 155; national work and employment relations systems 151–152; 'platform businesses' 152; 'sharing economy' 152; Swedish Arctic and Australian desert

mining 143–145; Swedish leadership 147–149; work organisation research, Sweden 149–150
Ridout, Heather 111–112
Roberts, Ben 50, 92, 138
Robertson, Geoffrey 27
Roosevelt, Franklin Delano (President of the USA) 156
Ross, Iain 113–114
Rotary Club of Lund 35–36
Rotary Foundation Graduate Scholarship 27
Rotary International Graduate Scholarship 18
Rowe, Les 13
Russell, Bertrand 34–35

Salinger, JD 14
Sandberg, Ake 114
Sandblom, Philip 36
'scattergun' approach 160
Senghor, Leopold (President of Senegal) 36
Senior Fulbright Scholarship 90–93
Shell Scholarship to Oxford University 21
Skills, Outlooks and Passions (Davies) 18
social cohesion 35
social contract at work: collective voice and representation 166–168; COVID-19 163; full employment commitment 164–165; labour market institutions 163; Nordic countries 164; vocational education and training 165–166
Social Democratic government 72, 115–116
'social partnership' approach 98–99
social reform approach 33
The Social Structure of the Restaurant (Whyte) 24
Social Theory and Social Structure (Merton) 32
social welfare policy 23
Soskice, D 132
Speaking Out (Triggs) 4
Spillane, Robert 79, 80; *Organisational Behaviour: The Australian Context* 81–82
Stern, James L 62, 71, 73
Strauss, George 65, 102, 153
Streeck, Wolfgang 93
Sudreau Report 71
Sun Yao Jun 83

superannuation reform 87
Svalastoga, Kaare 41
Swedish Centre for Worklife Research 1, 114–116
Swedish Communist Party 37
Swedish model 40, 51, 124, 147, 148
Swedish Social Democracy 22, 51–52, 71
Swedish suburban community 32
Swedner, Harald 32, 33, 35
Swinburne University 22
Sydney *see* Hawke/Keating era; University of Sydney

Tavistock Institute of Human Relations 46
Technical and Further Education (TAFE) 64, 67
Technical and Further Education Commission (TAFEC) 64–66
technological change, Sydney: German auto industry 93–94; retail distribution 96–97; socio-technical system 97; Sydney Distribution Centre 97
Thurley, Keith 45, 49–50, 64, 77, 92, 93, 141, 142
Ticket to Nowhere? Education, Training and Work in Australia (Gilmour and Lansbury) 65–67, 166
time-based management system 125
Trade Union Program 90
Trade Union Training Authority (TUTA) 60
Training Board Research Bulletin 48
Triggs, Gillian 20; *Speaking Out* 4
Trump, Donald 30

Union Debate 23
unions: employers and 56, 74, 75, 83, 85–87, 89, 94, 98, 100, 106–108, 136, 147, 148, 159; trade 23, 45, 47, 52, 55, 57, 60, 61, 67, 74, 87, 141
United States: Kent State University 28; *The Lonely Crowd: A Study of the Changing American Character* 29; NCC 29; UCLA 27–28
universities *see individual entries*
University of California Los Angeles (UCLA) 27–28
University of Chicago 29
University of Copenhagen, Denmark 40–43
University of Gothenburg 33

University of London 23
University of Lund 9, 16, 18
University of Melbourne 1, 2, 4, 8, 9, 16–18, 21, 27, 38–39
University of New South Wales (UNSW) 9, 79, 80, 121
University of Papua New Guinea 17–18
University of Sydney 4, 22; ACIRRT 106–107; Department of Industrial Relations 101; global employment relations 116–118; 'golden age,' industrial relations 102–104; in Hunter Valley 126–127; IBM, global HR strategies 120–122; IIRA 122–124; ILO 122–124; Industrial Relations Society 101; international automotive industrial relations project 118–119; power transformer industry 124–126; practitioners and policy makers, industrial relations 108–114; South Korea *vs.* Australia 119–120; Swedish Centre for Worklife Research 114–116; workplace industrial relations, Australia 104–105; workplace reform 107–108
University of Sydney Association of Professors (USAP) 128
University of Uppsala 32
University of Wisconsin-Madison 1

varieties of capitalism (VoC) approach 99, 132, 133
Victoria Lacrosse Association 9
Victorian Debating Association 21
Victorian Education Department 16, 24, 40
vocational training 87–88

Walker, Kenneth 70–71, 122
Walter, James 18
Walton, RE 135
Warner, Denis 19
Webb, Beatrice 3, 50, 52, 73

Webb, Sidney 3, 50, 52, 73
Weisz, Morris 71, 72
Wells, Murray 102, 103
Western market economies 158
Whitfield, Keith 102
Whitlam, Gough 54, 77
Whitlam Labor government 23, 51, 55, 57, 58, 60, 63, 66–68, 77
Whitley, R 133
Whyte, William Foote: *The Social Structure of the Restaurant* 24
Widernius, Hans 49
Wilenski, Peter 27
William Goodenough House (WGH) 45
Williams, Bruce 30, 101
Williams, Colin 29
Williams, Harvey 23
Wolnizer, Peter 103, 128–129
Womack, James P 118
Woodfull, Bill 12
Woodfull: Gentleman and Scholar (Gregory) 12
Wood, Stephen 50
Woolworths Limited 96, 97
Work and Organisational Studies (WOS) Discipline 104
work/workplace: democracy 73, 74, 116; industrial relations research, Australia 104–105; reforms 43, 64, 89, 107–108
Workplace Research Centre (WRC) 107
World University Service (WUS) 18, 20, 25, 26
Worrall, Graham 13
Wright, Chris F 99, 151, 155

Xi Jinping 85

Yerbury, Di 55–56, 79
Yeung, H 133
YMCA 14, 15